Crime and Society in Early Modern Seville

PUBLISHED BY THE UNIVERSITY PRESS OF NEW ENGLAND

HANOVER, NEW HAMPSHIRE AND LONDON, ENGLAND 1980

CRIME AND SOCIETY

IN EARLY MODERN SEVILLE

Mary Elizabeth Perry

Published with assistance from the
Andrew W. Mellon Foundation.

University Press of New England
Sponsoring Institutions
Brandeis University
Clark University
Dartmouth College
University of New Hampshire
University of Rhode Island
Tufts University
University of Vermont

TO RALPH, KATIE, AND DAN

Preface

A Fulbright-Hays Research Fellowship funded by the United States and Spanish governments made possible nine months of intensive research in Spain, and I am deeply grateful that my family and I were able to live in Seville while I worked in the archives of this fascinating city.

Special thanks are due several individuals who assisted my research in Spain. Doña Eulalia de la Cruz Bugallal, director of the *Archivo Municipal de Sevilla*, and her assistant, Doña Hermine Meós Gonzalez, were unerringly kind and helpful to me. At the *Biblioteca Capitular* of Seville, the director, Don Francisco Alvarez Leisdedos, and his assistant, Don José Jaén Santiago, assisted me with patience and tolerance. The director of the *Biblioteca Universitaria* in Granada, Doña María Pardo, permitted me to study the manuscripts of Pedro de León and to photocopy them. I appreciate very much help from the noted historian, Antonio Domínguez Ortiz, in finding these manuscripts. The Count of Peñaflor de Argamasilla, *Hermano Mayor* of the *Hermandad de la Santa Caridad,* kindly gave me permission to look through the collections of papers in the *Hospital de la Santa Caridad* in Seville. Doña Aurore Domínguez Guzmán assisted my search in this archive, and Don Tomás García sat with me while I read documents and helped me to photocopy them. Noël Diaz's assistance in preparing the maps and charts is greatly appreciated.

My thanks also go to several American scholars who have helped me with my work. William A. Christian, Jr., who has done extensive research in Spain, gave me many suggestions and unselfishly shared his notes and insights. Judith Walkowitz read an earlier version of the chapter on lost women and helped me improve it. Lutz Berkner and Richard Kagan gave me many valuable suggestions for converting an earlier version into the present book. Robert I. Burns, S.J., read the first chapter and shared his writing experience with me. Elizabeth Vodola, who gave her undivided attention to a thorough reading of the manuscript, suggested many improvements. Temma Kaplan has been a superlative guide in research, analysis, and writing. She has supported me with a marvelous balance of criticism and approval, and she has never run out of ideas to broaden and deepen my study of the underworld.

Finally, my husband and children have risen to the challenge of this entire project, and I am so thankful that they have shared in it with me.

Pasadena, California   *M.E.P*
August 1979

Contents

Illustrations

ABBREVIATIONS

AI   Archivo de las Indias
AMS   Archivo Municipal de Sevilla
BC   Biblioteca Capitular
BM   British Museum
HSC   Hospital de la Santa Caridad

Introduction

The Great Babylon of Spain

CRIME and politics are no strangers. Four hundred years ago they were uneasy partners in the city of Seville. A study of this city is essential to any investigation of the politics of crime in the early modern period, for Seville was the center of Hapsburg Spain, the greatest commercial empire of the sixteenth century. It was the seat of a permanent tribunal of the Inquisition, the scene of several demographic crises, and the site of the *Casa de Contratación,* a royal agency that administered trade and politics in the New World. With unique ties to the central monarchy, the fortunes of the city rose and fell with those of the Hapsburg rulers. Seville reveals in microcosm the relationship between city oligarchy and central monarchy and the tensions between political authority and those who defy it.

In 1503 the Crown of Castile decreed that all ships sailing between Europe and the New World should pass through Seville. This river port that became the capital of the Spanish commercial empire quickly developed into "the Great Babylon of Spain," as famous for crime as for trade.[1] New people and wealth poured into the city: merchants, bankers, shippers, soldiers, but also beggars, prostitutes, thugs, and thieves. Here thrived a subculture

---

1. Luís de Góngora, quoted in Francisco Rodríguez Marín, *Miscelánea de Andalucía* (Madrid, 1927), p. 11. The text in Spanish is: "Fénix del orbe,/que debajo de sus alas/tantos hoy lemos rocoge;/Gran Babilonia de España,/mapa de todas naciones,/donde el flamenco a su Gante,/y el inglés halla a su Londres;/escala del Nuevo Mundo,/cuyos ricos escalones,/enladrillados de plata,/son navios del alto borde."

of street people, the "people of low life" who were usually identified with crime.

Crime at this time was defined by a ruling alliance of the
Crown, aristocracy, and Church. Royal ordinances regulated
many local activities, from selling food to carrying weapons.
Through the city government, aristocrats decided who should be
allowed to beg and how prostitution could be legally practiced.
The Church censored public performances and preached a morality that condemned adultery, homosexuality, and abortion. Officials who enforced the laws and punished offenders were named
by the Crown, aristocracy, or Inquisition.

Diversities within the ruling alliance compounded the problems of defining crime. Until the reign of Isabella and Ferdinand
(1474–1516), the local aristocracy often split into "rivalries and
antagonisms of powerful men, assisted by their friends and families" in "scandalous and bloody skirmishes."[2] To counteract these
rivalries, Ferdinand and Isabella imposed the *Santa Hermandad,*
an agency to enforce royal justice against the aristocracy. They
also exploited these rivalries to justify increasing the power of
the *asistente,* a Crown-appointed noble from outside Seville who
directed the city's government. Throughout the early modern
period, the Crown of Castile followed the practice of appointing
outsiders as magistrates and heads of city governments. Directed
to carry out royal policies on crime and order, these officers
sometimes clashed with local traditions. Royal and city officials
were best able to overcome their differences by uniting against a
common enemy, such as people suspected of crime.

Vagabonds exploited aristocratic rivalries and the divisions
between the Crown, aristocracy, and Church. They sometimes
eluded the secular law by claiming special privilege as clerics or
lay officials of the Inquisition. Occasionally they escaped punishment in the jurisdictional confusion between the city government
and the *Santa Hermandad.* They looked to individual aristocrats
who consolidated their bodies of loyal retainers by intervening to

2. See the royal complaint of May 25, 1466, quoted in Joaquin Guichot y
Parody, *Historia del excmo. ayuntamiento de la muy leal, muy heróica,
é invicta ciudad de Sevilla* (Sevilla, 1896), 1:371.

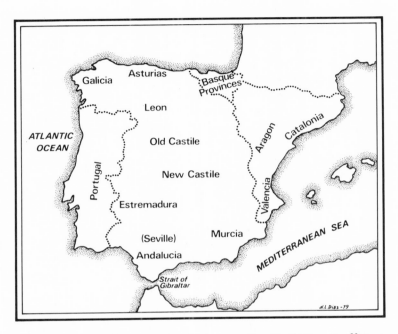

1 Kingdoms of the Iberian Peninsula. Prepared by Noël Diaz, Staff Cartographer, U.C.L.A.

protect them from prosecution by royal officials or other nobles.

Ferdinand and Isabella established a permanent tribunal of the Inquisition in Seville in 1480. At this time the Inquisition was concerned primarily with secret rites of judaizing that had been reported against several *Conversos* (Christianized Jews). Conversos and *Moriscos* (Christianized Moors) were suspected of false conversions, and Ferdinand and Isabella directed the Inquisition to prosecute those false converts who continued their old religious practices. Though some Conversos fled, others remained in the city and armed themselves against the Inquisition, which moved quickly against them, uncovered their caches of arms, and arrested them. Early in 1481, nine citizens were burned at the stake. Seville lost a chief magistrate in this fire, "and many other leading and very rich citizens."[3] In Seville the Inquisition found Conversos among churchmen, nobles, and commercial people.

By the mid-sixteenth century the Inquisition was as concerned with Protestant heretics as with false converts. One "furious crazy woman" in 1555 betrayed to the Inquisition in Seville more than three-hundred citizens suspected of Protestant heresies.[4] A secret Protestant sect was discovered in Seville, its members hiding in the Monastery of San Isidro and in the Convent of Santa Paula. Inquisition agents found copies of the New Testament printed in the Castillian language hidden in the home of Juan Ponce de León, son of the Count of Bailén. Constantino, a canon of the Cathedral in Seville, preached against the heresies of the Jesuits, but the Inquisition arrested him for Lutheran heresies. Although he died in prison, his bones were burned in 1560 by order of the Inquisition. According to one report, the prisons of the Inquisition processed more than 800 people during the prosecution of Protestant heretics in Seville from 1559 to 1560.[5] Later the Inquisition concentrated on prosecuting *Alumbrados*,

3. Henry Kamen, *The Spanish Inquisition* (New York, London, and Scarborough, Ont., 1965), pp. 44–46.

4. Marcelino Menéndez y Pelayo, *Historia de los heterodoxos españoles* (Madrid, 1928), p. 112.

5. Ibid., pp. 97–102, 112. AMS, Efemérides, "Noticias y casos." Diego Ortiz de Zuñiga, *Anales eclesiasticas y seculares de la muy noble y muy leal ciudad de Sevilla,* 1677 (Madrid, 1795), 4:517.

members of a religious sect that believed people could attain a mystical union with God without priestly intercession. Deviance was narrowly defined in this city, which had a strong institution for enforcing orthodoxy.

Religious orthodoxy was a bulwark of political authority as well as an article of faith. The Inquisition was theoretically independent of the Church and could even check the power of bishops. Ferdinand and Isabella had won for themselves and their successors the right to name Inquisitors, and they established a single Supreme Council of the Inquisition over both kingdoms of Castile and Aragon. The monarchy used the Inquisition as an agency to identify and prosecute deviance that would not be tolerated. In repressing heretics and false Christians, the Inquisition served to unify the diversity of the Iberian Peninsula into a social order favored by the Crown.

Demographic crises in Seville exposed power relations that remained invisible during periods of stability. The city's population more than doubled between 1520 and 1580, bringing it to at least ninety thousand. Seville was the largest city in Europe after Naples, Venice, and Paris. In the seventeenth century, population fell in the city as it did throughout most of the Iberian Peninsula. Emigration and military service contributed to the decline, as did seven major epidemics that struck Seville between 1520 and 1649. For this same period, nine famines or poor harvests were reported.[6] Bread riots in 1521 and 1652 became po-

6. Population estimates for Seville are available in Ramón Carande Thobar, *Carlos V y sus banqueros; La vida económica en Castilla 1516–1556* (Madrid, 1943), pp. 38–39; Antonio Domínguez Ortiz, *The Golden Age of Spain, 1516–1659* (London, 1971), pp. 134–136; Javier Ruiz Almansa, "La Población de España en el siglo XVI; Estudio sobre los recuentos de vecindario de 1594, llamados comúmente 'Censo de Tomás González,'" *Revista Internacional de Sociología*, 1 (1943), 136. Population for the Iberian Peninsula is discussed in Jorge Nadal, *La Población española, siglos XVI a XX* (Barcelona, 1966), pp. 37–90; and in John Elliott, *Imperial Spain, 1469–1716* (New York, 1964), p. 13. Epidemics were reported for the years 1520–22, 1562–63, 1581, 1588, 1599–1600, 1626, and 1649 in Antonio Astrain, *Historia de la Compañía de Jesús en la asistencia de España* (Madrid, 1912), 2:528–530; AMS, Efemérides, "Noticias y casos," No. 1; AMS, Siglo XVI, Sección 3, Escribanías de Cabildo, Tomo 7, Nos. 16, 17; Memorias eclesiásticas, 84-7-19; Diego Ignacio de Góngora, "Re-

litical rebellions. A comparison of these two rebellions shows a marked change in the positions of Church, aristocracy, and monarchy. It also shows that criminals and misfits helped to preserve the existing order during the crises, propping it up even as they tried to exploit it.

Strategic geographic location intensified the Crown's interest in Seville. The city was close to Granada and the Alpujarras, a mountainous region on the slopes of the Sierra Nevada, where Moriscos rebelled against the Crown in 1499 and 1569. Seville was also near the southern coast that was repeatedly attacked by English marauders in the late sixteenth century. It was the largest city close to the Portuguese border. From the time that Philip II claimed the throne of Portugal in the 1580's, the Portuguese were rebellious subjects, finally overthrowing their Spanish masters some sixty years later. Seville served the Crown as a base for operations as it tried to retain its rule over restless Portuguese and Morisco subjects, and to defend its coastline against the English.

The rise and decline of Seville parallels that of the Hapsburg monarchy. The city began to grow in population and wealth as Charles I (1520–1556) inherited the lands of the Hapsburgs from his father, Philip of Burgundy, and the dual crowns of Aragon and Castile from his mother, Juana, who was the heir of Ferdinand and Isabella. Charles successfully put down the *Comunero* revolts that broke out against him in several cities of Castile in 1520 and 1521. He also won election as Holy Roman Emperor and became Charles V. When Protestant princes rebelled in central Europe, he used the silver shipments that came to Seville from the New World as collateral for loans to finance his armies.

Philip II (1556–1598) inherited only part of the Hapsburg empire when his father abdicated in 1556. Charles V split the empire between his brother, Ferdinand, and his son, Philip II.

---

lación del contagio que padeció esta ciudad de Sevilla el año de 1649," Memorias de diferentes cosas, BC, 84-7-21. Famines and bread riots are discussed in Ortiz de Zuñiga, 4:504; AMS, Siglo XVI, Sección 3, Escribanías de Cabildo, Tomo 19, No. 19; AMS, Archivo General, Sección 1, Carpeta 27, No. 379; Memorias eclesiásticas, BC, 84-7-19; Guichot y Parody, 2:294.

As monarch of Spain, parts of Italy, the Netherlands, and the Atlantic empire, Philip II was able to assert Spain's position as a world power. He borrowed on the increasing silver shipments from the New World to carry out military campaigns against the rebellious Low Countries. Seville, continuing to grow in wealth and population, was able to raise the taxes and soldiers that he requested repeatedly. The Price Revolution, resulting from population growth and the increased amount of precious metals in circulation, raised prices in Seville before it affected other parts of Europe. It gave the appearance of growing prosperity.[7]

By the beginning of the seventeenth century, both Seville and the Hapsburg monarchy were in decline. Philip III (1598–1621) sent a letter to the city government in 1599 complaining that city officials "and other powerful and influential people" were using city income for illegal loans, amounting to more than 400,000 ducats.[8] The "poor administration" that Philip blamed for a loss of city income also meant a loss for the royal treasury. By 1607 this problem had become so acute that the royal government had to declare another bankruptcy. Attempts to reduce royal debts through increased taxation and monetary devaluation added to the economic misery in Seville, where wages could not keep up with the increased prices of the Price Revolution.

Misfortunes continued for Seville and the Hapsburg monarchy during the reign of Philip IV (1621–1665). Merchants of the city protested to the king in 1635 that losses by the fleet to the New World combined with extractions by the royal treasury had brought the commerce of the city to a "deplorable state."[9] When the Crown requested more money from Seville in May of 1637, a member of the city council replied that the king should be told of the depopulation of the city "and the great number of citizens, who for the past six years, have gone to live in foreign

7. A more complete discussion of the Price Revolution is in John Lynch, *Spain under the Hapsburgs* (New York, 1964), 1:124–127; and Elliott, p. 185.

8. Quoted in Guichot y Parody, 2:148–150.

9. Quoted ibid., p. 252.

kingdoms, and others have gone to the Indies." He implied that these people had left Spain in order to escape royal taxes, and he declared that "today the necessity and discomfort of this Republic and places of its kingdom are at a state in which one feels powerless to continue meeting the desires that with such love it has served and serves its king and natural lord."[10] The Crown's response was to request more soldiers and money to put down rebellions in Portugal and Catalonia, for the empire was slipping away. The peace settlement that ended the long revolt of the Low Countries in 1648 established an independent Netherlands, and Portuguese troops defeated the Spanish at Villaviciosa in June of 1665, only months before the death of Philip IV.

The commercial empire that had supported both the Hapsburg monarchy and the city of Seville was dissolving by the end of the seventeenth century. The last of the Hapsburg monarchs, Carlos II (1675–1700), was a child at the time of his father's death, but even as an adult he was unable to reconstruct a crumbling empire. He was a man so weak that he could neither feed himself nor produce an heir for the throne. Seville had retired into quiet oblivion. The value of shipments from New Spain had fallen to less than 5 percent of its high point in 1595.[11] Cadiz had gradually replaced Seville as the official port for trade with the New World. No longer did ships arrive in Seville laden with silver from the mines of Mexico and Peru. No longer did people flock to Seville, filling its streets with the colors and babbles of Babylon.

Many scholars have underestimated the importance of criminals in history. George Rudé, a distinguished historian of social protest, dismissed them as a "submerged group of poor" who played "little or no part in political protest movements (except possibly in food riots)." Since very little is known about this group, he advised against speculation and concluded it was best "to leave them out of further consideration."[12]

10. Quoted ibid., pp. 232–235.

11. Huguette and Pierre Chaunu, *Seville et l'Atlantique 1504–1650* (Paris, 1955–59), 2:464.

12. George Rudé, *Paris and London in the Eighteenth Century: Studies in Popular Protest* (New York, 1970), p. 51.

Evidence about criminals is limited but available. Since under-world people seldom left written records, historians must look to other sources. Documents of the city government tell of con-cerns about lawlessness, the Royal Prison, and abandoned child-ren. They also include ordinances on prostitution and lists of people who were licensed to beg. Chronicles describe charity, notable festivals, public executions, epidemics, bread riots, and *autos de fé,* ceremonies during which the Inquisition penanced its victims. Memoirs of prison chaplains and lawyers relate details about the Royal Prison and its inmates, while literature reveals attitudes about underworld people. *Romances germanescas,* traditional ballads that were passed on orally by vagabonds and street people, provide a basis for understanding their vocabulary and concerns. A detailed survey of the poor people of the city, which was made in 1667, explains how they lived and how they were identified. Paintings of the period suggest nuances in the relationship between rich and poor, weak and powerful.[13]

This evidence reveals an underworld that was far more than a colorful fringe group. It shows that they participated in the commerce and military life of the city. It describes them as spectators and actors in the rituals of justice and popular enter-tainments. It suggests a complex relationship with the Church and shows how their presence affected the city's system of charity. It shows that the areas in which criminals and other citizens interacted were community activities that became vehicles for expanding the power of the Crown and city oli-garchy.

The evidence reveals a paradoxical relationship between the underworld and political authority. On the one hand, they were antagonists. Underworld people challenged political authority, and government officials resolved to punish their defiance. On the other hand, they were partners. The underworld helped to legitimize the extension of political power. In misfits, prosti-tutes, criminals, and outcasts, political authority found a ra-tionale for imposing more control on the diversity and violence tolerated in the city. The underworld was a visible symbol of

13. For a more complete discussion of these sources, see below, pp. 262–270.

the opposite of respectability. It was a foil against which the rest of the community identified itself.

The political significance of the underworld directly affected the outcome of social protest movements. The underworld resisted political authority and sometimes defended local traditions against attempts to change them by imposing laws. Although they lacked a clearly stated political program, underworld people were not apolitical; their defiant gesture of thumbing the nose was as much a protest as passing out handbills. Criminals cannot be ignored simply because they do not fit into the usual categories of collective action. Their characteristic and unusual protest suggests another dimension in political power, and it raises another paradox: though underworld people added the strength of numbers to protest movements, they brought with them a fatal weakness. An underworld presence discredited protest movements and helped to consolidate opposition to them. Even as they defied political authority, the poor and the criminals helped to support it.

The following chapters, arranged chronologically, are organized around topics. They begin with a description of city fathers and a criminal subculture in the early sixteenth century. Commercial expansion quickly followed the opening of trade with the New World in 1503, and the next chapter describes the interaction of crime and respectability in commerce. Royal reforms in the 1550's affected both the city's system of justice and the Royal Prison, which are the subjects of Chapters 3 and 4. Because military urgencies became more frequent after 1580, the fifth chapter is concerned with the military and the underworld. By the end of the sixteenth century, the Protestant Reformation and the Counter Reformation had affected both the Church and popular entertainments, which are considered in Chapters 6 and 7. The seventeenth-century economic decline and depopulation of Seville are particularly evident in the city's system of charity and in the lives of the women and children of the streets, and the following three chapters discuss these topics. The last chapter describes epidemics and famines, since the relationship of city government and the underworld must be examined in times of disaster as well as in more peaceful periods. A comparison of two bread riots that became political rebellions in 1521 and 1652 shows that even though the city had changed, the criminal sub-culture still worked to conserve the political order. City govern-ment and street people survived together, mutually distrustful but mutually dependent.

1

City Fathers and Street People

A narrow winding street, the *Calle Sierpes*, led to the heart of early modern Seville. From the town palace of the Duke of Medina Sidonia, *Sierpes* wound past the Royal Prison, which received some 18,000 prisoners each year.[1] Not far from the prison, the street ended at the city hall and the major square of the city, the *Plaza de San Francisco*. Across this plaza and next to the Archbishop's palace stood the Cathedral, the third largest in all Christendom. Here on the steps leading down from the Cathedral merchants gathered to make business deals.

In *los Olmos* and *los Naranjos*, two patios immediately next to the Cathedral, a scruffier group of people congregated. Many were beggars, and a few carried secondhand clothing or fruits and vegetables, which they hawked in the streets. Most had a knife or other weapon; some carried marked cards and loaded dice. Few of these people appeared in a parish register in the city, for they were part of the large floating population that formed the underworld of Seville.

Seville was really two cities. It was the city of an oligarchy that included land-owning nobles, wealthy merchants, and leaders of the Church. It was also the city of an underworld that retained an identity separate from the dominant culture of the city. Any study of crime and society in Seville must begin with a discussion of these two groups.

1. Alonso Morgado, *Historia de Sevilla* (Sevilla, 1587), p. 194.

CITY FATHERS

The Reconquest produced a nobility in Seville which owed its strong position to the Crown. As the Crown of Castile led Christian forces southward against Moslem rulers in the thirteenth century, large areas of land in Andalusia suddenly fell into the hands of the Christians. The Crown awarded these areas intact, replacing the former Moslem overlords with a few Christian nobles and the three religious military orders. Here there was no need to establish settlements of small-holders, for the Moslem rulers were unable to resist the advancing armies of the Christians. The rapid capitulation of the Moslem rulers helped to ensure the continuation of a system of *latifundia,* or vast landholdings, which had persisted in southern Spain since Roman times.

Urban policy of the Crown of Castile during the Reconquest further strengthened the position of nobles loyal to the Crown. When Ferdinand III of Castile (1217–1252) entered Seville in 1248, he found a well-developed city that lacked only Christian overlords to rule in his name. Instead of having to found an outpost and buy its support against the Moslems with guarantees of special local rights, as the Crown had to do earlier in the North, Ferdinand III simply superimposed a Christian hierarchy over Moslem society. Just as Moslem mosques were converted into Christian churches, the urban oligarchy was transformed into a government by Christian nobles. Seville received from the Reconquest a nobility that was urban, loyal to the Crown, and dependent on the Crown for its position of strength.

A city council developed to govern the city. Luís Peraza, who wrote a description of the city's government in the mid-sixteenth century, listed city council members in the order of their importance: the asistente, a Crown-appointed mayor; the *alguacil mayor,* or chief sheriff; six *alcaldes mayores,* who were the head judicial officers; thirty-five *veinticuatros,* similar to senators, originally twenty-four; and fifty-six *jurados,* two representatives from each parish.[2] With the exception of the asistente, who,

2. Luís Peraza, *Justicia de Sevilla; Historia de esta ciudad* (n.p., n.d., ca. 1560), p. 1167.

as noted above, was a noble sent from another region to Seville, all of these positions were filled by local nobles. Before the reign of Philip II, these offices were granted by the Crown in thanks for special services that the nobles had performed. Offices of veinticuatros were usually granted in perpetuity, but the Crown attached certain conditions to other offices. For example, when the Marquis of Alcalá was appointed alcalde mayor in 1538, he complained because the king refused to allow him to assume the office with sword, a privilege that he had granted his predecessor, the Duke of Medina Sidonia.[3]

The wealthiest nobles of Seville lived off income received from leasing their lands. The Duke of Medina Sidonia controlled vast stretches of land and received annual income that was twice the amount of that of the next leading noble, the Marquis of Tarifa. As a large landholder, the Duke had recognized that the Crown's policies of taxation and land use favored his own interests. The Duke of Medina Sidonia put down the local *Comunero* revolt in 1520 and was rewarded by the Crown with additional lands. Later the Duke was commander of the king's army in Andalusia.

Lesser nobles made money through commerce. The noble Enriquez family received a substantial income from the production of soap, and the Espinosa family exported wine and oil. These commercial nobles mixed comfortably with the most prestigious merchant families of Seville, and there was intermarriage between the two groups.[4] Both merchants and commercial nobles used profit from trade to build magnificent palaces, courtyards, and gardens. The "incomparable and rich city of Seville" became world famous, noted for the grandeur and wealth of its merchants and nobles.[5]

Merchants, shippers, artisans, and bankers could be city fathers

3. Guichot y Parody, 2:34–36.

4. The soap industry is discussed in Antonio Domínguez Ortiz, *Orto y ocaso de Sevilla; Estudio sobre la prosperidad y decadencia de la ciudad durante los siglos XVI y XVII* (Sevilla, 1946), p. 19; and Morgado, p. 157. Domínguez Ortiz discussed the nobility and commerce in *Orto*, pp. 49–53. Intermarriage is discussed by Thomás de Mercado, *Summa de tratos y contratos* (Sevilla, 1571), Book II, p. 17.

5. Pedro de Texera, "Discripción de las costas y puertas de España," ca. 1619, BM, Add. 28497.

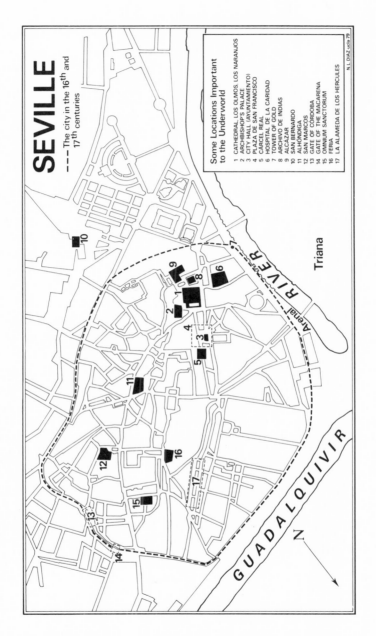

SEVILLE
--- The city in the 16th and 17th centuries

Some Locations Important to the Underworld

1 CATHEDRAL, LOS OLMOS, LOS NARANJOS
2 ARCHBISHOP'S PALACE
3 CITY HALL (AYUNTAMIENTO)
4 PLAZA DE SAN FRANCISCO
5 CARCEL REAL
6 HOSPITAL DE LA CARIDAD
7 TOWER OF GOLD
8 ARCHIVO DE INDIAS
9 ALCAZAR
10 SAN BERNARDO
11 ALHÓNDIGA
12 SAN MARCOS
13 GATE OF CÓRDOBA
14 GATE OF THE MACARENA
15 OMNIUM SANCTORUM
16 FERIA
17 LA ALAMEDA DE LOS HERCULES

N.L. DIAZ ucla 79

Triana

RIVER

Arenal

GUADALQUIVIR

N

2   The City of Seville in the sixteenth and seventeenth centuries. Prepared by Noël Diaz, Staff Cartographer, U.C.L.A.

in Seville, although bankers were usually held in low esteem. Some merchants bought noble status with the purchase of an office from the Crown. Others participated in the *Consulado,* an organization of the merchant families of long standing. Foreign merchants could hold no office, but the Crown granted them the right to have a representative who could protect their interests. They lived in palatial homes and were said to be well educated and wealthy.[6]

For several reasons people were willing to buy offices from the Crown. Some bought them strictly for the noble status that provided tax exemptions and the privilege of carrying arms. Offices were a source of income to other purchasers, such as the sheriffs, who were allowed to keep a percentage of the money or property that they confiscated for debts. Some used the purchase of office to build up their own local positions of power. Juan Gutierrez Tello bought an office from Philip II in the mid-sixteenth century by granting the royal treasury a loan free of interest. By continuing to grant these interest-free loans annually, he received the right to enter the city hall wearing "sword and dagger."[7] The Tello family genealogy emphasized the family's long tradition of holding city offices, but family members were probably as concerned with power positions as with community service.

The least wealthy nobles of Seville guarded their privileges very carefully, particularly tax exemptions. When they needed cash, they mortgaged any land they held and sold off family possessions. An impoverished noble in Quevedo's novel, *El Buscón,* lamented: "The only thing I've got left to sell is my *'don'* [a title of respectability], but my luck's so bad I can't find anyone to buy it."[8] There is reason to believe that some of these nobles were among the mutineers in the Comunero revolt in Seville in 1520. A contemporary reported that the Comunero rebels of

6. Peraza, pp. 1173–74. Bankers are discussed in Domínguez Ortiz, *Orto,* p. 38.

7. Luís Fernandaz Melgarejo, Discurso genealógico de la nobilissima y antigua casa de los Tellos de Sevilla, 1660, BC, 84-3-42.

8. Francisco de Quevedo Villegas, *Quevedo; The Choice Humorous and Satirical Works,* trans. Sir Roger L'Estrange and others (London, n.d.), p. 149.

Seville were city residents who most resented the rising fortunes of local Conversos.[9]

Noble families with dwindling estates often purchased clerical positions for younger sons. In sixteenth-century Seville there were two hundred chapels with positions for fifty-seven chaplains, as well as 3500 chapels and 611 simple benefices within the diocese of the Archbishopric.[10] These positions usually guaranteed an annual income.

A few churchmen received very large incomes from their clerical offices. A canon in the Cathedral of Seville received an annual income of 300 ducats in the beginning of the sixteenth century; by the end of the century this had grown to 2000 ducats. (Appendix I gives the comparative value of Spanish coins in this period.) At the beginning of the sixteenth century the Archbishop of Seville had an annual income of 24,000 ducats, which had grown to 80,000 by the end of the century.[11] The Archbishop's income gave him the appearance of considerable power, even though the money was always at the disposition of the needy.

Although churchmen rarely held secular offices in Seville, they can be considered city fathers. The Archbishop was a principal symbol of authority, and secular parish priests were often influential leaders in their neighborhoods. Monks who were preachers helped to form public opinion. The Monastery of San Pablo in the mid-sixteenth century was an order of preachers and contained eighty monks who were described as "very learned."[12] The Jesuits, who came to Seville in the early 1550's, founded a house and a school with the help of a rich relative of one of the members. They were tireless missionaries within the city, preaching on the streets and in the brothels, visiting prisoners, educating young boys, and training actors to dramatize religious stories.[13]

9. Anonymous, *Discurso de las Comunidad de Sevilla año 1520 q'escrivió un clérigo apassionado de la casa de Niebla* (Sevilla, 1881).

10. Antonio Domínguez Ortiz, *La Sociedad española en el siglo XVII*, Vol. 2, *El Estamento eclesiástico* (Madrid, 1970), pp. 60–61.

11. Domínguez Ortiz, *Orto,* pp. 54–55.

12. Peraza, p. 40.

13. Ortiz de Zuñiga, p. 512.

These civic leaders did not always agree with one another, and the rivalry between the noble families of Guzmán and Ponce flared openly in the Comunero revolt of 1520. Juan de Figueroa of the Ponce family led the mutiny in Seville. For a time he and his followers held the *Alcázar,* a Moorish palace that had become a stronghold in the city. The Duke of Medina Sidonia, a member of the Guzmán family, quickly rallied his own men, however, and those of other local nobles who were eager to prove their loyalty to the new king, Charles I. The Duke of Arcos sided with the loyalists, even though he was the brother of Juan de Figueroa and a long-time rival of the Duke of Medina Sidonia. The rebels were routed, and both the Duke of Medina Sidonia and the Duke of Arcos rode out to welcome Charles I and assure him of the city's loyalty when he visited the city some months later.

Other rivalries split the city oligarchy. Nobles with waning fortunes especially resented the growing wealth of merchants and bankers. Jesuits and Dominicans clashed over the proper preparation for death of a condemned man in the city's Royal Prison. Priests accused one another of heresies. Churchmen who were officers of the Inquisition in Seville challenged the jurisdiction of some secular officers. Justices of the *audiencia,* a court of Crown-appointed magistrates from outside Seville, feuded with the local nobles who were members of the city council.

Despite their many differences, city fathers considered themselves collectively as the governors of Seville. They agreed upon the traditional bases for this government: the *fueros* (rights) granted by the Crown of Castile in the thirteenth century, the code of law compiled under Alfonso X (1252–1284), the royal ordinances of successive Crowns of Castile, pronouncements of the Church, and regulations adopted by the city council. They agreed upon the traditional mechanisms for making policy through the Crown, Church, and city government. To preserve this system, they would look for some common ground when they disagreed; often this common ground was an alliance against an enemy, such as the vagabonds and people of "low life" in the city.

THE UNDERWORLD

Contemporaries commonly associated *la gente de mal vivir,* or underworld people, with particular occupations. Though frequently traveling actors, minstrels, puppeteers, palm-readers, and beggars, they were also slaughterhouse workers, soldiers, and sailors. City residents looked upon boatmen as potential criminals, for they knew that many underworld people were galley slaves and smugglers, using ships on the Guadalquivir River to enter and leave the city illegally.[14] Although these occupations were closely associated with the underworld, not all of those who followed them joined the criminal subculture. Prostitution, for example, was a common occupation in the underworld, but the well-dressed courtesan kept in luxury by a wealthy man belonged to another social group.

The underworld should not be confused with the poor of the city, for many poor citizens kept a marginal place in respectable society. Furthermore, to group the underworld in one class is to ignore the variety of its members. In Seville the underworld included defrocked churchmen, impoverished nobles, discharged soldiers, and hustling retailers, as well as beggars and unemployed day-laborers. Moreover, underworld people who got some

14. For general references to occupations and the underworld, see Antonio Ballesteros, *Sevilla en el Siglo XIII* (Madrid, 1913), pp. 191–193; Domínquez Ortiz, *Orto,* pp. 69–71. Specific references to slaughterhouse workers are in Juan de M. Carriazo, "Negros, esclavos y extranjeros en el barrio sevillano de San Bernardo (1617–1629)," *Archivo Hispalense,* Series 2, 20 (1954), 124; and Miguel de Cervantes Saavedra, "The Dogs' Colloquy," *Exemplary Stories,* trans. C. A. Jones (Middlesex, 1972), pp. 197–198. An example of city complaints about visiting soldiers is in Guichot y Parody, 2:117. A Captain's complaints about the treatment of his soldiers by city ruffians is in AMS, Siglo XVII, Sección 4, Escribanías de Cabildo, Tomo 16, No. 20. Galley slaves and crime are discussed in I. A. A. Thompson, "A Map of Crime in Sixteenth-Century Spain," *Economic History Review,* Series 2, 21 (1968), 244–267. The tough reputation of boatmen is reported in Tomás de la Torre, "Traveling in 1544 from Salamanca, Spain, to Ciudad Real, Chiapas, Mexico; The Travels and Trials of Bishop Bartolomé de las Casas and His Dominican Fathers," ed. and trans. Frans Blom in *Sewanee Review,* 81 (1972), 461.

money did not automatically use it to buy respectability. Innkeepers used theirs to buy stolen goods, and gamblers threw down large sums of money on the gaming tables. Many people in the underworld were very poor, but poverty is not a defining characteristic.

Another approach is to categorize inhabitants of the underworld as outlaws, not only because they engaged in criminal behavior, but also because they often were born, mated, procreated, and sometimes even died unrecognized and unregistered by the law.[15] One problem with this definition is that it fails to distinguish the underworld from gypsies, slaves, and Moriscos, who were also outlaws in early modern Seville but not necessarily part of the underworld. Gypsies lived in Triana, the suburb across the river from Seville, but there are no reports that they mingled with underworld people there. They were under special royal prohibitions, and they seemed to maintain their own distinctive culture, which further separated them from other people in the city.

Slaves, on the other hand, figured in several complaints about crime and the underworld. According to a sixteenth-century ecclesiastical census, slaves numbered 6327, in a total city population of 85,538.[16] A 1569 city ordinance prohibited any innkeeper from giving food and drink to slaves because so many got into trouble in the inns and began committing crimes.[17] Many slaves lived apart from their masters, and they usually lived in the parish of San Bernardo or Triana, neighborhoods also frequented by underworld people. Masters of incorrigible slaves frequently sent them to a workshop that produced items made from esparto grass. This workshop gained a reputation for being tough and was the scene of a murder committed by a mulatto in 1615.[18]

15. Louis Chevalier, *Laboring Classes and Dangerous Classes in Paris during the First Half of the Nineteenth Century*, trans. Frank Jellinek (New York, 1973), p. 310.

16. Ruth Pike, "Sevillian Society in the Sixteenth Century: Slaves and Freedmen," *Hispanic American Historical Review*, 47 (1967), 345.

17. Manuel Chaves, *Cosas nuevas y viejas (Apuntes sevillanos)* (Sevilla, 1904), pp. 37–38. For a broader discussion of slaves, see Pike, esp. p. 344.

18. Pedro de León, Compendio de algunas experiencias en los ministerios de que vsa la Comp^a de IESVS con q practicamente se muestra con algunos acaecimientos y documentos el buen acierto en ellos (Granada, 1619), Biblioteca Universitaria de Granada, Appendix 1 to Part II, Case 294.

Slaves were both white and black. One contemporary reported, "There is an infinite number of Negroes from all parts of Ethiopia and Guinea," brought to Seville from Portugal.[19] However, many slaves were white Moors or Moriscos, usually captured during war with the Turks. Most of them worked to earn money that could buy their freedom. At the beginning of the seventeenth century, a male slave was worth 100 ducats, a female slave, 50 ducats. Some masters granted freedom to their slaves, and these people either tried to return to their homelands or stayed in their own settlements within Seville.[20]

Free Moriscos in Seville often worked as carters, muleteers, and street vendors. After a Morisco uprising in the Sierra Bermeja near Granada in 1568, Philip II ordered their dispersal throughout Castile. More than 4000 were sent to Seville, where nervous city fathers imposed severe restrictions on them. Forbidden to live together or gather in city inns, they nonetheless formed little neighborhoods, particularly in San Marcos, a parish famous as the center of smugglers and fences.[21] Always suspected of being more loyal to the Turks than to the Christian masters who had forcibly baptized them, Moriscos were formally expelled from Spain in 1609. The royal decree of expulsion not only accused them of endangering the state, but also asserted that they had committed many murders and robberies against "old Christians."[22] Moriscos were often prosecuted for crimes in Seville, but this may reflect religious persecution as much as a genuine participation in a city underworld.

Too vague to distinguish underworld people, the term "outlaw" as a definition has other limitations. It implies that all other inhabitants of the city behaved legally, but studies have shown that illegal behavior was common in all parts of society in early

19. Peraza, p. 1175.

20. Domínguez Ortiz, *Orto*, p. 64.

21. For excellent discussions of *Moriscos* in Seville, see Domínguez Ortiz, *Orto*, pp. 57–58; Carriazo, p. 127; Celestino Lopez Martínez, *Mudéjares y moriscos sevillanos* (Sevilla, 1935), pp. 53–54, 58–59; and Ruth Pike, *Aristocrats and Traders; Sevillian Society in the Sixteenth Century* (Ithaca and London, 1972), pp. 154–155.

22. AMS, Siglo XVII, Sección 4, Escribanías de Cabildo, Tomo 23, No. 35.

modern Spain.[23] Furthermore, restricting the underworld to criminals presents a distorted picture, for information about criminals is usually obtained from judicial documents concerned only with the failures who had been caught.[24]

A better approach is to define the underworld as a subculture within the city. It grew up in a context of rapid urban development. It was spawned in congestion, commercial activity, and anonymity. As an alternative culture that spilled over from city to city, the underworld offered one solution to the social dislocations of rapid urbanization. Seville's population grew very rapidly in the sixteenth century. Figure 3 presents two estimates of population growth. The figures of Domínguez Ortiz are higher than those of Carande Thobar because Domínguez Ortiz includes an estimate of a floating population that represents the underworld and other people not appearing in official registers.

A parish census of 1588 indicates that population density grew unevenly among the parishes (see Appendix II). Even though these statistics may not include the underworld, they suggest that this subculture developed in a city in which population growth outstripped most housing and social services. Most reports on underworld activity come from the parishes of San Marcos, San Gil, and San Bernardo, as well as the Cathedral, the port, and Triana.

As an urban subculture, the underworld can be distinguished from banditry, which was a rural activity. Banditry has been characterized as a conservative reaction against the attempts of authorities to displace with a new order the traditional and popularly accepted concept of justice.[25] The social bandit makes a

23. For example, see José Deleito y Piñuela, *La mala vida en la España de Felipe IV* (Madrid, 1959), pp. 50–54; and Carlos Caro Petit, "La Cárcel Real de Sevilla," *Archivo Hispalense*, Series 2, 12 (1949), 41.

24. Porphyre Petrovitch (a pseudonymn for a group of historians), "Recherches sur la criminalité à Paris dans la seconde moitié du XVIIIe siècle," in A. Abbiateci and others, *Crimes et criminalité en France sous l'Ancien Régime 17e–18e siècles* (Paris, 1971), p. 261, discusses this problem.

25. E. J. Hobsbawm, *Social Bandits and Primitive Rebels: Studies in Archaic Forms of Social Movement in the Nineteenth and Twentieth Centuries* (Glencoe, Ill., 1959); José Antonio Gomez Marín, *Bandolerismo, santidad, y otras temas españoles* (Madrid, 1972), pp. 10, 25–26.

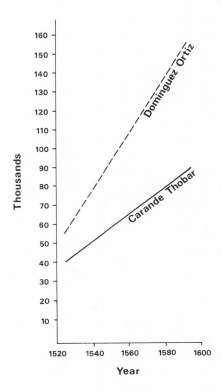

3 Two estimates of population growth in sixteenth-century Seville. According to Ramón Carande Thobar, *Carlos V y sus banqueros; La vida económica en Castilla 1516–1556,* Madrid, 1943; and Antonio Domínguez Ortiz, *The Golden Age of Spain, 1516–1659,* London, 1971.

gesture of defiance against the rich and is helped by the sympathetic or fearful poor of the countryside to escape the authorities. In the city, underworld people also defied the authorities, but their gestures of defiance were most commonly a deliberate violation of a commercial regulation. Francisco de Ariño, who wrote a chronicle of Seville in the late sixteenth century, described how one wily woman resold meat after she had colored it on the outside. The city's asistente had her arrested, sentenced her to 200 lashes, and drove her through the streets. "Her shrieks were terrific, and all the distributors of cargo remained wary, and their friends returned to advise them to watch out because they would not be able to help them."[26]

Police could be more effective in the city than in the countryside, as this anecdote shows. Even though fugitives could disappear into crowds and the mazes of narrow streets, the confines of the city helped to concentrate police power. Moreover, police had the support of city residents who objected less to the onerous retail regulations than to being cheated by meat retailers or having to compete with them. The anecdote told by Ariño suggests that underworld people would find help not so much in an appeal to the people against the authorities as in their own underground network of warnings.

The underworld was also distinguished by antisocial livelihoods. Opportunities for making a living in Seville were restricted because the city's guilds limited the numbers of people who could become skilled laborers or artisans. They also denied membership to Jews, Moriscos, and slaves. The merchant guilds were more powerful than all other guilds of the city, and trade rather than industry dominated the local economy. To the man with no money and no training, commerce offered few jobs; he could be a sailor, teamster, hawker, messenger, or domestic servant—jobs which could easily be combined with criminal activity.

Some rather large industries employed thousands of people in the city, but there is little evidence that underworld people worked in the city's workshops and factories producing soap,

26. Francisco de Ariño, *Sucesos de Sevilla de 1592 á 1604 recojidos de Francisco de Ariño, vecino de la ciudad en el barrio de Triana* (Sevilla, 1873), p. 57.

pottery, silk, and gunpowder. Long working hours in a factory may have used up the time and energy that could otherwise be spent in endeavor outside the law. Perhaps there was a more basic incompatibility in outlook between the man who would work in a pottery factory and the man who loved to gamble. An underworld conservatism seemed willing to exploit the traditional forms of commercial trickery, but unwilling to adapt to industrial production. Performing routine, monotonous tasks in a confined factory might provide a salary, but it would also reduce to a passive machine the man who delighted in living by his wits, outsmarting others in a good deal, and risking huge stakes.

People of the underworld favored three classes of activity that could be combined with crime. First, they employed a variety of retail ruses. Some specialized in quickly reselling stolen property, and others bought products like vinegar, oil, wine, sugar, honey, and wax which they adulterated and resold. One clever retailer sold to a noble a piece of a ewe which he disguised as a quarter of beef by sewing testicles on it. Unfortunately for the retailer, the noble's cook had sharper eyes than his master; the rascal was caught, whipped, and banished from the city.[27]

A second major underworld livelihood was begging. Many masqueraded as cripples or religious hermits, and it was difficult for city residents to distinguish them from the monks who begged alms for genuinely charitable purposes, such as support for the poor in prison. The city council finally decided in 1597 that they would have to examine and license each person who wanted to beg in Seville. They warned able-bodied beggars to get a job or leave town, and they threatened a whipping to anyone caught begging without a license.[28]

27. Secondhand clothing dealers are discussed in Ruth Pike, *Enterprise and Adventure: The Genoese in Seville and the Opening of the New World* (Ithaca, 1966), p. 23. Guichot y Parody, II, p. 156, suggests that innkeepers tried to corner the market on game and fish. The ewe-selling meat-retailer is described in Ariño, pp. 50–51.

28. Ariño, p. 47. A description of masquerades used by false beggars in Lyon is discussed by Natalie Zemon Davis, "Poor Relief, Humanism, and Heresy: The Case of Lyon," chapter 2 in *Society and Culture in Early Modern France: Eight Essays* (Stanford, 1975), also *Studies in Medieval and Renaissance History*, 45 (1968), 226–227. See below, pp. 163–189, for more discussion of beggars and vagabonds.

The many forms of entertainment were a third major livelihood of the underworld. Gambling was a favored occupation,
and prostitution brought money to both men and women. Many
underworld people performed as singers, dancers and actors,
professions that were commonly associated with theft and loose
women. City residents delighted in street satires, even while
suspecting actors of immoral and criminal behavior. They sought
out underworld people who could read palms, tell fortunes, and
sell potions and poisons.

Although the underworld can be considered antisocial, it had a
distinct sense of justice and honor that is evident in *romances
germanescas,* the folk poetry that had been transmitted orally in
Spain by street people and vagabonds. One poem describes a
young student, Pantoja, "very brave and inspired."[29] Dying from
a wound, he beckoned his friends to come close so he could tell
them his life story. He had left his "noble parents in their respected estate" when he was only seventeen years old. Once after
wounding a sheriff and a scribe in a knife fight and fighting with
another man over a "woman of style," he quickly enlisted in the
army. "Many wanted me, that is certain." He left the army in
another scuffle and survived five wounds, finally ariving in
Seville, "the abridged map for good and evil." There he kept
company with the most prestigious nobles until he killed a man
in a fight over another "woman of style." Thrown into prison
after informers had betrayed him to a city magistrate, Pantoja
found the prisoners divided between friends of the man he had
killed and people willing to side with him. He wrote to the Duke
of Arcos from prison, and finally got his freedom "through the
love of the Duchess." Pantoja promptly left prison and found
one of the informers who had betrayed him. "I killed him eating
supper in his house." Fleeing to Portugal, he was caught up in
another rivalry. "We both took out our knives; mine found its
mark first, and his after he had fallen. He fell dead in the sand
and I fell into a boat."

Pantoja's highest values were survival and personal honor. He
used violence and flight to survive, and he defended his honor

29. This poem is reprinted in John Hill, *Poesías Germanescas* (Bloomington, 1945), pp. 207–209.

with bravado and vengeance. He regarded women as objects to fight over or use for his own purposes. Other men were rivals, traitors, or people he could use. Pantoja's world was full of conflict, and he had no vision of a better world nor hope to improve this one. His fatalism is evident throughout the poem, for he knows that his end has come, that he is dying. He tells of seeking asylum in "the Church that has never failed me," but his listeners know that neither God nor Church can work a miracle now.

It is true that a similar attitude pervaded other groups in the city. It is also true that there were some loners in the underworld who shared no sense of honor with anyone. Nevertheless, it is possible to identify the underworld with a fatalistic world view, a code of ethics based on personal honor and survival, a concept of justice in which the weak are exploited by the strong and the crafty.

Although survival and honor suggest individualism, the underworld was not simply a collection of individuals; it was also a social organization with prescribed roles, an established hierarchy, and some social control over its members. One contemporary described it as a "religious fraternity."[30] Cervantes discussed underworld organization in his story of two boys, "Rinconete and Cortadillo."[31] These two young ruffians had drifted into Seville. Assuming that "stealing was a free trade," they quickly found that they had entered a very tightly controlled guild led by the fatherly Mr. Monipodio. This organization offered the boys some advantages in protection from the law and tips on good opportunities within the city. In return, the boys were expected to share their "earnings" with the organization and to report their activities to Monipodio. Citizens who had an old score to settle with an enemy contacted Monipodio to carry out a beating or vandalize a house. He kept a notebook listing each job, the person who got the assignment, and the payment received for it.

Monipodio granted the boys full membership in the organiza-

30. Vicente Espinel, quoted in Francisco Rodríguez Marín, critical edition of *Rinconete y Cortadillo* by Miguel de Cervantes Saavedra (Madrid, 1920), p. 73.

31. Cervantes, "Rinconete and Cortadillo," *Exemplary Stories*.

tion without the customary year of probation. This was a considerable privilege, since it meant that they would not have to pay half the proceeds of their first theft, nor do menial jobs all that year. They could drink wine without water in it and have a party whenever they wished without asking permission. Best of all, they could have a share right away in the winnings of the senior members of the brotherhood.

As he received the two boys into his organization, Monipodio gave them new names; Rincón became Rinconete, and Cortado became Cortadillo. He specified their occupations: "Rinconete, card sharper; Cortadillo, pickpocket." He also assigned definite territories to the new members, for "it's only right and proper that no one should encroach on someone else's territory." The two boys "kissed his hand for the kindnesses done to them, and promised him to carry out their duty faithfully and well, with all diligence and caution." In turn, Monipodio embraced them and gave them his blessing. The boys were reminded to return on Sunday when Monipodio would give them "an important lecture on matters concerning their craft."

Monipodio's organization is fictional, and Cervantes' motives in writing this story must be examined. Undoubtedly he wanted to delight his public as well as to describe in loving irony a society that he had known on the streets and in the Royal Prison of Seville. The many details he included and the evidence of criminal organization he amassed suggests that he was consciously trying to make a point about it. His story satirized a society in which each person had his role and his territory secure so long as he did not question the people above him who took a share of his earnings.

Other contemporary accounts corroborate the existence of underworld organization. Luís Zapata wrote in the late sixteenth century of a society of thieves in Seville. Its chief was called the "prior," a term often given to the head of a monastery, and other officers were "consuls," ordinarily titles for government representatives. Members of this society deposited their loot in a chest that was locked with three keys. There is also evidence that some prostitutes were organized in houses under the direction of bogus "abbesses." Another account reports that "hot" fugitives often accepted the role of servant to other underworld characters in return for some protection.[32] Organization must have been essential to the survival of an underworld character in a city swarming with other underworld people who were also trying to evade city regulations and city police.

The underworld not only worked together; it played together in distinctive forms of amusement that are another defining characteristic. Underworld people shared with other social groups in the city some amusements, such as gambling and street plays. Working class people undoubtedly enjoyed the Sunday gang fights at the gates of the city walls as much as the underworld. A Jesuit who worked among the poor people of the city from 1578 until 1616 described the people sitting on the city walls, lustily cheering their favorite gangs.[33] Bullfights in this period were still monopolized by the nobility, but underworld people joined other commoners in the city as eager spectators.

Underworld people might also enjoy drama in a theater. They could gather as noisy groups on nearby rooftops to watch the plays in the city's roofless theater, or they could sneak or strong-arm their way into the theater. Seville was notorious for the numbers of people who entered the theater without paying, sometimes provoking brawls and stabbings at the entrance.[34]

More exclusively an underworld amusement were the games that prisoners played among themselves in the Royal Prison. Pedro de León observed some of these when he was chaplain in the Royal Prison. He described a few, such as *la culebra* (the snake), in which prisoners walked about with a whip after lights were out and snapped it here and there among the other prisoners as a snake. In *la mariposa* (the butterfly), prisoners placed a thin stick between the fingers or toes of a sleeping prisoner,

32. Luís Zapata is quoted in Deleito y Piñeula, *Mala vida,* p. 197. Guichot y Parody, 1:375–377, discusses houses of prostitution. Underworld servants are discussed in Quevedo, p. 135, and note in appendix on p. 402.

33. Antonio Domíngues Ortiz, "Vida y obras del Padre de León," *Archivo Hispalense,* Series 2, 26–27 (1957), 165–166. For a theory that gang wars in nineteenth-century Paris were descendants of journeymen's violence in the countryside, see Chevalier, pp. 420–433.

34. Hugo Albert Rennert, *The Spanish Stage in the Time of Lope de Vega* (New York, 1963), pp. 51, 124–126, 281.

lighted it, and then let it burn down to waken the sleeping man.[35] Humor was cruel in underworld games, and laughter was usually cynical.

The prisoners' names for their games suggest another defining characteristic of the underworld: a distinctive vocabulary. In Cervantes' story, Rinconete and Cortadillo quickly learned the argot as they were initiated into the underworld. The basket boy who took them to Monipodio explained some of his terms: "a *cuatrero* [one who does something with a *cuatro,* a slang word for horse] is a horse-thief; *ansia* [anxiety] is a torture; *roznos* [small donkeys] are asses, speaking with respect; *primer disconcierto* [first discomfort] is the first twist of the rope."[36]

The nineteenth-century Spanish criminologist Rafael Salillas studied underworld vocabulary as an index to the physiognomy, psychology, and sociology of the underworld.[37] Using the vocabularies of picaresque literature and romances germanescas, Salillas speculated on the origins of specific words. He found 108 names that distinguished various kinds of thieves, and he listed a whole series of thieves' auxiliaries who had definite titles denoting prescribed roles. For example, the *levedor* (one who raises or weighs anchor) carried the loot stolen by the thief; the *polidor* (one with many qualities or interests) sold stolen goods; and the *garitero* (gambler, master of gambling den) provided shelter for thieves.[38] These titles suggest not only a vocabulary characteristic of the underworld, but also a well-defined organization based on a division of labor.

Underworld jargon assumed many forms in the different cities of Spain. One form juxtaposed letters of the alphabet, altering the initial consonants of syllables or changing the places of these letters to make them read from right to left. Other forms postponed letters or placed them before words in order to make them difficult to understand. A common form in seventeenth-century Spain simply "frenchified" words by dropping

35. Pedro de León, Part II.

36. Cervantes, "Rinconete," pp. 95–96.

37. Rafael Salillas, *El delincuente español; El lenguaje (estudio, filológico y sociológico) con dos vocabularios jergales* (Madrid, 1896).

38. Ibid., pp. 103, 126–127.

the last syllable of each word and speaking very rapidly.[39]
Underworld people often combined the specific words of their
vocabulary into characteristic metaphors. The rascal Guzmán de
Alfarache of Alemán's novel described the Royal Prison of Seville
in the following terms:

a fire that consumes everything, converting it into its own
substance
a windmill
child's play
a miller or grindstone
a toy
a nursery that sometimes deals with murderers and highwaymen
a paradise of fools
a tardy repentance
a short inferno, long death
a port of sighs
a valley of tears
a house of crazy people in which each one cries and is concerned only with his own madness.[40]

Guzmán's metaphors imply violence (fire, grindstone), rural as-
sociations (as the windmill, miller), childhood concerns (child's
play, toy, nursery), religion (paradise, repentance, inferno), and
unhappiness (sighs, tears, madness). These metaphors were written by a picaresque novelist, and they may be more colorful
than ordinary underworld speech. Nevertheless, their implica-
tions of violence, religion, and unhappiness echo the metaphors
that Pantoja used to tell the story of his life.

Underworld language reveals a cynical humor in its word sub-
stitutions. In addition to Guzmán's metaphors, underworld people referred to the prison as *madrastra*, or stepmother. Pimps
were called *padres*; procuresses were *madres*. One word, *coto*,
referred to both a cemetery and a hospital. *Corredor* referred
either to the person in charge of coordinating a theft or to a
minor officer of justice. Salillas suggests that these officers may
have been so described because they worked together to prosecute

39. Rodríguez Marín, *Miscelánea*, pp. 78–80.
40. Mateo Alemán, *Guzmán de Alfarache* (Strasburgo, 1699), Part III,
p. 394.

prisoners, but underworld people may have seen a closer parallel between their own coordinators of theft and lesser city officials.[41]

The underworld was a fluid subculture. Although these people could be distinguished from the dominant culture of the city by vocabulary, social attitude, economic activities, social organization, ideology, and amusements, their world was not an isolated enclave. People were constantly moving from one place to another as drifters, emigrants, and soldiers. They also moved in and out of respectable society. In commerce, military life, religion, popular entertainments, the judicial system, and charity, the underworld and the city's dominant culture met and mingled. The margin between criminality and respectability continually shifted. Rather than a distinct line, there was a marginal area that included activities like street-hawking, military service, begging, and prostitution. The underworld was a parallel culture running through all classes, actively participating in the life of the city.

41. Salillas, pp. 126–127, 172, 174.

2

Merchants and Street Hawkers

EVILLE had been at the center of a regional market for hundreds of years, but in the sixteenth century the city became a world commercial center. With the opening of trade with the New World, business was so good that hundreds of people came to Seville to share in its fortunes. One of *las Gradas*, the steps of the Cathedral where merchants closed business deals, was reputed to be worth more than "the entire world."[1]

Before the end of the century, this open and highly visible commercial center on the Cathedral steps was replaced by proud new buildings: the *Lonja* (businessmen's exchange), the *Casa de Contratación* (board of trade), and the *Casa de Moneda* (mint). Much of the city's commerce remained in the streets and plazas, but another part reached far beyond las Gradas to the markets of the New World.

Commercial expansion affected people from all classes in Seville, and it increased tensions between those who made fortunes and those who did not. A commercial ethic and a growing number of regulations accompanied the development of trade. Crimes were defined differently within this developing commercial order, and boundaries changed for the commercial activities in which both underworld and respectable citizens participated.

1. Alonso Sanchez Gordillo, "Recopilacion de las cosas seculares de Sevilla," Memorial de historia eclesiástica de la ciudad de Sevilla, BC., 82-6-19, 1612, folios 20-20ᵛ. Also, see the prologue by Antonio María Fabié in Ariño, p. xxvi.

PEOPLE OF COMMERCE

The rapid growth of trade with the New World in the sixteenth century required many more merchants, shippers, and bankers in the city. Trade continued to be dominated by the Consulado, a corporation of the wealthiest merchant families in Seville, but it also opened to others. Attracted by the wealth of the trade with the New World, merchants and shippers flocked to Seville from northern Spain and Italy. Artisans and less skilled workers came from France and Portugal. The Consulado tried to preserve its commercial monopoly, but it could not prevent the influx of outsiders. Some, like Claudio Irunza and Juan Antonio Corzo Vicentelo de Leca, became very wealthy. So many outsiders arrived in Seville to seek their fortunes that the city became known as "the mother of foreigners."[2]

Bankers assumed new significance as Seville's commerce extended to many parts of the world. Merchants needed a banking system that had international connections. The greater distances and larger cargoes involved in trade with the New World required a substantial credit system that could make longer-term loans. Since Spain used no paper money at this time, merchants turned to bankers for letters of credit and bills of exchange to replace increasingly cumbersome metallic coins. The factors of time and geography increased the need for a reliable credit system and credit ethic, but at the same time they increased the opportunities for fraud. People of the underworld who had some education specialized in forging letters of credit. Merchants and bankers hesitated to expose these frauds because the mere acknowledgment that they had been fooled could bring down their entire credit structure.[3]

Foreigners or Conversos usually provided banking services, for banking was stigmatized as a form of usury in this period. The Genoese and the Fugger family of Germany were bankers for sixteenth-century Seville, but their participation waned with

2. Peraza, pp. 1173–74. Sanchez Gordillo, folio 23^V. Domínguez Ortiz, *Golden Age*, pp. 140–41. Domínguez Ortiz, *Orto*, p. 47.

3. See the commercial frauds described by Pedro de León, Part II, chapter 25, folios 193–197.

the bankruptcies declared by the government of Philip II. By 1595 so few bankers were available in Seville that the Espinosa family was named to provide public banking even though it had been previously involved in a counterfeiting case and was primarily interested in exporting to the New World the oil and wine produced on its estates. This bank failed in 1601, and merchants of the city had to report in 1616 that the money owed for an export tax was not available, nor could it be gathered together in a year. Portuguese Converso bankers had participated in the city's commerce, but they fell victim to the Inquisition after 1640. No longer protected by the Count-Duke of Olivares or any other royal minister who understood their importance to financing the military requirements of the Crown, their banking services in Seville declined abruptly.[4]

The numbers of people involved in shipping increased rapidly in the sixteenth century. Figures 4 and 5 show that both the numbers of ships and the value of shipping grew very rapidly when trade with the New World increased. Seville never became a center for ship building, probably because the province lacked the necessary wood, but the port employed thousands to maintain and repair ships. Trained ships' pilots were in great demand— so scarce were they in fact that shipowners called for them throughout Seville and the nearby towns. Unable to find enough, they got permission to use unlicensed pilots and hoped that convoys would solve the problem of untrained pilots as well as that of marauders.[5]

As the threat from French and English corsairs grew, the armaments industry also employed many people to manufacture the explosives and arms that could help protect the ships sailing to New Spain. The loss of a fleet between Spain and the New World would disrupt the entire life of the city. Commercial houses suspended payment, rich men declared bankruptcy, the wealthy reduced their charity and style of living, everyone had less money

4. Antonio Domínquez Ortiz and Francisco Aguilar Piñal, *El Barroco y la Ilustracion; Historia de Sevilla*, Vol. 4 (Sevilla, 1976), pp. 73–74. Kamen, p. 220.

5. Luís Navarro García, "Pilotos, maestres y señores de naos en la Carrera de las Indias," *Archivo Hispalense*, Series 2, 46–47 (1967), 275–276.

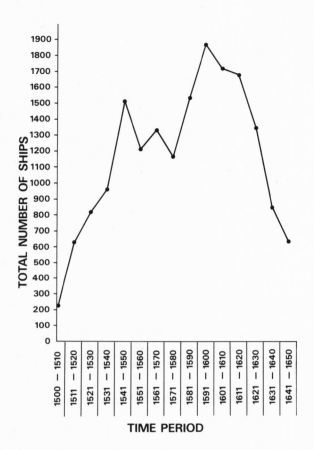

4   Total number of ships in Spain–New World routes, by decade, 1500–
1650. Based on Pierre Chaunu and Huguette Chaunu, *Seville et l'Atlantique 1504–1650,* Paris, 1955–59, Vol. 6, pp. 160–167.

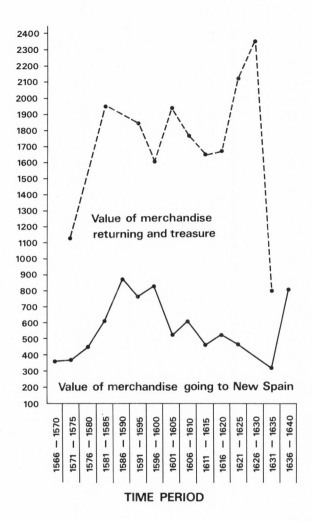

5 Estimated value of shipping between Spain and New Spain, 1566–1640.
Based on Pierre Chaunu and Huguette Chaunu, *Seville et l'Atlantique
1504–1650,* Paris, 1955–59, Vol. 6, p. 468.

for purchases, and churches filled with people seeking asylum from imprisonment for debt. To protect their fleets from the weather and marauders, merchants and shipowners agreed to sail in convoys with smaller military ships. The cost of defense was raised by an export tax (*avería*) that grew from 1.7 percent in 1585 to 8 percent in 1591.[6]

Defense was also needed on land, for the precious metals entering Seville from the New World tempted a variety of thieves. Some infiltrated the mint where the silver was stamped into coins, and others attacked armed land convoys taking the coins into interior Spain.[7] The wealthy silk and silver quarter of the city had its own set of guards and a gate that was locked each night, defenses that helped to prevent theft by outsiders but were ineffective against inside jobs. A silver dealer who needed money in 1581 killed the servant of another silver dealer and stole the gold he was carrying. The guards and gate of the quarter had not prevented the crime, but they helped to expose it, for the murderer had to get the body of his victim past the gate. He put it into a sack and told the guard that it was to be thrown on the rubbish heap outside the city walls. The guard, suspicious of such heavy rubbish, looked inside the sack and called the city sheriffs.[8]

The convoy system used in trade with the New World led to moments of sudden frantic commercial activity followed by long periods of inactivity. The simple task of providing a ship with the biscuit needed for its voyage became gigantic when a whole fleet of ships had to be provided in time for the annual crossing. One study estimated that the ovens of Seville had to work constantly for four months to produce all the biscuit needed for a fleet going to the New World. When the fleet could not wait four months for provisions, shipowners got part of their biscuit supply from

6. Antonio Domínguez Ortiz, "Una relación de la pérdida de la Armada de don Juan de Hoyos," *Archivo Hispalense* (1967), 299–307. Lynch, 1:157, 165–66.

7. AMS, Papeles del Conde de Aguila, Efemérides, Cuadro 2. AMS, Siglo XVII, Sección 4, Escribanías de Cabildo, Tomo 23, No. 9.

8. Pedro de León, appendix 1 to Part II, Case 60.

Cadiz and El Puerto.[9] The irregularity of bursts of intense activity followed by long interludes of inactivity hardly promoted a middle-class ethic of steady, honest work. Many laborers in Seville were underemployed or unemployed during slack periods, and many were caught up in the feverish work of active periods.

City officials noted another problem in provisioning fleets. In 1579 they asked the king to order ships to get their provisions in Malaga rather than Seville. "Because this city is so large and there is usually in it a great crowd of people, natives and foreigners, and they get here provisions for the commercial ships that enter and leave, and since the bread is almost all transported from the surrounding areas, it has been seen through experience, that after they have gotten their provisions here, they have raised very much the price of wheat, even though the harvests are plentiful." This price increase, they wrote, was "an obvious injury, especially to the poor, also to the landowners."[10]

When a fleet arrived in Seville carrying millions of silver bars from New Spain or Peru, the mint came under intense pressure to convert the silver into money very quickly. One result was that money was often printed in large denominations, and this led to a shortage of the smaller coins and a depreciation of money. Seville's mint enjoyed a near monopoly on converting the silver because merchants were reluctant to pay to transport the silver to other mints. They were also impatient with any delays in converting the silver to money and preferred to have it laboriously stamped by hand in the Sevillian mint than to wait for it be stamped by the more efficient water mill or horse-turned mill in the mint of Segovia. Counterfeiters obviously favored the Sevillian mint because it was easier to counterfeit hand-printed coins.

As the number of ships sailing between Seville and the New World grew from three in 1504 to 283 in 1608, shippers needed greater numbers of day-laborers to load and unload them.[11]

9. Domínguez Ortiz and Aguilar Piñal, p. 75.

10. Guichot y Parody, 2:89–90.

11. Domínguez Ortiz, *Orto*, p. 16. Luís Navarro García, "El puerto de Sevilla a fines del siglo XVI," *Archivo Hispalense*, Series 2, 44–45 (1966), 166–176. Domínguez Ortiz, *Golden Age*, p. 183. Chaunu, 6:116–157.

There is some evidence that workers tried to limit their own numbers so that they could enjoy more continuous employment and higher wages. City ordinances limited to fourteen the companies for loading and unloading ships, a provision that rankled city officials concerned with the growing independence of these laborers in the late sixteenth century.[12] Shipowners and merchants wanted many laborers available to load and unload their ships quickly, and they wanted to pay them as little as possible. They gladly used the underworld toughs who were willing to work occasionally, a pool of surplus labor that brought into line the licensed day-laborers.

Because two of the major exports from the city were wine and oil, the container-makers played a significant commercial role. Cask-makers had a guild strong enough to insist that the city prohibit the use of casks manufactured outside Seville. As the numbers of cask-makers increased in the sixteenth century, the membership of this guild appeared to decline in quality. City records reported a quarrel that two young cask-makers had in 1599 with another young man over a woman. They stalked him openly through the city streets with drawn swords until he turned into an alleyway, where they ran him through.[13]

On a smaller scale, ceramic containers were also used for transporting oil and wine from the city. By the mid-sixteenth century there were some fifty earthenware workshops in Triana. Earthenware was so cheap and plentiful here that merchants bought large quantities to take to France, Flanders, and England. One problem was that the clay was gathered from the river banks along the *Tablada,* a pastureland, and the small islands in the river. Continuous gathering of clay undermined the pastureland rented out by the city in these areas and provoked many complaints. After investigating the problem in 1567, the city council posted guards to prevent the potters of Triana from gathering clay near the pasturelands. Conflicts continued into the seventeenth century, with city merchants arguing that pottery containers were essential to their trade and the potters'

12. Navarro García, "El puerto," pp. 176–177.
13. Domínguez Ortiz, *Orto,* p. 18, AI, Casa de Contratación, Seccion 2, Legajo 64.

guild complaining that the city's action against them was hurting the 5000 people involved in clay-gathering and pottery manufacture.[14] In this case, merchants, artisans, and workers shared a common interest against the landholding city council.

Commerce also involved local producers, but most were unable to keep up with the greatly increased demands triggered by the opening of trade with New Spain. Costs were higher here, for the influx of precious metals from the New World and the great population increase of the sixteenth century were felt most directly in Andalucia, where they pushed up prices sooner than in many other areas of Europe. Merchants in Seville turned to the producers from Flanders, Germany, and northern Spain to buy the cargoes for the ships that they sent to the Indies. The Sevillian producers of soap, gloves, cloth, printed books, and swords continued to produce for export, but there is no evidence that trade with the New World stimulated a markedly increased production.[15]

Agricultural producers were more important to the export trade of Andalucia. Wine and olive oil were especially profitable in the markets of the New World, with wine selling in American markets for nearly twice the price that it got in Spain.[16] Some land around Seville that had been cultivated with cereals, fruits, or vegetables was converted to the more profitable olive and vine production. At the same time, population growth increased demands for agricultural products. Prices rose and agricultural producers began to cultivate more marginal land, a further impetus to higher prices for agricultural products.

14. Domínguez Ortiz, *Orto,* p. 15, Navarro García, "El puerto," pp. 162–165.

15. Domínguez Ortiz, *Orto,* esp. pp. 12 and 27, is the best single source for local producers. See also Morgado, p. 157, for the soap industry. The city's ordinances in AMS, *Ordenanzas,* suggest the great variety of local producers in Seville. Tomás de la Torre, p. 460, describes the many products purchased in Seville to outfit his ship. The sixteenth-century Price Revolution is discussed in Earl J. Hamilton, *American Treasure and the Price Revolution in Spain* (Cambridge, Mass., 1934), and J. Nadal, "La Revolución de los Precios españoles en el siglo XVII; Estado actual de la cuestion," *Hispania,* 19 (1959), 503–529.

16. Carande Thobar, pp. 83–84.

Noble families, the Church, and military orders owned most of the land around Seville, but usually they did not exploit it directly. They rented it out for money. Small agricultural producers who rented small parcels of land were unable to keep up with rising prices and increasing rents. Many of them abandoned agriculture and tried other occupations in the city. Larger agricultural producers fared better, cultivating more of the land abandoned by the smaller farmers. They faced a shortage of agricultural labor, however, a problem that some contemporary economists believed could be solved by relocating vagabonds and other idle people in agricultural colonies.[17]

Sevillian commerce was also open to the lowly *regatones* (street hawkers), and *pregoneros* (vendors). Both of these groups of people made their living through retail, but pregoneros had a special status. According to city ordinances of 1632, only thirteen pregoneros were authorized for the city, and each had his own territory within the city. These men were occasionally required to make public announcements, but their major economic role was to buy and sell secondhand goods. When a resident needed money quickly, he took one of his belongings to the pregonero, who would sell it for him. The pregonero was supposed to keep no more than 2 percent, or a maximum of 100 *maravedís,* from the selling price.[18]

Regatones, on the other hand, were very numerous in the city and enjoyed no special status. Most sold food, but some also sold soap, pottery, and charcoal. Many had customary selling routes in the streets and plazas of their neighborhoods, although some regatones sold only from their houses. People of all ages worked as regatones, and both men and women found that they could combine this work with other jobs. Underworld people combined street retailing with prostitution, gambling,

17. Domínguez Ortiz, *Orto,* p. 51. Carmelo Viñas Mey, *El problema de la tierra en la España de los siglos XVI y XVII* (Madrid, 1941), pp. 24–28, 123, 139, 191–192. Olwen Hufton, *Bayeux in the Late Eighteenth Century; A Social Study* (Oxford, 1967), pp. 11–15, found a similar response to agricultural crisis in Bayeux.

18. AMS, Ordenanzas de Sevilla, recopiladas, Archivo de Privilegios, 1632, "Titulo: De los Pregoneros," folios 132–135.

and theft. Regatones were noted for their tough manners and gutter language.[19]

Underworld attitude toward commerce was a cynical admiration. Underworld people used merchants' terms for their own enterprises. To underworld people the *aduana* referred not to the customs house but to the brothel or the place where thieves deposit their loot. They recognized the practicality of commercial regulation through a customs house and adapted it to their own economic activities. Because prostitution could be subjected to controls similar to those in banking houses, underworld people called the brothel a *cambio* (exchange). A *pagote* (payee) was the person guarding the women to be sure that clients paid them.[20] Thieves' societies were reported to deposit loot in a box locked with three keys, the same system used by the Casa de Contratación.

Although underworld people used the terms and systems of successful merchants, they resisted the developing commercial ethic. Debt was nothing to them but a tool used by the more powerful against the weak, a snare to be evaded. Underworld people viewed commercial fortunes as the result of lucky speculations rather than hard work, and their vocabulary reflected a characteristic attitude toward money and work. In the underworld language the usual word for work, *trabajo,* referred to the prison or galleys. Money was called *sangre* (blood) or *amigos* (friends). A bag of money was called a *pelota* (ball).[21] Money did not seem to be the wages for labor to these people, but a plaything, a friend, the vital substance of living.

COMMERCIAL REGULATIONS

Trade with the New World brought Madrid and royal bureaucracy into the commerce of Seville. Eager to control relations with the newly discovered territories, the Crown established the Council of the Indies to make policy and the Casa de Contratación to administer the policy. International policies of the

19. Ariño, pp. 79–92.
20. Hill, pp. 107, 119, 122, 124.
21. Ibid., p. 119.

Spanish Crown directly affected Sevillian commerce. The Spanish Hapsburgs' wars with France, Holland, and England closed several foreign ports to Sevillian merchants. In addition, the defeat of the Armada in 1588 lost countless ships and trained seamen needed for commerce.

The Casa de Contratación was closely tied to the Consulado through family and friendship, but it was a separate institution and required its own bureaucracy. According to one contemporary, the officers of the Casa included a president, administrator, treasurer, accountant, assessor, fiscal reporter, secretary, scribes, sheriffs, porters, warden of the Casa's prison, head pilot, cosmographers, boat inspectors, professor of astrology, professor of cosmography, receiver of export duties, accountant of duties, and lawyers. Some of these offices were only parttime. The presidency of the Casa did not become a continuous office until 1579, and in 1598 it was reserved for nobility of the blood.[22]

Regulatory duties of the Casa became more complex as the size of commercial ships increased and the Guadalquivir River filled with silt and became less navigable. When trade with the Indies began in the sixteenth century, the average size of ships was 100 tons. By 1650 the average size was 250 tons, and some were as large as 500.[23] Because the sandbar at Sanlucar was especially difficult for the larger ships to cross, they were often partly loaded or unloaded at Sanlucar, El Puerto de Santa Maria, or Cadiz. The Casa de Contratación had to send representatives to these ports, and the city council of Seville had to oversee a fleet of smaller boats that could link the city with the larger ships unable to pass up the river to Seville. In 1717 Cadiz formally replaced Seville as the site of the Casa de Contratación, but the replacement was actually a long gradual procedure throughout the seventeenth century. During this period people who wanted to avoid trade regulations exploited the confusion of overlapping port authorities in and around Seville.

The Crown regulated commerce in Seville in order to raise money. In addition to the *alcabalá,* the traditional sales tax, the Crown found several other sources for revenue in the com-

22. Ortiz de Zuñiga, 4:559. Morgado, p. 166.
23. Chaunu, 4:334–336.

merce of the city. Some royal prerogatives brought in rather small amounts of revenue but still played a major role in the city's economy. An example is the tax of 360,000 maravedís which Seville paid to the Crown each year for permission to use the income from a nearby salt works.[24] Much more important in the amount of revenue it produced was the *almojarifazgo* (import duty). In exchange for the periodic payment of lump sums, the Crown leased the right to collect import duties in the port of Seville. With the growing New World trade it was able to divide this privilege into the *almojarifazgo major* and the *almojarifazgo de Indias* (import duties on all items brought from the New World, or the Indies, as this area was commonly called). The latter was especially profitable, and its growth was estimated at 600 percent in the last half of the sixteenth century.[25]

As a royal prerogative the collection of import duties was supervised by the *Aduana* (customs house), an institution independent of the Casa de Contratación. The Aduana had its own set of officials, accountants, inspectors, and porters—as many as 250 employees.[26] Ironically, the Aduana brought into play an even greater number of smugglers, forgers, fences, and counterfeiters. To avoid paying an import duty, merchants and shippers bribed inspectors and paid teamsters to hide merchandise. Passengers entering Seville from the Indies hired sailors to smuggle precious metals or jewels through the customs inspection. If legitimate merchants hesitated to handle contraband merchandise, smugglers knew many fences in the city. A letter of 1651 from a Franciscan friar in Seville complained that the parish of San Marcos was a center for contraband trade. A group of *gente de mal vivir* (bad people) freely bought and sold contraband merchandise in their houses in this parish, he reported, and they had become very rich and insolent. They

24. AMS, Ordenanzas, "Titulo: Sumario de los privilegios de Sevilla," folio 132.

25. Fernand Braudel, *The Mediterranean and the Mediterranean World in the Age of Philip II*, trans. Sian Reynolds (New York, 1972), 1:293–294. See also Chaunu, Vol. 6.

26. Ortiz de Zuñiga, 4:564–565.

nearly killed a customs judge who got in their way, and other officials of the city were either afraid of them or respected them.[27]

Stung by countless smuggling ruses, the royal government increased the penalties on smugglers. Boatmen or shipowners caught smuggling were to lose their vessels. Merchants who proclaimed their innocence of trying to smuggle valuable merchandise concealed in loads of less valuable products were to lose all concealed merchandise, as well as the beasts carrying it. When contraband merchandise was discovered and seized, duties were first extracted. The value of the remainder was divided, with one quarter going to the denouncer, one quarter to the royal officers of contraband, and one half to the royal treasury.[28]

Since the Crown wanted to use the gold and silver coming into Seville as collateral for foreign loans, it directed city officials to register all money withdrawn from Seville. This regulation, as city officials noted in 1579, was "very prejudicial and harmful for the citizens of this city, and for the foreigners who come here for business, who receive so many vexations and so much bother that commerce could decline to a great extent, because thieves and highwaymen learn and take notice of those who withdraw money, whenever and wherever they go, in order to rob and kill them, as has been seen many times."[29]

The monarchy imposed commercial rules to safeguard its authority. The privileges it granted would have meant very little without their economic advantages, such as exemption from

27. Antonio Domínguez Ortiz, "Documentos para la historia de Sevilla y su Antiguo Reino," *Archivo Hispalense*, Series 2, 44–45 (1966), 74–75. AMS, *Archivo General*, Sección 1, Carpeta 26, No. 310, AI, Indiferente General, Sección 5, Legajo 2003, "Libro de documentos que vinieron y de cartas escritas a S. M. por los Jueces de la Contratación y otras personas de Sevilla y otras partes años 1563 y 1564," describes the arrival of a fleet from New Spain in 1564 and the imprisonment of people attempting to smuggle precious metals and jewels into the port.

28. AMS, Papeles del Conde de Aguila, Sección Especial, Tomo 29 en folio, No. 13. Navarro García, "El puerto," pp. 176–177. Navarro García, "Pilotos," pp. 241–243, 279–280, 293–295. Domínguez Ortiz, *Golden Age*, pp. 142–143. Domínguez Ortiz, *Orto*, p. 115. Peraza, pp. 1170–74. Guichot y Parody, 2:288–290.

29. Guichot y Parody, 2:91.

certain taxes or commercial restrictions. From the sale of noble titles, the Crown gained income and support of the newly appointed nobles, who now enjoyed some economic advantages. What is more, the Crown demonstrated that it was the source of privilege and advantage.

The Crown was not above making commercial deals in return for money. Urgently needing money for its wars in Flanders and Portugal and its campaigns against France and England, the Crown turned to foreign bankers for loans. It granted the Fuggers the administration of the mercury mines of Almaden and the silver mines of Guadalcanal in southern Spain in return for loans. Some Genoese bankers loaned money to the Spanish Crown and were rewarded with a monopoly on the sale of playing cards in Spain, as well as the control of salt works in Andalucia.

Royal policies discouraged merchants from reinvesting their profits in commercial enterprise in Spain. Some remained in the Indies or other foreign ports, where they could continue trading without paying high import duties and other taxes to the Spanish Crown. Periodic monetary devaluation outraged some merchants, who refused to sell at old prices for the new devalued currency. Foreign wars increased the risks of overseas trade, but the Crown seemed deaf to merchants' pleas for peace. Drake's raid on Cadiz in 1587 destroyed the fleet of New Spain that was in port, and with it the confidence of Spanish merchants who had invested large sums in the Indies trade.[30]

One reaction was to blame all these problems on foreigners. Spain, declared contemporary economist Martínez de Mata, was the "Indies of Europe" because it provided markets and profits for foreign manufacturers.[31] In response to Sevillian merchants' complaints about foreigners, Philip III decreed in 1608 that

30. Ibid., pp. 215–218, 232–233. Domínguez Ortiz, *Orto,* pp. 73–75. Lynch, 1:166.

31. Gonzalo Anes Alvarez, ed., *Memoriales y discursos de Francisco Martínez de Mata* (Madrid, 1971), p. 60. A similar statement is in Cristóval Suarez de Figueroa, *El Passagero,* 1617 (Madrid, 1914), p. 20. Two contemporary historians, Barbara and Stanley Stein, discuss this argument in their thoughtful study *The Colonial Heritage of Latin America: Essays on Economic Dependence in Perspective* (New York, 1970).

foreigners should have no part in the trade with the Indies.[32] This was obviously impossible to enforce, because the profitability of the Indies trade depended on the exchange of goods and money between the Indies and all parts of the world. Furthermore, the Crown had borrowed so heavily from foreign creditors that profits from trade with the Indies frequently went directly into the coffers of foreign lenders. One citizen of Seville estimated that one third of all the value of precious metals from the Indies went to foreigners. His complaint to the king was not that the Crown was spending too much, but that foreigners were taking too much—a clear example of xenophobia defusing internal tensions and deflecting them to outsiders.[33]

The city government imposed commercial regulations to raise revenue. To pay the obligatory "donations" that the city had to pay to the Crown, the city government usually estimated and paid a sales tax to the Crown before it was actually collected. The city then used several ways to collect the tax, such as duties on food and merchandise brought into the city for resale. Sales taxes became so complicated that the city in 1515 decided to combine many of them into the *blanca de carne,* a tax of approximately two maravedís for each pound of meat sold in the public meat markets. Any person who bought meat in the city automatically paid the blanca in the selling price. Nobles, clergymen, and certain other privileged groups were exempt from this tax, but they had to petition the city council to return the tax to them after they had paid it.[34]

Social order was another motive in the regulations imposed by city government on the sale of food. The stability of any government depends to some degree on its ability to provide food

32. AMS, Archivo General, Sección 1, Carpeta 8, No. 149.

33. "Papeles varios," BM, Add. 14015. Note, however, that the Steins have argued that the ruling elite in Spain actually favored economic dependence on the rest of Europe, because this facilitated the survival of their traditional life-style; see esp. their p. 26.

34. Guichot y Parody, 1:204–205; 2:336–337. An example of a petition by a noble for the return of the blanca is in AMS, Siglo XVI, Sección 3, Escribanías de Cabildo, Tomo 4, No. 44. An account of the blanca for 1573 is given ibid., Tomo 3, No. 40. A description of the tax and those exempt is in Memorias eclesiásticas, BC, 84-7-19, folios 114v–115.

for its people at a price they can afford. The city government had been charged with this responsibility since the eleventh century, although the Crown occasionally interfered. Millers, bakers, innkeepers, and food-retailers were required to post official prices, and they were prosecuted for charging more than these prices.[35]

In order to enforce price controls, the city government regulated weights and measures used in the city and limited the places where food could be sold within the city. Food retailers were required to sell in plazas where they could be more effectively policed than in the mazes of narrow back streets. Meat could only be sold in the licensed meat markets, a regulation of even more significance because the tax on meat sales was crucial to the city. Innkeepers and secondhand dealers were very closely regulated because they were notorious for violating price controls, as well as for selling stolen property. The city's ancient ordinances warned of innkeepers who bought and sold game at high prices, a complaint repeated frequently before the more stringent regulations of 1629.[36]

When the Count of Puñoenrostro (Francisco Arias de Bobadilla) was named head of the city council in the last years of the sixteenth century, he decided to enforce city regulations on price ceilings.[37] He directed a pregonero to announce in the main squares that people breaking price regulations would be severely punished. Very soon he had arrested and punished several street hawkers, but, significantly, more substantial merchants were not prosecuted for price violations. This may indicate

35. See the laws proclaimed by the city asistente in 1629, reported in Guichot y Parody, 2:210–211. Ariño described the price regulations of 1597, pp. 91–92. See also E. P. Thompson, "The Moral Economy of the English Crowd in the Eighteenth Century," *Past and Present,* No. 50, February 1971. The best description of the just merchant and moral economy by a Spaniard in the early modern period is in Thomás de Mercado, Book II, pp. 20, 33–35. See also "Food Supply and Public Order in Modern Europe," in Charles Tilly, ed., *The Formation of National States in Western Europe* (Princeton, 1975), pp. 380–455.

36. AMS, Ordenanzas, "Titulo: De los tabernos y mesoneros," folios 88–89. Guichot y Parody, 2:156, 210–211.

37. Ariño, pp. 91–92.

that merchants were trying to observe the traditional commercial ethic, or that street hawkers were prosecuted in order to deflect popular indignation about prices away from the "big fish" and on to the "small fish" who were certainly more visible to most city residents.

An example of a small fish was Francisca Gamarra, a well-known old vegetable seller. When the Count moved to arrest her for selling vegetables above the price ceiling, she and her son fled the city. After a few days they were found hiding under a fig tree in an orchard. The Count sentenced the son to a whipping and ten years in the galleys. He marched La Gamarra through the streets with pieces of squash tied around her neck. As city officials gave her the prescribed two hundred strokes, other street hawkers gathered to watch and shout. Some smiled and some cursed. Two weeks after the uproar, La Gamarra was back selling vegetables. People passing her door said, "Look how little shame she has. She was whipped yesterday, and now she is here selling." La Gamarra retorted, "Look out for your necks, suckers, some sucker is watching me." The Count merely said that it was a pity that the old hawker had not been exiled.[38]

The Count's crusade created a clamorous public uproar in the city, especially in the case of Maria de la O, a soap vendor who was accused of price gouging. When she was arrested, she appealed to the audiencia. Already feuding with the Count, the gentlemen of the audiencia rose to her defense, locking themselves in prison with her so the Count could not whip her. The Count and his men quickly broke into prison, clapped the members of the audiencia into irons, and drove Maria de la O through the city streets on an ass, stripped to the waist for a public whipping.[39]

Some of the uproar between the Count and audiencia took the form of verses that circulated through the city. Since most were favorable to the Count, the audiencia arrested three verse-makers; they were later freed on order from Madrid. The chronicler who recorded the verses favored the Count, and his sympathies colored his report. Nevertheless, the verses he

38. Ibid., pp. 79–92.
39. Ibid., pp. 67–79.

recorded indicate the attitudes of local authorities about the moral commerical order. One verse depicted the Count as a hero who had saved Seville from the "unreason" of the abusive street hawkers:

When Seville was infested
By street hawkers
And their shameful abuses,
The famous Bobadilla
Got rid of the creeps.[40]

Another verse emphasized the contrast between the "just and holy" order and the street hawkers who had been frightened away by the Count's opposition:

All Seville sings to you
A thousand honorable hymns.
Because the street hawker has been frightened
The just and holy justice
Preserves you well here.[41]

Street hawkers were reviled in the verses, and one woman retailer was described as having many of the traits associated with the underworld:

She has these positions:
First, she keeps a tavern,
A perfume shop and soap shop,
She is a procuress of fornications
And does a little black magic.[42]

Maria de la O and other women hawkers may not have had anything to do with witchcraft or prostitution, but it is significant that the verses, representative of the position of city

40. Ibid., pp. 76-79, 82. The Spanish text is, "Pues, cuando estaba Sevilla/vencida de regatones/y de abusos, que es mancilla,/el famoso Bobadilla/se ha opuesto a sus sinrazones."
41. Ibid., p. 87. The Spanish verse is, "Toda Sevilla te canta/mil himnos dignos de ti/porque el regaton se espanta/la justicia justa y santa/te conserve mucho aquí."
42. Ibid. The Spanish text is, "Ella tenía estos oficios:/el primero tabernera,/perfumera y jabonera,/coberta de fornicios/y un poquito hechicera."

authorities, wanted people to believe so. City authorities tried to discredit street hawkers in order to demonstrate the government's ability to feed the people and control the food sellers.

In this account the chronicler deliberately undercut any hints that these women were popular heroines. He had to report that Maria de la O was showered with bouquets and attention when she returned home after her whipping, but he added that she spoke insultingly, calling the Count and other officials cuckolds and fornicators.[43] The arrogant tongue of Maria de la O must have delighted many people, from members of the audiencia to the lowest thief of the underworld. Price-gouging may be anti-social, but defying government regulations and sassing the authorities are popular gestures that are especially appreciated by people who are afraid to speak out. By depicting Maria de la O as a filthy-mouthed scold, the city authorities could discredit her protests against them.

The Count's crusade, which identified street hawkers as immoral violators of a just economy, defused tensions and deflected antagonisms within Seville. The city depended upon the success of wealthy merchants, and the city oligarchy rested upon an alliance of nobles, churchmen, artisans, and merchants. Nevertheless, the merchants' success provoked much resentment. Nobles resented the newly rich bankers and merchants from whom they had to borrow money. They feared that the power of money would undercut their position. One seventeenth-century poet played on the names of coins as he suggested the power of money to buy ancestry:

> *Cruzados* make crusaders,
> *Escudos* paint armorial shields,
> And very shabby gamblers
> Make earldoms with their dice;
> Ducats produce dukedoms
> And *coronas* true
> Majesty.[44]

43. Ibid., p. 79.
44. Quoted by Julio Caro Baroja, "Honour and Shame," in J. G. Peristiany, ed., *Honour and Shame: The Values of Mediterranean Society*

More simply and sardonically, Quevedo wrote:

A powerful gentleman
Is Mr. Money.[45]

Underworld people, so often associated with street hawkers in Seville, served as scapegoats in the commercial order. City officials used them to discredit street hawkers and justify more stringent government regulation. They also used the underworld as a symbol for commercial immorality. Against this symbol they could define a moral commercial order that minimized class conflicts and united workers, artisans, merchants, bankers, churchmen, and nobles.

(London, 1965), p. 105. In Spanish the poem is, "Cruzados hacen cruzados,/escudos pintan escudos,/y tahures muy desnudos/con dados hacen condados;/ducados dejan decados/y coronas majestad/verdad."

45. Ibid., p. 106. "Poderoso caballero/es don Dinero."

3

Lawmen and Crooks

IN the mid-sixteenth century Philip II received so many complaints about the local administration of justice in Seville that he sent three royal judges to replace judicial officers of the city council. The first action of the new royal judges was to sentence on the steps of the Cathedral a merchant who had gone bankrupt, losing the estates of several other people. Significantly, this man was sentenced to hang, not by the traditional order of the chief justice of the city council but by order of the king.[1]

Royal justice, of course, was not new to Seville. A favorite legend of the city described the justice of Peter I, who was King of Castile from 1350 to 1369. Known in history as "Pedro the Cruel," this eccentric ruler liked to wander the streets of Seville disguised as a common citizen, defending the humble against the proud. When he heard that a priest who had murdered a shoemaker was excused by an ecclesiastical court with only a twelve-month suspension from his sacerdotal duties, Peter decreed that henceforth any tradesman who killed a priest would be punished merely by losing the exercise of his trade for twelve months.[2]

Both of these accounts illustrate how rulers have used justice as an instrument of power, but their descriptions of royal justice differ considerably. Peter I was presented as a champion of the common people, meting out justice directly, insisting

1. Ortiz de Zuñiga, 4:511.
2. Albert F. Calvert, *An Historical and Descriptive Account of "The Pearl of Andalucia"* (New York, 1913), p. 41.

that it should be applied equally to privileged groups and common people. Philip II, on the other hand, carried out justice through a bureaucracy that he had appointed and imposed on Seville. He sent nobles from other parts of Spain to reform the local administration of justice. In addition, his justice was not directed against privileged groups immune to ordinary law but against a merchant who had cheated several people and fallen into bankruptcy.

It is true that Philip II was a very different person from Peter I, but personality cannot explain all the differences in their styles of justice. More significant are the changes in Castile and Seville between the fourteenth century of Peter I and the sixteenth century of Philip II, illustrating that justice was functioning within a specific social context. When early modern Seville became the site for the royal agency to control trade with the Indies, it also became a focus of royal concern. Local traditions of justice waned as royal influence grew, and the crooks who were prosecuted for crimes and the lawmen who administered justice increasingly reflected royal concerns. A discussion of crime and justice in this city reveals, above all, changing power relations that directly involved the underworld.

LAWMEN

The administration of justice in Seville had a long tradition of conflicting, overlapping jurisdictions that became even more complex in the sixteenth and seventeenth centuries. In the early sixteenth century conflicts in the administration of justice stemmed from the bitter rivalries between powerful aristocrats, such as those of the Guzmán and Ponce families who took opposite sides in the local Comunero rebellion in 1520 and 1521. Members of both of these families held the office of chief justice for Seville at various times. Nobles who received offices from the Crown often received the privilege to name lesser judicial officers. When the Duke of Alcalá bought the office of alguacil mayor in 1589, he bought with it the right to name the assistant to this office, the warden of the Royal Prison, several magistrates in Triana, and several judicial officers in charge of handing over prisoners.[3] Nobles used their control of these judicial offices to acquire more power and supporters in the local rivalries.

Royal unification introduced another pattern of conflict in the administration of justice when Ferdinand and Isabella revived a medieval brotherhood, the *hermandad*, placed it under the central direction of a Crown-appointed bishop, and charged it to maintain order among feuding nobles and local factions. The Duke of Medina Sidonia and other powerful nobles tried to keep this central law enforcement agency out of Seville because they feared that it would limit their own privileges. In addition, they disliked the annual levy of 18,000 maravedís for every one hundred residents that was imposed on the nobility to finance it. Ferdinand and Isabella persevered, however, and the Santa Hermandad became an institution of justice in Seville with its own court, law officers, and prison.

Inevitably, there were many cases of overlapping jurisdiction between the city's courts and that of the Santa Hermandad. In 1597 a woman was captured by the Santa Hermandad for stealing in the fields, but the city's ordinary justice also claimed jurisdiction over her. A dispute arose over how she should be executed because the Santa Hermandad and the city followed different practices. Evidently the forms of local justice prevailed, for she was taken to be hanged in the Plaza de San Francisco rather than killed in the field, as the Santa Hermandad proposed. Moreover, the procession taking her to the gallows was led by the *Pendon Verde*, a green flag captured from the Moors and used as a local symbol in contrast to the royal flag.[4]

Local resistance to the Santa Hermandad developed into a broader resistance to the Crown's increasing attempts to influence local administration of justice. The tradition of some royal supervision over local government was long-established, but royal reforms in the last half of the sixteenth century greatly strengthened the position of the Crown in the local administration

3. Ortiz de Zuñiga, 4:574.
4. Morgado, p. 190. Guichot y Parody, 1:177. Pedro de León, appendix 1 to Part II, Case 229. The Pendon Verde is discussed as a popular symbol in Chaves, p. 29, and Guichot y Parody, 2:16–17.

of justice. Charles I revived the custom of appointing a com-
mittee of local officials to oversee the city's government, and he
tightened royal control through the audiencia, a royal court in
Seville. By a decree of January 10, 1556, this court was reduced
to six judges and a chief judge *(regente)*, and it was given major
judicial jurisdiction for Seville and the surrounding area within
a radius of five leagues. These judges were to be appointed by
the Crown and could not be natives of the city. All civil cases
were to go to the audiencia, and criminal cases were to be judged
by the alcaldes mayores of the city council. In cases of jurisdictional dispute, the regente was to settle the question with the
oldest judge and alcalde mayor.[5]

Philip II further strengthened the royal audiencia as the seat of
judicial power in Seville. Irritated by the growing number of
complaints about local judges, he abolished the judging functions
of alcaldes mayores and substituted three crown-appointed
judges who were to be non-local nobles.[6] The rivalry among
local nobles provided Philip with an excuse for assuming more
control over justice in Seville, a lesson that alerted the nobles
of the city council. When the alguacil mayor of the city complained in 1566 that the sheriffs of the audiencia were usurping
his position, taking the fees that he should receive for confiscating arms or attaching property for debts, the city council
agreed to stand firmly with him. The Crown backed down and
ordered the audiencia to respect the jurisdictions of the city
government. In 1573 and again in 1579 Philip II prohibited the
audiencia from meddling with city ordinances relating to granaries, bread, the slaughterhouse and meat markets, prices, the
administration of the city's estates, expenditures, bills of exchange, and elections. The audiencia was to act only when
some person claimed that the city had wronged him.[7]

Conflicts between royal and local judicial officials continued,
however, magnified by the Crown's increasing commercial

5. AMS, Ordenanzas, "Titulo: De los fieles executores," folios 47–48.
Ortiz de Zuñga 4:513–515. Guichot y Parody, 2:39–48.

6. Guichot y Parody, 2:38.

7. Ibid., pp. 65–66. AMS, Siglo XVI, Sección 3, Escribanías de Cabildo,
Tomo 2, No. 17. Guichot y Parody, 2:81–86.

interest in Seville. The Crown established a mint, a customs house, and the Casa de Contratación to regulate trade with the Indies. Each of these institutions had its own sheriffs and guards. The Casa had its own judicial system and prison.

Much to the consternation of Seville's oligarchy, the Crown sold increasing numbers of offices. The city council wrote to Philip II in 1586 complaining that their building was not even large enough to hold all the new officers he had appointed. In 1589 city council members were alarmed by rumors that Philip II planned to create the new office of alguacil mayor of the audiencia, and nine years later they complained that rich merchants were buying up noble titles and offices. Money spoke more loudly than complaining letters, however, and Philip II was grateful for the 7000 ducats he received for each office of veinticuatro, as well as the 170,000 ducats he received for the office of alguacil mayor.[8]

Despite complaints from local nobles about the increasing numbers of officials, they must have recognized the need for more judges and constables as the population mushroomed and regulations multiplied. The growing numbers of judges, lawyers, scribes, inspectors, and constables had certain interests in common. Their offices and livelihood depended to some extent on the existence of crime in the city, and the position of each of them depended upon preserving the existing social order. As the city's fortunes declined in the seventeenth century, their security became more precarious. Creditors would pay the customary fee to a sheriff for confiscating a debtor's property, but who would pay the sheriff's fee for confiscating illegal arms? During epidemics and famine, lesser officials often abandoned their offices. A witness to the 1652 bread riot wrote that the sheriffs were "invisible" and the offices of the city at a standstill.[9]

8. AMS, Papeles Importantes, Siglo XVI, Tomo 12, No. 13. AMS, Siglo XVI, Sección 3, Escribanías de Cabildo, Tomo 2, No. 19. Santiago Montoto, *Sevilla en el Imperio, Siglo XVI* (Sevilla, 1937), pp. 60–61. Ortiz de Zuñiga, 4:574.

9. "Casos del tumulto de Sevilla de 22 de mayo del año de 1652," Papeles varios, BC, 83-7-14, folios 181–182.

The quality of officials decreased as their numbers grew during this period. Some flagrantly misused the powers of their offices. In 1636 the city council drew up sixteen complaints against one magistrate, Roque Simon. Witnesses testified that he had caused many people to be arrested and imprisoned for his "own particular ends" and only on his own authority. He had taken merchandise by force and would only pay his own price for food. He had arrested a baker because, he said, the baker was cheating him with his prices, but the assistant to the mayor rushed to the aid of the baker and had Roque arrested. Many people testified that he had insulted them and imposed huge fines on them. Witnesses described his "scandalous living" and accused him of residing unmarried with a woman. Although he defended himself and his crusades against retail cheaters and criminals, his case was decided from the moment it was learned that he had also insulted judges of the city.[10] The judicial bureaucracy could tolerate many failings among its members, but certainly not that.

Improper conduct among judicial officers and local nobles permitted even more royal intervention in local justice. When two local nobles fought in 1628 over the protocol of placing a chair, the regente ordered both men under house arrest, and the Crown sent a special justice from Madrid to try the case.[11] The brutal behavior of arresting officers who broke into houses and injured suspects prompted the Crown to impose further control over local justice. When a person broke a law for which there was only a pecuniary penalty, judges were directed to send for the accused and order him to pay the fine. Only if he refused to pay was he to be imprisoned, and then he was to be taken without breaking down the door of his house.[12] Finally, the audiencia wrote to the king in 1678 that its own judicial officers had to make the rounds of the city because local officials had left them to lawyers and sheriffs who were unable to stop the repeated robberies and scandalous murders. City residents lived in "notorious danger" with no security in their homes, lives, or estates, the judges wrote, and added pointedly that in

10. AMS, Papeles Importantes, Siglo XVII, Tomo 3, No. 17.
11. Algunas memorias, BC, 84–7–21, folios 228^V.–229.
12. AMS, Ordenanzas, "Titulo: De las alcaldes de la tierra," folio 53.

1556 the Crown had taken away some of the legal jurisdiction of local justices who were not carrying out the obligations of their office.[13]

Other conflicts arose from the overlapping jurisdictions between secular and ecclesiastical courts. Secular authorities had long chafed at the fact that clerics were usually immune to secular justice and that ordinary criminals could find asylum from them in churches. Ferdinand and Isabella sent to the city in 1493 an ordinance prohibiting anyone from harboring fugitives from royal justice in churches. Complaining that criminals sometimes escaped royal courts by declaring they were clergy, the Crown also ordered the city to draw up a list of those who claimed they were clergy, together with the crimes they had committed and the testimony against them.[14]

The question of asylum sometimes created a great public uproar. In 1582 Francisco de Castillo killed another man in a quarrel and fled to the nearest church, San Jorge. Unfortunately for him, a justice of the audiencia who was passing through the church spied the fugitive and dragged him outside. He was sentenced immediately to hang within twenty-four hours. Pedro de León protested that this speed would not give him time as chaplain to prepare the man for communion. While others died of old age in prison, waiting for sentence, this man had been summarily sentenced because the audiencia realized there were questions of its jurisdiction over a man found in church. The judge remained adamant, but while the chaplain was walking with the victim to the gallows, some kind people found the widow, who agreed to pardon the killer of her husband for a payment of 200 ducats. However, this pardon required assent from the audiencia, and the condemned man had to proceed to the gallows. Just as the hangman was setting the noose about his neck, a roar went up from the crowd. A messenger arrived with the news that the audiencia had agreed to commutation. The fugitive could be returned to the church where

13. AMS, Siglo XVII, Sección 4, Escribanías de Cabildo, Tomo 31, No. 24.

14. AMS, Ordenanzas, "Titulo: De los que deven gozar la Corona," folio 68.

he had sought refuge, the judges agreed, because his crime had not been "perfidious" and, therefore, the secular authorities lacked the right to capture him in a church.[15]

Jurisdictional disputes between Church and secular authorities were probably all the more conspicuous because these two groups usually agreed on matters of justice. Clergymen arrested for serious crimes were often tried by an ecclesiastical court, defrocked, and then turned over to secular authorities for execution. When a clergyman was arrested with a layman in 1623 for killing a sacristan and his brother, the clergyman was tried by ecclesiastical courts, and the layman by the secular courts. Both were hanged by the secular authorities, although the clergyman was first publicly defrocked in the square before the archbishop's palace. After they were hanged, the head of the layman was cut off and placed in the house where he had murdered the men. The clergyman was merely cut down from the gallows and buried in the monastery of San Lorenzo.[16] Both secular and Church authorities had agreed that these men should be punished, and they had also agreed that the procedure for punishment could vary slightly.

As asistente at the end of the sixteenth century, the Count of Puñoenrostro wanted to enforce secular laws more stringently, especially at the expense of pretentious churchmen. Once he met a beautiful young woman in an inn and asked her what she was doing there. She told him that she had come there "looking for her life" after she had been seduced and abandoned by a canon of the Cathedral. The Count summoned the canon to appear before him the next day. Arriving in style on the back of a fine mule, the canon first denied the story and then admitted it. He agreed to pay the girl one hundred ducats, but the Count told him that he would keep his mule as security until the canon brought the money to him for the girl. The canon had no recourse but to set off on foot to get the money, and the Count had the satisfaction of giving a lesson in humility to this churchman.[17]

15. Pedro de León, appendix 1 to Part II, Case 75.
16. "1616–1634," Papeles varios, BC, 85-4-11.
17. Ariño, pp. 52–55.

The Inquisition added another dimension to the jurisdictional disputes between secular and Church authorities. Technically, it was an institution independent of the Church, promoted by the Crown to prosecute false Christians and heretics. In fact, the Inquisition was not limited to matters of spirit. It was empowered to confiscate the property and titles of accused apostates and heretics, and it could demand that prisoners of secular justice be turned over to its courts for examination on matters of faith. In addition, it could excommunicate secular authorities who denied the jurisdiction of the Inquisition. In 1655, for example, two men were arrested for committing thefts up and down the Guadalquivir River. When they were sentenced to death, the Inquisition demanded to examine them on spiritual matters. The sheriff believed the Inquisition was more interested in the property of his prisoners than in their faith. He refused to release the prisoners to the Inquisition and posted guards around them. Enraged, the Inquisition arrested the sheriff and excommunicated two secular officials. The thieves were finally hanged, a year later.[18]

During the early modern period the Inquisition grew in independence as its bureaucracy and financial transactions increased. Because it had to pay increasing numbers of its own officials, it could justify keeping larger amounts from the property it confiscated. In addition, the Holy Office had to keep money from the confiscations to pay the expenses of keeping prisoners and of presenting autos de fé. Sometimes the Holy Office concealed confiscations, thus adding to its financial independence from the Crown.[19]

Privileges claimed by officials of the Inquisition could lead to disputes with secular authorities. Inquisition officials declared that they had the right to carry weapons and were exempt from inspection of goods or papers that they carried through

18. Memorias eclesiásticas, BC, 84–7–19, folio 205[v].
19. "Relacion de la translacion de la imagen," Papeles varios, BC, 85–4–13, folio 159, lists the great variety of Inquisition officials; Kamen, *Inquisition*, p. 195, discusses the costs of autos. Henry C. Lea, *A History of the Inquisition of Spain* (New York, 1922), 1:328–334, reports on concealment of confiscations from the Crown.

the city gates. They also claimed that their houses were exempt from entry and search by secular officials, for they frequently detained prisoners in their houses and wanted to maintain secrecy about them. In 1540, however, the Inspector General of the Inquisition wrote the Sevillian Inquisition to rebuke them for allowing murderers to enjoy asylum in the Castle of Triana. He directed that the gates of the castle be kept shut so that criminals could not find refuge there. Inquisition officials also agreed to let secular authorities enter their houses to pursue fugitives whom they had just seen committing a crime.[20]

In the atmosphere of jealousy over serious jurisdictional disputes, some squabbles erupted over trivial matters. In 1637, for example, a great uproar ensued when an Inquisition official refused to help some judges of the audiencia dismount from their carriage, which had just broken down. Furious, the judges fined him 200 ducats. The Inquisition asked them to explain this fine, and the asistente and his justices jumped into the fray. They sent fifty soldiers to the houses of the Inquisition to support them while they confiscated property to cover the fine. The Inquisition thundered back with excommunications of six judicial officers. Nine days later, however, the order came from Madrid to cancel the excommunications and lower the fine to fifty ducats.[21] Evidently, both royal and Inquisition officials in Madrid recognized the advantages of preventing an open rupture.

Although the Inquisition later opposed royal power, it helped to buttress the Crown in the sixteenth and seventeenth centuries. Because all officials and nobles had to pledge an oath of obedience and assistance whenever an Inquisitor came to set up a tribunal, the Inquisition could weaken local independence and impose more central authority. A royal decree of 1523 prohibited any municipality or other group from passing laws that would limit the Inquisition. The Crown seemed willing to tolerate a more independent Holy Office if it could limit the independence of local nobles and was willing to undertake tasks as mundane as prosecuting counterfeiters. In a decree of 1627 that conferred this task on the Holy Office, the Crown acknowledged

20. Lea, pp. 422–423.
21. Memorias eclesiásticas, BC, 84–7–19, folios 206ᵛ.–207.

the criticism that the Inquisition was being used "more for reasons of State than for those of the faith." It added, however, that leaders of the Inquisition had agreed that counterfeiting was not only harming Spain, but "enriching and increasing the power of the enemies of God and of men in common offense against the Catholic cause."[22]

Justice in early modern Seville was administered by a coalition of local nobles, royal officials, rising bureaucrats, Inquisition officials, and churchmen. They generally agreed on how to administer justice to people as flagrantly criminal as underworld murderers and highway robbers. The underworld in this sense unified the coalition. Their squabbles over prestige and jurisdiction sometimes masked a genuine power struggle, however, and they freely used the administration of justice to extend their own powers. This reinforced the underworld's cynical view that justice was not a blindfolded lady holding a scales, but a wanton woman whom they could woo and use. Again and again underworld people used the conflicts within the judicial establishment for their own purposes—for example, when they shouted atrocious blasphemies in the Royal Prison, hoping to place themselves in the hands of the Inquisition and thus escape the secular authorities.[23]

Underworld people found many opportunities for profit in the city's system of justice, for the proliferation of judicial offices resulted in a great confusion of responsibility and a decline in the character of judicial officials. Some lower judicial officers became identified very closely with professional criminals.[24] One city lawyer described the profitable practice by which an unscrupulous lawyer would take a constable and a scribe to arrest an unsuspecting citizen, who would then agree to pay the lawyer to defend him.[25] Not many people in the underworld were equipped to act as lawyers, but many were prepared to work as paid false witnesses for corrupt lawyers and judges. A few could even pose as Inquisitors empowered to

22. Quoted in Domínguez Ortiz, *Estamento,* pp. 232–233.
23. Pedro de León, appendix 1 to Part II, Case 22.
24. Petrovitch, p. 195, discusses this problem.
25. Cristóbal de Chaves, "Relación de las cosas de la cárcel de Sevilla y su trato," Papeles del Conde del Aguila, AMS, Tomo B-C, Part II.

arrest people and confiscate their goods. One false Inquisitor at the end of the sixteenth century had his own band of bogus sheriffs. Before he and his lieutenants were found out, they had escaped to the Indies.[26]

The old system whereby one constable was elected from each parish to work under the chief constable in patrolling the city had the advantage of providing law enforcement officers who were easily recognizable and accountable to the people of their neighborhoods. This relationship changed as a result of the growing need for constables in the sixteenth century. By the end of this century the original twenty constables were no longer elected but were nominated by the Crown. One chronicler said that so many more judicial officers were now appointed that the city was full of them.[27] The status and authority of law enforcement officers fell as their numbers grew, and this happened when the city and Crown were trying to reserve to their law enforcement officials the exclusive right to use violence. The underworld found many ways to exploit this problem and involve constables in crime. In Cervantes' story Monipodio reminded his fellow criminals of the importance of keeping the constable's friendship.[28] Fictional accounts of constables implicated in crime are substantiated in many actual cases, such as that of the alguacil mayor condemned for murdering his wife in 1597, and the constable arrested with a group of highway robbers in 1615.[29]

In addition to exploiting city justice, underworld people performed roles that helped to complement the city's imperfect system of justice and defuse the tensions arising from it. Like the men whom Cervantes described in Monipodio's organization,

26. For false witnesses, see Alemán, also quoted in Pike, *Enterprise,* p. 36. Pedro de León describes a false inquisitor in his Compendio, Part II, Chapter 26, folios 197–198.

27. Morgado, pp. 183–184. The old system of elected constables in each neighborhood is in AMS, Ordenanzas, "Titulo: Del alguazil mayor, y de los otros alguaziles."

28. Cervantes, "Rinconete," p. 102.

29. Pedro de León, appendix 1 to Part II, Case 302. Another example is in Ariño, pp. 42–45, who discusses the 1597 arrest and trial of an alguacil mayor for murder.

they were hired to "settle old scores," to impose a justice more swift and certain, more in tune with traditional concepts of honor than the "legality" of the city's courts. They also acted as vigilantes in executing their own kind of justice, a role performed by a gang called the Esquiveles, who killed a man in 1628 for insulting a woman.[30]

By the first quarter of the seventeenth century, the condition of justice in Seville had provoked many complaints. One citizen wrote a scathing description of his city in which there was

> no administration of justice, rare truth, little honor and fear of God, and less trust; neither does anyone attain his rights without buying them or collect his estate without giving a tenth to the receiver . . . here there are no whippings unless one lacks a bodyguard, nor are people condemned to the galleys unless they lack arms; neither does anyone appear delinquent unless he is without money and can't pay scribes, lawyers, and judges. For six years I have not seen a thief hung in Seville, nor will such a thing be seen, since there are swarms of them like bees . . . the majority in Seville are bullies, pimps, false beggars, ruffians, assassins, moneylenders, hucksters, vagabonds that scrape a living from Mohammed and from those that play and rob in gambling houses and at gaming tables, for we pass from 300 gambling houses to 3000 brothels.[31]

With less exaggeration but equal concern, the jurados of Seville wrote to Philip IV in 1621 of the "bad office and administration of justice" in their city. They blamed this problem on the sale of office, on negligent veinticuatros, and on the numbers of vagabonds "that gather here from all over the kingdom."[32]

30. AMS, Efemérides, "Noticias y casos," Tomo 20, folio 22. Cervantes, "Rinconete," pp. 115–116. Julian Pitt-Rivers found a similar contrast between traditional popular concepts of honor and state-imposed legality in a twentiety-century Spanish village. See his *The People of the Sierra* (Chicago and London, 1971), pp. 129–130, 159; also his essay "Honour and Social Status," in Peristiany, ed., pp. 30–31.

31. Porras de la Cámara, quoted in Domínguez Ortiz, *Orto*, p. 68.

32. "Informe de las Jurados de Sevilla a Felipe IV," quoted ibid.

Justice in Seville had become a confusion of lawmen and crooks.

CROOKS

Available evidence is inadequate for a statistical study of crime and criminals, but it provides rich details about the people most likely to be branded criminals in early modern Seville. The overwhelming majority of people punished for crimes were young and middle-aged males. Some women were whipped and publicly humiliated for retail cheating, one was hanged for causing a "respectable woman" to have an abortion, and a few were executed for theft, adultery, killing their husbands, or other murders. Law enforcers usually went after male violators, however, an indication that women violators appeared less threatening, perhaps better constrained by marriage, convents, or social mores.

Germanesca ballads and picaresque novels of this period emphasize the youth of their criminally inclined antiheroes. Rinconete and Cortadillo were only teen-agers in Cervantes' story, although their criminal companions were somewhat older. Unfortunately, statistics do not reveal the ages of most criminals. Pedro de León did not record the age for each of the people he attended as prison chaplain between 1578 and 1616, but he did note sixteen cases in which the offender was between sixteen and twenty years, or a "youth," and he recorded one case in which the offender was sixty years old. The only juveniles younger than sixteen years who appear in criminal records are accomplices in sodomy.

Most criminals were native to Spain.[33] Of the 309 people whom Pedro de León attended before their executions, only one was a gypsy, seventeen were foreigners, and forty-two were Moriscos, Negroes, or mulattos. One reason that Moriscos do not figure more prominently in crime is that they were expelled from Spain in 1609. Another reason is that the Inquisition could go after many as heretics or false Christians. Societies with agencies to enforce religious orthodoxy do not

33. See the excellent study in I. A. A. Thompson.

have to rely solely on criminal prosecution to attack enemies.

Many accounts of criminals do not mention any profession or occupation other than the crime for which they were prosecuted. Pedro de León's list includes two oil merchants and the son of a wealthy merchant. Other sources report lawyers who were convicted of crimes.[34] Two schoolmasters were convicted of sodomy, and soldiers who had deserted their companies were sometimes turned over to civilian authorities who prosecuted them for rape, theft, highway robbery, and murder.[35] Clerics who committed especially heinous crimes were defrocked and turned over to secular authorities for punishment. Pedro de León attended only seven condemned clerics between 1578 and 1616, one for forgery, one for murder, and the others for sodomy. Condemned clerics appear more frequently in city and ecclesiastical records in the seventeenth century, especially for sodomy and counterfeiting.[36]

Many people convicted of crimes were poor. Pedro de León wrote with great sympathy of the numbers of men imprisoned for debts, and he tried to convince creditors to write off these debts or accept a lesser amount in payment.[37] Sometimes wealthy benefactors paid off debts for these prisoners before they died from illness or malnutrition in the prison. Poverty undoubtedly drove some people to commit theft. The chief justice (regente) reported a great number of thefts in 1639, and he attributed many of them to the economic hardships suffered because the fleet from the Indies had not yet arrived.[38]

The system of justice ensured the more stringent prosecution of poor people because it permitted the purchase of pardon for some crimes from the person who had been harmed. Highway

34. "Algunas cosas notables sucedidas en Sevilla," BC, 84-7-19, folio 101.

35. Pedro de León, appendix 1 to Part II, Case 112.

36. See for example, Joseph Maldonado Danila y Saavedra, "Tratado verdadero del motín que hubo en esta ciudad este año de 1652," BC, 84-7-21, folio 133[V].

37. Pedro de León, Part II, Chapter 5, folios 118-120.

38. Antonio Domínguez Ortiz, "Documentos para la historia de Sevilla," *Archivo Hispalense,* Series 2, 32-33 (1960), 73-74.

robbery and treason were excluded from this system, but widows and mothers pardoned the murderers of their husbands or sons in exchange for a payment. Not all recorded criminals were poor, however; some were nobles, and some quite wealthy. Authorities made examples of some nobles to restrain others from committing the same crimes. Usually these people had been accused of murder or sodomy.

The offense most likely to receive capital punishment was murder, accounting for 104 of the 309 cases in Pedro de León's list. Some murders were committed in conjunction with theft, highway robbery, passion, or "other crimes." Murders considered most serious involved highway robbery or adultery. Others resulted from brawls, vendettas, and the use of hired killers to settle old scores. One man was hanged for "imagined murder" after he had plotted to kill his master with poison.[39] Murder threatened not only the Crown's ability to preserve law and order, but also its attempt to monopolize all forms of violence. The Crown had long forbidden commoners to walk the streets of Seville armed with anything other than a small knife. Pointing out the threats to the city and Crown from armed ruffians, the Crown increased penalties for violation of arms regulations.[40]

The city government was not willing to give the Crown exclusive power to decide who should carry arms. In the sixteenth century the council decided that city residents who went to work at night or before the sunrise should be permitted to carry arms and that the arms previously taken from them should be restored.[41] Moreover, city government distributed arms to nobles and citizens to hand out to their families and "entirely satisfactory neighbors" during political uprisings. In 1642, for example, the city council distributed arms throughout the parishes during an uprising set off by the presence of many Portuguese in Seville.[42]

Traditionally, nobles had the right to enter Seville's city hall

---

39. Pedro de León, appendix 1 to Part II, Case 72.

40. Guichot y Parody, 1:372. AMS, Ordenanzas, "Titulo: De los vandos y armes y de los omes de mal vivir," folios 62–63.

41. AMS, Archivo General, Sección 1, Carpeta 25, No. 220.

42. "Algunas memorias," BC, 84-7-21, folio 261ᵛ.

bearing arms, but Philip II succeeded in reserving this privilege for nobles who made handsome loans to him. In a letter of April 21, 1570, Philip II granted to Juan Gutierrez Tello the right to enter the city hall with "sword and dagger," stating that this was the privilege he customarily granted to those who loaned him 8000 ducats for one year without interest.[43]

Even though both the Crown and city government tried to limit arms-bearing, they were unable to control violence. In the last quarter of the sixteenth century, Pedro de León found widespread violence in Seville which neither the Crown-appointed asistente nor the city's sheriffs could control. Everyone in the city feared the "famous" thugs, and every feast day or Sunday was marked by murders and casualties. Boys came by the scores to settle grievances from the week past. Gang fights continued despite efforts of the authorities to stop them, "such was the strength of this barbarous people, indomitable and irrational." When the priest was able to divert some of the boys to the Jesuits' house, he collected from them slings, knives, skewers, small shields, and "other warlike instruments."[44]

One reason that violence continued in Seville was that so many people claimed the right to bear arms that city officials must have found it impossible to enforce the prohibition on weapons. Men who had been in the army frequently drifted into Seville, still wearing the sword that was once the symbol of prestigious employment. Many guards were employed in Seville's customs house, markets, mint, and prisons, and all of these men were armed.

Ironically, the city's and Crown's attempts to limit arms encouraged the development of an illegal violent elite. If ordinary citizens were forbidden to carry arms, they would look to the thugs and ruffians who were willing to carry out violence for them. These hired bullies and killers could command a higher price as the severity of law enforcement against them increased. Men resisting arrest directly challenged the government's attempt to monopolize violence. The famous ruffian Damián de Carmona resisted so vigorously that he was subdued only after a pitched

43. Quoted in Fernandez Melgarejo, B.C. 84-3-42.
44. Pedro de León, Part I, chapter 3, folios 6-9.

battle with one hundred lawmen.[45] After he was hanged for murder, his hands and head were cut off and displayed to warn other ruffians of the consequences of defying authority.

Theft and highway robbery were the next most commonly prosecuted crimes after murder. Some thieves were whipped or exiled from the city, but those who were suspected of committing several thefts were executed as "famous thieves." House-breaking, horse theft, and other simple forms of theft by individuals were not prosecuted as often as highway robbery, a crime that seriously threatened the efforts of the Crown to preserve order and control violence on the roads of the empire. The implication of a city sheriff in one of the highway robbery gangs intensified Crown reluctance to leave law and order to local authorities. Moreover, highway robbery interfered with the activities of wealthy merchants who provided the major tax base for the Crown. When one highway gang nabbed 15,000 ducats in merchandise and money in a single attack, the Crown suffered not only a blow to its political authority, but also a severe loss in taxable wealth.[46]

Another reason why highway robbery was taken so seriously is that it was usually carried out by gangs. Pedro de León reported that many active gangs of highwaymen met in the little food stands along the river in Seville to plan their attacks on travelers taking the roads out of the city. These gangs and other thieves' organizations would have been too visible in rural villages, but they easily blended into the crowds of the city. Population growth in Seville promoted anonymity and weakened traditional social restraints, so that groups of young thugs felt much freer to bully, terrorize, and rob. One historian has interpreted these offenses as collective retorts to society.[47]

The high proportion of people executed for sex crimes is

45. Ibid., appendix 1 to Part II, Case 207.

46. Ibid., Cases 207, 213, 214, 300, 301, 302, 304.

47. For a higher visibility of crime in rural areas, see William A. Christian, Jr., *Person and God in a Spanish Valley* (New York and London, 1972), p. 163. Yves Castan, "Mentalités rurale et urbaine à la fin de l'Ancien Régime dans le ressort du Parlement de Toulouse d'après les sacs à procès criminels (1730–1790)," in Abbiateci, et al., p. 165, discusses crime as a collective retort.

striking. Pedro de León reported two cases of adultery, two of bestiality, four of rape, and fifty-two of sodomy. The far greater number of sodomy convictions implies that these offenses were reported more often than rape or adultery and that they were considered more serious. The method of execution supports this conclusion, for sodomizers were executed by burning, while rapists were hanged. One man convicted of bestiality was burned, while the burro that was his partner in this offense was hanged. In 1604 authorities burned for sodomy an old street vendor of Triana, "fat, deaf, and blind," hardly a threatening figure.[48]

Sodomy had traditionally been treated as a sin against nature, but its criminal prosecution in this period suggests that it was also an offense to the political order. The prevailing moral system controlled female sexuality through convent, marriage, or licensed brothel; but sexuality in men was not so neatly contained. Evidently their deviant behavior could not be treated as merely a sin, a problem between man and God. It was considered an offense against the moral order that was imposed by an alliance of the Crown, Church, and city oligarchy.

Crimes of fraud account for many prosecutions in this period, particularly frauds against royal prerogatives. Two oil merchants, for example, were accused of cheating on the royal tenth taken from all oil sold in the city. A clergyman was hanged for forging royal decrees, and another man was executed because he used fraudulent playing cards. His crime was not an offense against a gambling ethic so much as a violation of the royal monopoly on playing cards. Violators of price ceilings were vigorously prosecuted, for they were not just cheating city residents, they were challenging the right of the city government to set and enforce price ceilings. Forgers of letters of credit and other commercial papers also challenged the commercial order. They had to be stopped if the city oligarchy was to establish a climate in which merchants and shippers could do business together.

There is evidence that commercial crimes increased in the seventeenth century. One reason is that the Crown began to require the use of stamped paper in this period, and forgery of

48. Pedro de León, appendix 1 to Part II, Case 13. AMS, Efemérides, "Noticias y casos," No. 1.

stamped paper became a rather common white collar crime, often carried out by clergymen. During this century, the Crown also decreed the frequent restamping of coins. Counterfeiting thrived, and the problem became so grave that the Crown sent a special judicial officer to Seville in 1641 to investigate and prosecute counterfeiters. Among those he arrested were several lawyers and the chief assistant to the head of the city council. Many people were imprisoned, and almost all of them, under torture, confessed to the crime. Twenty-five were sent to the galleys, and six were hanged.[49] Economic distress increased the numbers of people who were willing to risk counterfeiting. In 1652 some poor people with only a few *reales* desperately restamped them to show higher denominations. The royal prosecutor hanged one man who had restamped seven reales.[50]

Prosecutions for smuggling also increased in the seventeenth century, reflecting an increasing economic distress and a growing royal determination to control trade. The customs house of Seville was finished in 1587, and all merchandise entering the port was required to pass through it. More than 250 people worked here as receivers, administrators, guards, scribes, stampers, and wardens. Surrounded by wealth and paid small salaries, these officials were excellent targets for people willing to pay bribes in order to "facilitate" the importing of merchandise. For these small officials, many boatmen and sailors, smuggling was an ordinary way to increase their incomes.[51]

Royal officials especially considered smuggling a serious crime, and the Crown frequently urged customs officials to prosecute offenders more vigorously. In 1638, for example, Philip IV directed a royal judge in Seville to prosecute very severely certain men accused of smuggling tobacco into the city.[52] Smuggling in

49. "Diferentes casos," Memorias eclesiásticas, BC, 84-7-19, folios 215ᵛ–216ᵛ.

50. See the letter from Fray Juan de los Santos of Seville, April 23, 1652 in the appendix of Antonio Domínguez Ortiz, *Alteraciones andaluzas* (Madrid, 1973), pp. 205–207.

51. Cf. Cal Winslow's discussion of smuggling in Douglas Hay, et al., *Albion's Fatal Tree; Crime and Society in Eighteenth-Century England* (New York, 1975), pp. 149–150.

52. AMS, Archivo General, Sección 1, Carpeta 148, No. 211; and Carpeta 10, No. 169.

the eyes of the Crown was much more serious than simply evading a tax at the city gates; not only was it a violation of royal directive, a challenge to royal efforts to use commerce for its own benefit, but it threatened royal income, for the Crown received hundreds of thousands of ducats by granting the right to collect import duties. If smugglers were not prosecuted, the privilege would have no economic value and no one would be willing to buy it from the Crown. Despite royal severity, this crime flourished. City records describe a well-organized group in the mid-seventeenth century that dealt only in contraband, led by "princes of the blood" and several lesser nobles.[53]

The acts defined as crime were those which posed a challenge to the social order. Authorities in sixteenth-century Seville considered murder, moral crimes, and highway robbery to be the most serious challenges. Later in the seventeenth century, commercial crimes of counterfeiting and smuggling became particularly serious. The prosecutions reveal an on-going struggle in power relations in the city between armed men and government officials who wanted to control violence; a struggle between sexual deviants and an oligarchy that wanted to preserve its position through enforcing a moral order; a conflict between a revenue-seeking Crown and city residents who wanted to evade import duties and monetary devaluation.

Underworld people were useful in these struggles. On the one hand, they personified crime and provided a target against which royal officials, city notables, and lowly residents could unite. On the other hand, they buffered some of the antagonisms built into the system of justice. They acted as the hired thugs, pimps, and smugglers so useful to many city residents. Crime was not a monopoly of the underworld, for seemingly respectable citizens and underworld people alike found that certain crimes were useful and profitable, and they often found that they could work together. Citizens unwilling to break laws could use people of the underworld who were willing to commit crimes for a price. The partnership was not always easy, but it persisted, and it fed on the tensions between local traditions of justice and the definitions of crime which increasingly reflected royal interests.

53. Domínguez Ortiz, "Documentos," pp. 74–75.

4

Prisoners, Wardens, and Trusties

HEN lawmen caught crooks in Seville, they usually took them to the Royal Prison, an institution colorfully described in Spanish literature of the sixteenth and seventeenth centuries. Picaresque novelists emphasized its bizarre and ribald aspects.[1] Miguel Cervantes, who was imprisoned there twice at the end of the sixteenth century, described it poignantly as a place "where every discomfort has its seat and every dismal sound its habitation."[2] In contrast, a chronicler of late sixteenth-century Seville, Alonso Morgado, described the Royal Prison as evidence of the grandeur and power of the city oligarchy, a symbol of authority to be admired and preserved.[3] Cristóbal de Chaves, a lawyer for the royal court in late sixteenth-century Seville, reported its extraordinary characteristics—the exotic, the horrible, and the unbelievable.[4]

The most complete description was written by Pedro de León, a Jesuit who worked with the poor people of Seville and acted as prison chaplain during most of the years between 1578 and 1616.[5] His *Compendio* contains a detailed account of Sevillian

1. For example, Alemán, Part II, pp. 394–397.
2. Miguel de Cervantes Saavedra, *The Adventures of Don Quixote,* trans. J. M. Cohen (Middlesex, 1970), p. 25. Francisco Rodríguez Marín, *La cárcel en que se engendró el "Quijote" por* . . . (Madrid, 1916), p. 21.
3. Morgado, pp. 191–202.
4. C. Chaves.
5. Pedro de León. One copy of the manuscript is in the Biblioteca

society, the Royal Prison in Seville, and a list of the condemned criminals whom he attended just before their executions. Where Chaves reported the scandalous behavior in the prisons with ill-concealed delight, Pedro de León recorded prison life with the resignation of a man wise to human weakness.

The composite picture of the Royal Prison which emerged from these different sources shows much more than a large building for confining criminals. It reveals, first, that the prison was a flourishing business, profiting both inmates and authorities. Second, it presents a picture of a great central meeting place in which the underworld mingled with other groups of the city and nurtured its own culture. Finally, the prison emerges as an institution that supported but also resisted political authority.

THE PRISON AS A BUSINESS

The three doors of Seville's Royal Prison were popularly called the golden door, the copper door, and the silver door—a sardonic reference to the power of money. A new prisoner first entered the golden door, where an assistant warden recorded his name, his offense, the names of the lawmen involved in his case, and, especially, whether he had any money. If he had little or was not well known, he was sent upstairs to the copper door, to enter the section which took the left-overs from the golden door. If he was to be held in maximum security, he was sent to the silver door, which led to the three strongest cells of the prison. Only those able to raise a considerable amount of silver would be able to escape from these cells.[6]

The place of money in the prison was also recognized by members of the city council, who believed that the prison should be as self-supporting as possible. They did not look upon it as an institution to rehabilitate citizens or confine them permanently in order to protect society. They used it to hold criminals while

---

Universitaria, Granada, and the other is in the Biblioteca de la Universidad de Salamanca. Most names have been inked out in the appendix of both copies.

6. C. Chaves, Part I.

they were being examined, processed by the machinery of justice, and sentenced to punishments far more effective as moral retribution than long-term confinement. They used city income to pay for the building and to pay some officials, but they would not pay to feed social misfits. People who could not pay their own room and board in the prison literally starved to death. In the sixteenth and seventeenth centuries the problem became so acute that monks went through the streets begging alms for poor prisoners. The city council appointed special administrators to provide funds for the prisoners in "extreme necessity."[7]

For some, prison was a money-making business. The assistant warden had up to 400 special cells that he could rent for fourteen or fifteen reales a month. He rented beds curtained off by blankets in the large cells, into which 300 or 400 men were crowded; they were dens of disease and bad smells. He also collected three reales each day from each of the taverns and little stores that were leased out in the prison. Prisoners had few ways to get food and drink except to buy it for very high prices from the prison stores and taverns. When city officials came to inspect the wines sold to prisoners, the storekeepers showed them special containers of very good wine, much better than the "pure bile" that they sold to the prisoners.[8] Prisoners who saw the parallel between this exploitative commerce and that on the outside called the prison a bank and the warden a banker.[9]

City-paid salaries provided only a small part of the income of prison officials and lawyers, most of whom bought their offices or obtained them as special favors for services they had performed. Appointed by the chief constable of Seville, the warden of the Royal Prison held the right to name subordinate officers and sold offices to the highest bidders in a process similar to

7. AMS, Siglo XVI, Sección 3, Escribanías de Cabildo, Tomo 5, No. 19. AMS, Ordenanzas, "Titulo: De los presos, y carceleros," folios 70–72. Most people in Europe in this period believed that prisoners should pay for their room and board in prison.

8. C. Chaves, Part II. Carlos Caro Petit, "La Cárcel Real de Sevilla," *Archivo Hispalense*, Series 2, 11–12 (1949), 342–344. Pedro de León, Part II, chapter 3, folio 113.

9. Salillas, p. 272.

a public auction.[10] The city council appointed notaries and lawyers to represent poor prisoners, as well as a chaplain, pharmacist, and doctor. These offices were granted as privileges, and their salaries were not expected to be much more than an honorarium.

Lawyers and notaries were especially notorious for finding ways to get money from the prisoners. Some promised quick releases to those who could raise 500 reales. Others continued to take money from prisoners, explaining that just one more legal plea had to be presented. Prisoners literally sold the shirts off their backs in order to pay these officials, and they often failed to hear from them again after the last maravedí had been extracted. Not surprisingly, the lawyers and notaries were called "rats of the prison."[11] One administrator of poor prisoners suggested that city-provided lawyers would work more diligently for the poor if they received a larger salary, but the problem remained. By the last decade of the sixteenth century one chronicler had reported more than seventy criminal lawyers, each with his office on the Plaza de San Francisco and each depending for a part of his livelihood on the needs of criminals.[12] Lawyers and notaries continued to regard the prison as a commercial enterprise, and complained that the Jesuits were taking away their means of livelihood by interceding with judges on behalf of poor prisoners.[13]

Although the city council regarded the prison as a business lucrative enough to support most of its officials, it did not expect the prisoners to labor productively. During epidemics or military crises, prisoners sometimes received commutations to serve in the army or to help care for the sick and the dead. As a general rule, however, prisoners were rigidly separated from the laborers of the city. This undoubtedly pleased some guilds that wanted to protect wages by limiting the numbers of people providing their form of labor or service, but it also served the interests of

10. Caro Petit, p. 40.

11. Pedro de León, Part II, chapter 5, folio 120.

12. AMS, Siglo XVI, Sección 3, Escribanías de Cabildo, Tomo 5, No. 18. Morgado, pp. 188–189.

13. Pedro de León, Part II, chapter 6, folio 123.

the city government, which wanted full employment of all able-bodied men. This practice reflected the prevailing attitude that criminals were not to be "saved" or channeled into useful lives, but were to be punished in such a way that the entire community would recognize their immorality. Idleness was regarded as an evil for which a person was to be confined and punished in prison.[14]

Although prisoners were often exploited in the business of the prison, they also acted as the exploiters. Demonstrating an underworld pragmatism, these people accepted their situation and turned it to advantage. Some became prison trusties and received special privileges for acting as night guards or internal police. *Porteros* were prisoners entrusted with the keys so they could lock up the newly arrived prisoners. They carefully distributed new prisoners among the cells, charging each four reales, keeping half for themselves and giving the other half to the prisoners already living in the cells. Some prisoners charged visitors a small sum for running to find the prisoner to be visited.[15]

Pawnbrokers and moneylenders thrived because prisoners needed money to buy food and legal help. Some prison officials played these roles, but prisoners did too. Pregoneros sold or auctioned items pawned by other prisoners. Frequently they passed these things to friends on the outside, who resold the pawned or stolen items. Prisoners who had some money would loan it at a high interest rate, rarely letting a fraternal feeling for fellow prisoners interfere with sound business practice.[16]

Some enterprising prisoners stood guard at an entrance to the prison latrine and charged prisoners a small amount to use the stepping stones they had placed there to pass through the filth. Others charged a fee for providing a support that helped make more bearable the punishment of suspension by wrist shackles high above the ground. Prisoners who could write and draw charged other prisoners for writing letters and decorating notes. Sometimes they used their talents for forgeries and counterfeiting.

14. Michel Foucault, *Discipline and Punishment; The Birth of the Prison,* trans. Alan Sheridan (New York, 1977), develops this theory.
15. C. Chaves, Part I. Caro Petit, pp. 41–42.
16. C. Chaves, Part I.

A few even made money through honest skills. Somehow they got the materials they needed, such as wood or wool or esparto grass, and then paid a portero to sell their crafts for them. Chaves reported that one man had earned 1300 ducats by the time he was transferred from prison to the galleys.[17]

Even the beggars who begged alms for poor prisoners found a way to profit. They brought three-pound loaves of bread to the prison to distribute among the prisoners, but instead of dividing each loaf into three one-pound portions for the prisoners, the beggars kept a quarter of each loaf for themselves. These beggars were popularly known as *animeros,* beggars who got alms in return for praying for the souls of the dead. An anonymous poem about the Royal Prison of Seville described their enterprise:

> One loaf for three,
> And the one who divides it,
> In payment for his work
> Takes a piece from the middle.
> To this they call the spirit,
> And some *animero* has such an
> Evil spirit that he wants to take
> Half the bread for himself from the middle.[18]

While such enterprise had long thrived in Seville's prison, it seemed to reflect in the early modern period a changing consciousness triggered by economic developments. As the site of the Indies trade-regulating Casa de Contratación, Seville, by the middle of the sixteenth century, had become a world monetary center. Great fortunes had been made and lost in this city, and the power of money was evident in the numbers of wealthy merchants who had been able to buy nobility and privilege. Value was now measured in money rather than by traditional

17. Ibid., Parts I, II, III.
18. Quoted in Rodríguez Marín, *La cárcel,* p. 25. The Spanish text is: "Entre tres una hogaza,/y hay uno que va partiendo,/y en pago de su trabajo/saca vn pedaço de un media./A éste el ánima le llaman,/y tiene algún animero/tan mal ánima, que quiera/llevarse del pan el medio."

service or bloodlines. Money meant power, and to the prisoners it meant survival, as well.

The Royal Prison was a successful social institution in the sense that it provided and supported its own functionaries. Here were money-making opportunities for wardens, assistant wardens, guards, barbers, surgeons, pharmacists, torturers, lawyers, clerks, storekeepers, wine-sellers, and the prisoners themselves, who needed money to buy food and legal assistance. Here also were the victims, confined and forced to serve the money-making purposes of the exploiters.

A CULTURAL MEETING PLACE

At one point in his report, Pedro de León called the Royal Prison a "great Babylon that is one of the marvels of the world."[19] More than 18,000 people passed through this building as prisoners each year, and many more thousands came as visitors, lawyers, priests, or hawkers. Their amazing variety in dress and manner, their shouts and babble and shrieks and groans, must indeed have filled the prison with all the sights and sounds of Babylon. If the prison was a flourishing business, it was also a great market, a central meeting place for cultural exchange and development.

Consider first the influence of outsiders coming into contact with prisoners. Prison doors were not locked until 10:00 P.M., and a steady procession of men and women entered and left the prison during the day. Friends and relatives brought the prisoners food, clothing, bedding, money, and even weapons. Often part of the underworld culture of the outside, these visitors maintained underworld links between those inside and outside. In many cases they were the difference between life and death for the prisoners.[20]

Lawyers, notaries, and other judicial officers also linked prisoners and the outside world. Some took advantage, but others helped these often illiterate and penniless people to understand and respond to the language of the judge. Their

19. Pedro de León, Part II, chapter 29, folio 208^V.
20. C. Chaves, Part I.

helpless dependence reinforced the prisoners' feelings that corrupt and merciless lawyers were the rats of the prison, but helpful lawyers were *amparos* (sanctuaries) or *alivios* (relievers).[21]

Clergymen and charitable lay people helped. One pious woman provided meat and bread for all poor prisoners twice a week. She also gave money so that converted women could leave prison for an "honest life," and she provided clothing for naked prisoners. Another wealthy noble woman, whom one chronicler called "the true mother of the poor," gave money so that debtors could pay off their debts and be released.[22] Chaplains interceded on behalf of imprisoned debtors and complained to the city council that prisoners were not getting medicines because the pharmacist assigned to distribute medicine to prisoners was neglecting his job. A *beata* (holy woman) assigned to the Royal Prison asked the city council to repair the walls—not to prevent escapes, but because their crumbling conditions endangered the prisoners.[23]

Most of those who engaged in pious works of charity were helpful but provided only temporary relief. They held no promise for a better world or a more just social order. In fact, they were as supportive of the established order as of the prisoners. A beata was assigned to women prisoners to provide spiritual help, but she was also required to police them, particularly in preventing them from meeting male friends at the prison door. If chaplains provided music and special food for religious festivals in the prison, they also prepared prisoners to die as victims of the social order.[24] Since religious people aligned themselves with the authorities who had taken the prisoners by force, it is not surprising that prisoners ridiculed their spiritual "supporters." Chaves described a mock church ceremony in which

21. Salillas, p. 268.
22. Morgado, pp. 195–196. Pedro de León, Part II, chapter 5, folios 117v–118.
23. AMS, Siglo XVII, Sección 4, Escribanías de Cabildo, Tomo 10, Nos. 30, 26.
24. Pedro de León, Part II, Chapter 12, folio 142v, and chapter 8, folios 128–128v.

one prisoner played the priest with a whip in his hand to control his unruly congregation.[25]

As a meeting place for prisoners and outside groups, the prison emphasized the subordination of prisoners to the larger society and their dependence on outside support, but it also provided a meeting place for the variety of people who came together as prisoners. They were from Portugal, Italy, and most parts of Spain. They were between fourteen and eighty years of age. Many were penniless, a few were wealthy—although the wealthy prisoners often kept to their own better quarters. Some, as Lope Ponce, came from well-known noble families.[26] In no other place in Spain could so many varieties of people meet together to enrich and reinforce an underworld culture.

This was no great melting-pot democracy, however. When a prisoner first entered the prison, the prisoner-porteros ran to receive him, giving him two blows if he was wounded or penitent, three blows if he resisted, and four blows if he was a thief. The lucky portero to whom he was entrusted took him "as though his spirit were possessed by the devil," happily leading him to pay homage to prisoner chieftains.[27] New prisoners had to meet these leaders, acknowledge their positions, and give them presents. Chaves told of one prisoner chieftain, Gomez de Faran, who had such a comfortable fiefdom in the prison that he refused to leave it when the judges decided he should be returned to the church where he had sought asylum when he was arrested four years earlier.[28]

Violent fights settled many questions of hierarchy among prisoners. In addition to the weapons smuggled into prison, prisoners used sharpened sticks they called *pastorcillos* (little shepherds). Some died after being stabbed with them. Others recovered from wounds and swore revenge, or simply accepted an inferior position among the prisoners.[29] The flock of prisoners

25. C. Chaves, Part II.
26. Pedro de León, Part II, chapter 29, folio 208[v].
27. C. Chaves, Part I.
28. Ibid. Part III.
29. Ibid., Part I.

must have recognized *pastorcillos* as staffs of authority as well as the useful tools of herdsmen. Daring, speed, and cunning separated the sheep from the shepherds in the prison.

Authorities isolated prisoners convicted of sodomy, prohibiting them from leaving their cells or sleeping with other prisoners.[30] Segregation did not solve the problem of homosexuality in the prison, however. In 1567 one prisoner accused of sodomy was found committing the same act with a young man who was imprisoned with him.[31] Some homosexual offenders became legends of the prison, discussed with as much delight as revulsion. Chaves, for example, described a merchant who was imprisoned because he had fashioned himself an artificial organ with which he sodomized himself.[32] He died from a whipping in prison, punished for what he had done to himself. Sexual crimes were considered not physical offenses against other people as much as moral offenses against a social order enforced by prison authorities.

Lesbians were also severely punished in the prison. According to Chaves, the women in prison spoke the same tough language as underworld men. Many of them appeared to want to be men, strutting about and crowing like roosters. Some made artificial male genitalia; those who were discovered were given 200 lashes and permanently exiled from Seville.[33]

Despite the variety of inmates, the prison emphasized many things they had in common. As in most European countries, prison fostered a solidarity among prisoners because it separated them from the rest of society. It provided enforced leisure time and opportunities to play rough games. *La mariposa*, the game of placing a lighted stick between the toes of a sleeping prisoner, was a collective sport; it was only fun because many other prisoners would gather around to roar in delight when the sleeping victim awakened with a shriek.[34]

---

30. Ibid., Part II.
31. AMS, Efemérides, "Noticias y casos."
32. C. Chaves, Part I.
33. Ibid.
34. Pedro de León, Part II, chapter 3.

Prisoners were rarely alone. They gambled together, fought together, drank together, and told stories together. They developed a ritual greeting in which each touched his own sword or knife arm and then his own face.[35] Countless social contacts facilitated the development of a prisoners' language. Based on word substitution, their jargon enabled them to express shared attitudes and fostered a collective identity distinct from the rest of society. Chaves told of women in the prison singing *germanesca* songs that celebrated underworld heroes or lamented the human tragedies of this imperfect world. Pedro de León described the women prisoners as communicating through another common language—the rites of black magic. Witches and "famous procuresses" in prison used black and white beans to tell fortunes and call on devils.[36]

Prisoners felt an intense collective identity because so many of them faced death. Sometimes prisoners made a burlesque of accompanying their companions to the gallows, but many times they drew together to move seriously through the rites preparing a prisoner for execution. Chaves described how the women of the prison would gather around a prostitute condemned to death. Some cried out as if they were her lovers; a few fainted in the arms of companions. They listened tearfully as a condemned woman asked that they not take away her clothing, and they agreed when she asked them to wash her quickly after she was dead so that she wouldn't remain as other dead paupers. "Even in death there is cleanliness," she cried, "Polish me well."[37]

Here in the Royal Prison of Seville an underworld culture thrived, as it did in most other contemporary prisons. If a prisoner had known little of the underworld on the outside, prison quickly initiated him. Prison surrounded him with underworld language and customs. It forced him to identify with this culture and depend on it. A prisoner was not only confined within the four walls of his prison; he was confined within a flourishing underworld culture.

35. C. Chaves, Part I.
36. Ibid. Pedro de León, Part II, chapter 12, folio 143.
37. C. Chaves, Part I.

POLITICAL SIGNIFICANCE

When the Royal Prison was rebuilt by the city in the 1560's, the inscription over the entrance of the building piously suggested that the purpose of this magnificent project was to preserve the "holy quiet of the republic."[38] A figure of justice over the door held a sword in its right hand and a scale in its left. These symbols suggest that holy quiet would be the result of not only a particular kind of justice, but also of the enforcement of this justice by an arms-bearing dominant culture. The prison was an agency of coercion, forcing people to obey the laws or suffer the penalties. It was a tool of cultural domination, a symbol of authority that permitted a ruling oligarchy to pose as the legitimate source and guardian of justice. Finally, the prison provided a carefully controlled arena for playing out rituals of conflict. Though Crown, nobles, and churchmen could never abolish all opposition to their rule in early modern Seville, they could channel these conflicts into the regulated rituals of imprisonment, torture, and execution.

Because city council members recognized the political utility of the prison, they were willing to spend thousands of reales for it. In 1563 the city government undertook a major rebuilding of the Royal Prison, its money well spent according to the inscription on the reconstructed building: "The illustrious senate and people of Seville, with the inspiration of Jesus Christ, attending with great providence to the holy quiet of the republic, which is often disturbed by the boldness of evil people, cared to raise from the foundations and magnificently restore and expand at public expense this prison . . ."[39] Although the city government did not buy food for inmates, it did pay salaries for a doctor, surgeon, pharmacist, barber, and several lawyers who represented the poor prisoners. It also paid to maintain the building, some 900 ducats every three years to clean it, and varying amounts for repairs. Between May 1644 and November 1648, a list of expenses for the city included 10,000 reales to repair the Royal

38. Guichot y Parody, 2:59–60.
39. Ibid., p. 335. Morgado, pp. 191–195.

Prison.[40] When the city council lacked public funds, its members believed the prison was so crucial to their social order that they were willing to support it with their own salaries and meat-tax rebates.[41]

The prison provided a defensive strategy against the violators of the laws that royal and city officials believed were most essential. It held prisoners until justice could be executed, but debtors posed a particular problem because imprisonment prevented many from raising money to pay off debts for which they had been sent to prison. The city council in 1534 had ordered that all prisoners judged to be poor should not be kept in prison to pay costs for which they had no money. Nevertheless, Pedro de León found that the problem still existed some sixty years later, and he often tried to intercede with creditors on behalf of debtors in prison. One debtor, desperate for a way to get out of prison to raise nine reales, wangled his release by leaving his infant in the prison as a security. Evidently he was successful, but not before his baby kept most of the prisoners awake for a night and a day with his hungry wails.[42] Prison inmates must have longed for the "holy quiet of the republic" that was promised in the inscription over the prison entrance.

Prison supported the attempts of political authority to monopolize violence, for prison authorities had license to commit violence against prisoners and hold them defenseless while they took away their very lives. At the end of the sixteenth century, six or eight people were whipped and hanged each week, and many died from the whippings. Prisoners were sent by the fifties to the galleys, a cruel service that usually ended in death.[43] The violence of the prison system was institutionalized, a routine matter accepted without question by most people of the community.

40. Guichot y Parody, 2:334–335.
41. AMS, Siglo XVI, Sección 3, Escribanías de Cabildo, Tomo 5, No. 17.
42. The council's directive is in AMS, Archivo General, Sección 1, Carpeta 25, No. 221. Pedro de León, Part II, chapter 5, folios 118–120, discussed imprisoned debtors. His description of the infant pledged by the debtor is ibid., Part II, chapter 22, folios 177–178.
43. C. Chaves, Part I.

Torture was a standard method for examining prisoners to extract confessions and information from them. The systematic practice of torture by prison authorities reinforced their appearance of power and filled some prisoners with terror. Some were so broken physically that they required medical attention. Chaves described them crawling painfully "like ants" to the prison doctor, unable to pull themselves up when the doctor told them to get up. The doctor had to get down on the floor beside them to examine their wounds and administer a poultice. One doctor at the end of the sixteenth century developed a cure for flesh that had been torn off the sinews of the arm. Before this treatment was developed, Chaves wrote, there were many maimed left arms in prison.[44] Pedro de León, noting that women were less likely to confess under torture than men, estimated that for every twenty women tortured, eighteen did not confess. Moreover, when women were stripped, they still did not confess—did not have anything to confess, he believed, because they would rather confess than be stripped.[45]

Prison authorities fell short of monopolizing all the violence in prison, however. Fights with weapons were common. According to Pedro de León, prisoners fought continually "like animals" with knives, daggers, and swords that they hid under their beds after their female friends had smuggled them into the prison.[46] Generally prisoners used these weapons only among themselves, but one enraged prisoner wounded the warden with a knife and seized a sword after his appeal had been denied. Officials who heard the commotion came running, but had to take refuge under chairs as the prisoner turned on them. Their shouts that they were being killed brought more help, and they hanged the attacking prisoner within thirty minutes of getting his sword away from him. They also cut off his hand, and put it, still encircled by a manacle, above the entrance to the prison.[47]

The officials' authority and opportunity to beat, torture,

44. Ibid., Part II.

45. Pedro de León, appendix 1 to Part II, folio 367ᵛ.

46. Ibid., Part II, chapter 3, folio 112.

47. AMS, Efemérides, "Noticias y casos," No. 1. This same case is reported in "Desde 1616 asta el de 1634," Papeles varios, BC, 85-4-11.

imprison, and execute were potent weapons. It is even more remarkable, then, that underworld people were able to laugh at the prison. Chaves reported an episode in which the prisoners taunted a judge who was determined to stop them from keeping women in their cells. Hearing that more than 500 women were spending the night with the prisoners in one of the largest rooms, he ran to the prison and threw open the cell door, only to find no women. After poking and inspecting, he left in disappointment. Some prisoners ran after him and assured him that his information was correct. Once more he dashed to the room, threw open the door, and again found no women. Finally, after returning a third time, he made the prisoners get out of bed and remove their bed clothes—and he found the women.[48]

Another sport of the prisoners was to tease the judges and scribes who came to question them. In vain the assistant warden tried to get the prisoners to show the proper respect and attention. Some prisoners pretended to be insane or half-witted in order to win compassion, but many were less concerned with compassion than with the fun of twitting authority. They pretended to leave the room or not to understand where they were ordered to stand. They rolled their eyes to disconcert the judicial officers, or they kept trembling or slightly raising one foot in the air. According to Chaves, the prisoners called this sport their "task" (faena), and they cheered happily when they succeeded in ridiculing the officials.[49]

Ingenious prisoners fooled the authorities who could pronounce sentence on them. Some men condemned to the galleys pleaded physical inability, and the warden had to call in doctors to examine them. The sentence of those whom the doctors designated physically unfit was commuted to a whipping and exile. Many left the prison so designated, only to recover with amazing speed. A thief who faked a crippled left hand fooled the examiners and quickly returned to his former occupation, stealing with his left hand as well as his right.[50]

Many prisoners feigned insanity so that authorities would send

48. C. Chaves, Part I.
49. Ibid., Part II.
50. Ibid., Part III.

them to a hospital rather than the galleys or gallows. One counterfeiter who had been condemned to death went into a trance after saying he wanted to prepare for execution by confessing to a priest. The priest asked the judge to delay execution until the prisoner was able to confess. For two months the prisoner remained immobile in prison while doctors examined him. Finally after studying him for thirty days, a doctor pronounced him insane with an "incurable mania." The prisoner maintained the trance for another nine months in prison, and then was moved to the Casa de Locos, an institution for the mentally ill. Nineteen months later he broke a window, tied together the strips of a blanket, and escaped. Not all prisoners were able to feign insanity for such a long period, but prisoners knew the ruse well and called it "the sanest insanity in the world."[51]

Inmates used a variety of tricks to escape. Many dressed themselves as women or priests in clothing smuggled into the prison by friends. Although some were caught and whipped, many escaped in successful masquerades. Escapes often depended on team work. Women prisoners got the key to their door and pretended to play catch with it while actually getting an impression of it in a roll. They asked outside friends to make a key from the impression, and then easily escaped over the roof at night with the cooperation of a trusty guard. An even larger group of prisoners escaped on the day of Saint John. Days before the festival prisoners dug a hole in the lower cells, removing the dirt in their hats and depositing it in the prison latrine. Faking piety, they got permission from the warden on the day of the festival to decoate some staffs and make a presentation for the other prisoners. Under this pretext, they gathered in the lower cells and more than forty slipped through the hole, two by two. Although people outside the prison saw them, they did not report them to authorities. It is not surprising that city council records frequently mention the repairing of holes in the prison's walls.[52]

Sometimes prisoners seemed less interested in actually escap-

51. Ibid., Part I.
52. Pedro de León, Part II, chapter 30, folios 211 ff. C. Chaves, Parts I, II. An example of a request to repair prison walls after an escape attempt is in AMS, Siglo XVII, Sección 4, Escribanías de Cabildo, Tomo 10, No. 33.

ing than in confounding the authorities. While they were being transported to the galleys in the nearby Port of Santa Maria, thirty-six prisoners removed their shackles and escaped from the two constables guarding them. The constables were able to capture twenty-four of the fugitives, but then decided that it would be worse for them to appear with only twenty-four prisoners than not to appear at all. The constables fled, and the twenty-four prisoners made their way back to the Royal Prison. Chaves suggested that they returned to prison because they enjoyed very comfortable lives there, but we can also imagine the prisoners' delight in reporting to the warden the escape of their constables.[53]

A very different kind of team work was involved in escaping prison through the *palabrilla* (little word). According to Pedro de León, thousands of prisoners were able to leave prison after a small word on their behalf was spoken to a scribe, judge, or lawyer. An exchange of money or other arguments for the respectability of the prisoner convinced judicial officers to release him.[54]

Some groups were exempt from the power of the prison. Clergy accused of crimes were usually turned over to ecclesiastical authorities. Children younger than fourteen were not considered legally responsible and were rarely turned over to the Royal Prison. The traditional code of law protected nobles from imprisonment with common prisoners. Usually they were placed under house arrest, but occasionally they were held in the Royal Prison, where the warden rented out special quarters to them. One famous noble, Lope Ponce, literally held court in the Royal Prison for more than four years. His high connections prompted prison officials to let him come and go freely, to keep his woman with him, and to live as a minor despot in the prison.[55]

Prison authority over women visitors was also limited. Chaves reported that more than one hundred prostitutes slept each

53. C. Chaves, Part III.

54. Pedro de León, Part II, chapter 24, folios 189ff.

55. Samuel Parsons Scott, trans., *Las Siete Partidas* (Chicago, New York, and Washington, 1931), Seventh Partida, Title XXIX, Law IV, p. 1453. Pedro de León, appendix 1 to Part II, Case 200.

night in the prison, welcomed by the prisoners and tolerated by the prison authorities.[56] In the prison the poorest women found shelter at no cost and an occasional paying customer. Sometimes wealthier women came, attracted by a few dashing prisoners who promised adventure. Chaves described one woman who came each feast day and Sunday to the prison. Using the pretext of going to church, she would leave her house well dressed, accompanied by servants and a page. At church she excused herself quickly and went to a friend's house, where she changed clothing and slipped away to meet a lover in prison.[57]

Women were imprisoned for abortion, prostitution, theft or adultery, but not for debt or civil crimes. Although they did manage estates and run businesses in Seville at this time, male relatives or husbands were customarily considered responsible for their indebtedness and civil agreements. In addition, women could escape imprisonment for prostitution by declaring that they were married, for married women were subject to their husband's authority, and their sexual misbehavior was prosecuted as adultery.[58]

Finally, the indomitable spirit of some prisoners limited the power of the prison. Two highwaymen, Diego Mesa and Juan de la Cruz, became legends because they maintained their swaggering bravado up to the moment they were hanged and quartered. Juan de la Cruz entertained the entire prison with stories of his amazing exploits, and he even managed to divert his torturers. Twirling their mustaches and tossing off jokes, these two men never crawled like ants. If the power of the prison was sufficient to hand them over to the hangman, it was never able to kill off the legends of their exploits and bravado in the face of authority.[59]

Some local officials treated the Royal Prison as a private fiefdom rather than an agency of the Crown and city government.

56. C. Chaves, Part I.
57. Ibid., Part III.
58. Pedro de León, Part II, chapter 2, folio 111^v; chapter 12, folio 142^v. The death penalty was provided for a woman who aborted herself; see Scott, Seventh Partida, Title VIII, Law VIII, pp. 1346–47.
59. Pedro de León, appendix 1 to Part II, Cases 213, 214.

The warden wielded considerable political influence. He appointed many officials of the prison, and he administered a lucrative business. Empowered to receive donations for poor prisoners and to disperse letters of payment, he was detained from "robbing the world" only by his own conscience.[60] Evidently Chaves did not believe that a personal conscience was much restraint, for he reported that the warden demanded more than all other justices and used his authority to a greater degree than the king.[61]

Despite his powerful position, the warden was not permitted to administer the prison free from outside interference. The Crown had long insisted that city officials should visit the prison regularly to ensure its proper administration, and it specifically ordered the asistente and his assistants to visit the prison each Saturday.[62] According to Morgado, two judges of the royal court and the chief constable were also required to visit the prison one day a week.[63] These visits protected the lives and welfare of poor prisoners, and also checked the power of prison officials. A report to the city council in 1615, for example, reiterated the need for jurados to visit the prison regularly, and it also suggested that all donations for poor prisoners should be kept in a special iron box with three keys, one key for each of three administering jurados.[64]

As a political tool, the prison was not wholly successful. Rather than molding criminals into useful citizens, as nineteenth-century reformers would later propose, the prison was a primary breeding ground for the underworld. Rituals of violence inside controlled conflicts and emphasized the strength and unity of officials, but even the most systematic terror could not cow some prisoners. Inmates taunted judicial officials and made sport of

60. Ibid., Part II, chapter 4, folio 116ᵛ.

61. C. Chaves, Part I.

62. AMS, Ordenanzas, "Titulo: Del cabildo y regimiento de Sevilla;" "De los jurados," and "Del asistente y de sus tenientes." Guichot y Parody, discussed a royal decree on the prison of Seville in 1337, 1:221.

63. Morgado, p. 194.

64. Concern for poor prisoners is in the ordinances approved by the city council in 1549, AMS, Archivo General, Sección 1, Carpeta 15, No. 18. The proposal for the iron box to be held by jurados is in AMS, Siglo XVII, Sección 4, Escribanías de Cabildo, Tomo 10, No. 24.

escaping from them. They quarreled and fought despite efforts of prison officials to monopolize the use of violence. The prison was not much more successful as a smaller sphere of political power, for both Crown and city government restrained the warden from ruling it as his own fief.

The variety of efforts to prevent the prison from being a successful political tool suggests the complexity of developing political power in Seville. The underworld was not alone in resisting an all-powerful Royal Prison. The Crown and most city fathers were also concerned to control it and curb its potential power. While prisoners used mockery and dirty tricks to resist the power of the prison, city officials used careful visiting committees and reports—very different tactics for a similar objective.

5

Soldiers and Picaros

IN the sixteenth and seventeenth centuries requests for soldiers bombarded the city of Seville as the military needs of the Crown of Castile increased. Seville in 1570 raised 3000 armed men and Triana 500 to help the Crown quell a mutiny of Moors in the southern provinces.[1] In an effort to preserve his Hapsburg empire, Philip II increased his Army of Flanders from 13,000 in 1572 to 85,000 in 1574.[2] Philip also needed soldiers for Portugal, and Seville sent in 1580 at the king's request 1500 infantrymen and 200 horses to support his claim to the Portuguese throne. In addition, the city had to provide forty pikesmen and sixty soldiers armed with arquebuses for every one hundred foot soldiers, requirements of the *tercio* method of warfare. In this pattern, pikesmen formed a protective square around swordsmen, and both were supported by the artillery of arquebusiers.

The Spanish army was an awesome military force in Europe during the sixteenth and seventeenth centuries. Its tough professional soldiers marched in precision and fought with discipline. They were well-trained and well-equipped, proudly wearing the uniform of the king's elite. The Spanish soldier in Velazquez' painting "The Lancers" holds his lance with pride. He stands straight, sits tall, and looks any man directly in the eye.

1. Guichot y Parody, 2:73.
2. Geoffrey Parker, *The Army of Flanders and the Spanish Road 1567–1659; The Logistics of Spanish Victory and Defeat in the Low Countries' War* (Cambridge, 1972), p. 27.

The contrast between this soldier and a thieving, shifty rogue could not be greater. In early modern Seville, however, much to the consternation of city residents, a soldier who entered Seville was as likely to be an antisocial ruffian as a defender of the state. Local citizens complained repeatedly of thefts, murders, and other outrages suffered at the hands of soldiers.

Chronicles and documents from the archives of Seville explain the close relationship between the soldier and the picaro, a migrant, clever rogue. Military problems and requirements of this period forced the Crown and city government to accept underworld people into an army that became an agency for renewal of the underworld as well as an arm of political authority. Both officials and underworld used the army, and each tolerated the other in an uneasy partnership.

MILITARY REQUIREMENTS AND PROBLEMS

The military needs of Philip II continued, even after he had secured the Portuguese throne. He was particularly concerned with the English, who harassed his coasts and ships on the Atlantic. In 1588 he directed Seville to defend itself and its immediate coastline. The city was to draw up a list of all men between the ages of twenty and fifty years who would be "useful for warfare," and it was to impose this order on all villages within its jurisdiction. Any noncomplying village would be fined 20,000 maravedís.[3]

English threats to Cadiz and other parts of the coast near Seville maintained pressure on Seville to obey. When the English attacked Cadiz in 1596, Seville sent twenty-four companies of infantrymen. One year later the Crown requested that the city send 2500 armed soldiers immediately to man the galleys patrolling the coasts. The Duke of Medina Sidonia, who was captain-general of troops in this area, replied that sending this number of men would leave Seville completely defenseless. The king answered that he understood the hardship, but the need for soldiers to patrol the coast was critical. Grudgingly, the city council

3. AMS, Siglo XVI, Sección 3, Escribanías de Cabildo, Tomo 17, No. 20.

6 "The Surrender of Breda," also called "The Lancers." Diego Rodriguez
de Silva Velazquez.

agreed to raise 800 more men. When the English again threatened Cadiz in 1625, Seville sent 1700 armed infantrymen. In 1635 the Crown directed Seville to send 200 infantrymen to guard the coasts, and ten years later another royal levy required 400 men from Seville to man the fleet sailing for the New World.[4]

Portuguese rebellions in the late 1630's and 1640 also required many soldiers from Seville. In 1637 the king wrote to the city council, directing it to help him in Portugal with "the greatest number of armed men that is possible."[5] The head of the city council took three companies of infantrymen and ten companies of cavalrymen to join the Duke of Medina Sidonia in Badajoz, close to the Portuguese border. The soldiers returned to Seville in a few days, after hanging the leaders of a rebellion that had been triggered by new royal impositions on the Portuguese. Evidently Seville frequently maintained a military force in Badajoz, for the city reported in 1643 that it had 150 cavalrymen and 300 infantrymen in the army at Badajoz. By 1657 a city chronicle reported that Seville had raised four tercios of infantrymen for the war against Portugal.[6]

The growing need for military manpower came at a time when monetary depreciation inflated the costs for keeping arms and a horse and reduced the numbers of nobles available for military service. In 1492 Ferdinand and Isabella had decreed that all subjects with an annual income of 50,000 maravedís were obligated to provide military service. In 1564 the minimum income for obligatory military service was raised to 1000 ducats, and in 1600 it was raised still further to 2000 ducats. The city could not find enough men who were able to support themselves in military service to the Crown, and the cost to the city became staggering. The city council reported that the city had to pay

4. Ortiz de Zuñiga, 4:581–582. Pablo Antón Solé, "El saqueo de Cádiz por los Ingleses," *Archivo Hispalense,* Series 2, 54 (1971–72), 219. Ariño, pp. 169–173. Guichot y Parody, 2:193. AMS, Siglo XVII, Sección 4, Escribanías de Cabildo, Tomo 21, No. 4.

5. Guichot y Parody, 2:238.

6. Ibid., pp. 238–239, 252–253. Ortiz de Zuñiga, 4:757.

10,000 ducats to cover expenses of its armed force of 450 men in the army of Badajoz in 1643.[7]

Nobles with a military obligation sometimes resisted royal requests. In 1642 so many nobles failed to respond to the Crown's call to arms against rebels in Portugal and Catalonia that crown officials had to write repeatedly to the city and invoke a fine of 20,000 ducats for noncompliance. Some nobles contributed money or provided infantrymen so that they would be excused from military service. The city council complained that sending all their nobles to serve in the royal army would abandon Seville to the many Portuguese and foreigners who were living here, but the king's military needs deafened him to these complaints. Some nobles were arrested and fined for not providing military service. Other noncomplying nobles were threatened with losing their noble privileges. Any person filing a publicly executed paper in Seville was required to sign an oath that he had remained in Seville because he was not of noble status and was therefore exempt from military service. Many nobles avoided this trap by refusing to execute any public papers, a ploy that caused "much damage" to business in the city.[8] When this coercion failed to bring nobles into the army, the royal audiencia listed 57 members of the city council and directed them to form a company to assist the king in Portugal and Catalonia.[9]

The methods of warfare used by the Spanish Crown in this period also affected the quality and quantity of the military manpower it needed. The wider use of infantry rather than cavalry meant that some soldiers did not need a horse, although infantry tactics often required a greater number of men, particularly in siege warfare. An infantry duel in Flanders tied down

7. Domínguez Ortiz, *Orto,* p. 56. Nicholás Tenorio, "Las milicias de Sevilla," *Revista de Archivos, Bibliotecas y Museos,* Series 2, 17 (1907), 243. Guichot y Parody, 2:252–253.

8. "Diferentes casos," Memorias eclesiásticas, BC, 84-7-19, folio 220[V]. "Algunas memorias, Memorias de diferentes cosas, BC, 84-7-21, folios 258–259[V].

9. AMS, Siglo XVII, Sección 4, Escribanías de Cabildo, Tomo 22, No. 52.

30,000 men to one garrison.[10] Arming the ships that patrolled the coasts and defended the Spanish fleets tied up thousands of other soldiers. The Crown's wish to secure its claims on the New World kept even more soldiers occupied, far from the arenas of battle in Europe.

While the Crown called for more and more soldiers from Seville, the city lost many people in the eight major epidemics reported in chronicles between 1520 and 1649.[11] It is true that epidemics usually take the very young and very old first, rather than men of military service age; in addition, the estimates of deaths may have been exaggerated. Nevertheless, these demographic crises placed an even greater burden on the city at times when it was ordered to send more of its men to serve in the king's army. In 1657, for example, Seville had to send four tercios of soldiers to fight in Portugal, and this was only seven years after the epidemic of 1649, which was estimated to have taken 300,000 lives.[12]

At times the city had no difficulty in filling its military quotas. A chronicler wrote that in 1596 the twenty-four companies raised by Seville to defend Cadiz were unpaid soldiers, most of them young and boisterous and quick to respond to the call to arms. Members of the city council volunteered to go as captains, eager to protect the fleet from New Spain that had anchored in Cadiz, as well as to perform a patriotic duty close to home.[13]

More often, recruiters had to work very hard to fill their lists. The usual procedure was to commission a captain who went from village to village to enlist men. If he had a paymaster with him, he had less difficulty, for there was no shortage of unemployed or dissatisfied men eager to sign up for an instant payday. When the captain entered a village, he ordered the usual public proclamation, placed his banner in the window of the inn where he was

10. Parker, p. 11.

11. AMS, Efemérides, "Noticias y casos," No. 1. Ignacio de Góngora, "Relacion del contagio de 1649," Memorias de diferentes cosas, BC 84-7-21. AMS, Siglo XVI, Sección 3, Escribanías de Cabildo, Tomo 7, No. 16, 17.

12. Góngora, Guichot y Parody, 2:266.

13. Ortiz de Zuñiga, 4:581–582.

staying, and prominently displayed his paymaster. Without the promise of immediate pay, however, the recruiter had to rely on lists of eligible men drawn up by local parishes. In 1580 Francisco Tello of Seville reported the difficulty of raising soldiers through parish lists, and he suggested a drawing of names from a box. Evidently recruiters without paymasters were unpopular. In 1636 Luís de Lazana, who had been sent to register men and arms, was stabbed to death in the parish of San Vicente.[14]

Royal orders to raise a large number of men so often, and frequently on very short notice, led recruiters to accept any able-bodied man, regardless of his background or lack of equipment. Not surprisingly, then, many companies raised by Seville included gamblers, ruffians, and drifters. A chronicler described a company of soldiers from Seville in 1569 which included nobles, naturalized foreigners, and quarrelsome gambling men. Most men recruited into the army in Seville, he said, were people who had come to the city from other regions and had found no other occupation.[15] The decreasing quality of men enlisted in the army prompted the Duke of Alva to write to Philip II pleading for "men of substance," so that the army would not be left "in the hands of laborers and lackeys."[16]

The city council noted the problems of accepting men of lesser quality into the army. In a letter of August 1640, the council complained to the Council of Castile that it had provided more than 8000 men to serve in Cadiz, Lisbon, and Catalonia, despite the difficulty nobles had in finding substitutes. They paid 150 ducats for each infantry substitute, and 500 ducats for a cavalry substitute. Even when they had paid these amounts, however, the substitutes frequently absconded with the money, forsaking their obligation to military service.[17]

14. Rodríguez Marín, *Miscelánea*, p. 52. Parker, p. 37. AMS, Siglo XVI, Sección 3, Escribanías de Cabildo, Tomo 17, No. 17. Memorias eclesiásticas, BC, 84-7-19, folio 206^v.

15. Ortiz de Zuñiga, 4:534.

16. Quoted in Parker, p. 41.

17. Quoted in Antonio Domínguez Ortiz, "Documentos para la historia de Sevilla y su Antiguo Reino," *Archivo Hispalense*, Series 2, 44-45 (1966), 265-266.

In times of military urgencies, prison sentences for "non-heinous" offenses were commuted to military service. When the English attacked Cadiz in 1596, the chief justice of the audiencia in Seville ordered that many prisoners from the Royal Prison be pardoned and sent to defend Cadiz. Even the famous Diego Lopez, a thug with a cut-off nose, was sent to the army, and the notorious highwayman Gonzalo Xenis marched at the head of one of the companies sent to Cadiz. Extreme military necessity in 1647 prompted the royal government to advise army captains: "If there are any men in the prisons of the Kingdom of a suitable age for service, provided that they are not there for heinous offenses, they may be set free, commuting their sentences to service in these companies for a limited period."[18] Underworld people must have sensed the irony of receiving arms and a commutation from a royal government that at other times vigorously tried to impose its own justice on them and monopolize all use of violence.

One key military job unsuitable to nobles was the backbreaking job of rowing the galleys, a task left to slaves or convicts. Since the numbers of galley rowers depended on the Crown's military needs, prison officials were often asked to transport their prisoners and increase the numbers sentenced to the galleys. In May of 1633, for example, the head of Seville's city council was directed to transport 170 galley slaves from the prison of Toledo to the Port of Santa Maria, and another noble was ordered to gather all available galley slaves from the prisons in the province of Seville. Galley needs were so urgent that royal directives in both 1637 and 1639 ordered all slaves within twelve leagues of the sea to be taken to the prisons for transfer to galley service. Owners resisted the orders and tried to hide their slaves, but many were found and taken in chains.[19]

18. Quoted in Parker, p. 46. Ariño, p. 38.

19. Domínguez Ortiz, *Orto*, p. 64. "Diferentes casos sucedidos en Sevilla en diversas mate[as]," Memorias eclesiásticas, BC, 84-7-19, folio 207[v]. AMS, Siglo XVII, Sección 4, Escribanías de Cabildo, Tomo 16, No. 38. Eugene L. Asher, *The Resistance to the Maritime Classes: The Survival of Feudalism in the France of Colbert* (Berkeley and Los Angeles, 1960), p. 7, discusses galley slaves in seventeenth-century France. I. A. A. Thompson gives a more complete description of galley slaves in Spain.

Military levies provided only intermittent employment, and this further reinforced the connection between underworld and military. Local military leaders sometimes spent time and money to raise a company for a military campaign only to find the campaign had ended before their men had left for active military duty. What happened to the men who were discharged? The social and economic dislocations of frequent military levies were enormous, but the cost and problems of maintaining a large permanent army seemed even greater. In 1598 the city council wrote to the king asking permission to dismantle its militia. There were no pressing enemies, the council wrote. Moreover, members of the militia had indulged in gambling and had committed murders and robberies, in addition to costing the city a large sum in expenses.[20]

Few soldiers dismissed with the thanks of their commanders at the end of a campaign had a secure job awaiting them in the civilian world. Many had joined in the first place because they had no other livelihood. Unemployed soldiers were often left to their own devices to return to civilian life as best they could, and they frequently found their way to cities like Seville which promised quick money or opportunity. The Marquis of Aytona described the plight of discharged soldiers in the mid-seventeenth century:

Some return indignant to their lands, trusting to a relative, resolved to put up with the most abject poverty rather than re-enlist. Others go back in despair to the army, and not only do they become trouble-makers in the ranks since they have so little inclination to serve, but I have been assured that this caused more than one and a half thousand veterans and 200 men relieved of duty to go off to serve in Venice and in Florence, and elsewhere in the years 1644, 1645, and 1646; and many take sides with our enemies. Others fall by the wayside and take menial jobs to live. Many have recourse to vice. Others seek alms in the convents, even in the streets, and others perish of want.[21]

20. AMS, Siglo XVI, Sección 3, Escribanías de Cabildo, Tomo 5, No. 12. Guichot y Parody, 2:131–132.

21. Quoted in Domínguez Ortiz, *Golden Age*, p. 37.

The temporary nature of military service compounded one of the most onerous problems of the military—how to provide soldiers with food, shelter, arms, and discipline. A small, permanent, and professional army was conditioned to accept military discipline and a regular system for provisions. Moreover, the war in Flanders lasted for such a long period of time that the army devised a system for moving money and supplies to its men.[22] Many of the men who joined in Seville, however, were formed into temporary armies that had little time for training recruits in the fine points of military discipline or for devising efficient ways to provide them with food, shelter, and arms.

The most common solution to the problem of provisioning soldiers was for the military commander of the area to direct the city government to provide his soldiers with bed and board, and sometimes with arms. In 1580 the city council was directed to pay half the expenses of the soldiers it was required to send to the Portuguese campaign. When the city replied that it lacked enough money to pay these expenses, the king granted the city council permission to take out a loan of 20,000 ducats. Through his captain-general, the Duke of Medina Sidonia, the king repeated a few months later the order that the city was to provide for the soldiers they had raised for the Portuguese campaign. The expenses of provisioning soldiers provoked conflicts between military leaders and the city government of Seville, but the city council usually acquiesced. In 1643 the council agreed not only to pay for the soldiers sent to Badajoz, but also to pay two reales each day to wives of these men, or three reales each day to wives who had children.[23]

When the city was unable to pay expenses for its soldiers in 1653, the Crown proposed that it raise this money through a sales tax on wine and live cattle.[24] Most residents would have

22. This is a central theme of Parker; see esp. his discussion of provisions by contract, pp. 162–164.

23. Guichot y Parody, 2:96–97, 213. AMS, Siglo XVI, Sección 3, Escribanías de Cabildo, Tomo 2, No. 38. AMS, Siglo XVII, Sección 4, Escribanías de Cabildo, Tomo 4, No. 16. "Diferentes casos," Memorias eclesiásticas, BC, 84-7-19, folio 230.

24. AMS, Siglo XVII, Sección 4, Escribanías de Cabildo, Tomo 36, No. 40.

tolerated this sales tax if they had not been forced, in addition, to provide for soldiers who were quartered with them. Soldiers frequently spent their daily allowance on gambling and carousing and then expected local residents to feed and board them without charge. When the city council complained of this practice to the Duke of Medina Sidonia in 1582, he defended the army, pointing out that it gave one real to each soldier every day to pay for his food. Nevertheless, he agreed to quarter soldiers on both sides of the river in Seville and thus relieve some of the pressure of boarding and feeding soldiers. Eight years later the king issued new rules to correct "disorders and excesses that some captains, officers, and soldiers . . . have committed against the people." The daily allowance was raised to one and one-half reales for each soldier, and they were to move in groups of 25, led by one who was charged with keeping order and discipline.[25]

A sixteenth-century resident of Triana, the suburb across the river from Seville, described one of the incidents that turned townspeople against soldiers. A shipmaster came to get bread in Triana for the soldiers and sailors on his ship, and he asked a baker for twenty loaves. When the baker gave him the bread and asked him to pay, he asked how much. "Six reales," answered the baker. The shipmaster, who felt that the baker was trying to get more than his usual price, pretended to look in his sack for the money. Suddenly he rushed the baker, shouting, "This stick is your money." He whacked the baker in the ribs and fled with the bread. Many people from the neighborhood and a sheriff who had been nearby pursued the shipmaster. Shielding himself with a large earthenware jar, he lunged and thrust so well with his sword that no one could arrest him. Although wounded in the arm, he escaped to the ship, still without paying for the bread.[26]

Local residents not only had to pay to feed and board these soldiers; they also had to endure violence and insults from them. Their trees were cut and their fruit stolen. Citizens complained repeatedly of "great vexations," robberies, and murders at the

25. AMS, Siglo XVI, Sección 3, Escribanías de Cabildo, Tomo 17, No. 14; AMS, Papeles Importantes, Siglo XVI, Tomo 9, No. 50.

26. Ariño, pp. 28–29. Ambrosias de la Cuesta y Saavedra, Memorias historicas sevillanas, BC, 82–5–21, folios 198ff.

hands of undisciplined soldiers. In 1631 they asked that all soldiers be quartered in *quartels* "where they be contained in military discipline, in view of their superiors, and having there the necessary provisions."[27] Despite attempts to improve the provisioning and discipline of soldiers, these problems remained a sore point between the military and the people.

The mobility of the army also promoted a close association between the underworld and the military. If the men enlisted in Seville had been kept as a local militia in the immediate area, they would have been recognizable to the citizens, who could have held them more accountable for their behavior. In most cases, however, soldiers were sent to Portugal, Catalonia, Flanders, or even the New World. They looked upon the army as a means to escape the law or obligations at home. Far from home, they treated civilians with less respect and felt less restraint about exploiting them.

The particular military needs of the Crown for a large army raised in haste and for short periods of time to serve in many different places increased the likelihood that underworld people would serve in the military. At the same time, these requirements diminished the possibility that the military could promote a cultural unity favorable to the Crown. An unemployed farm laborer who was conscripted to defend Cadiz in 1596 would scarcely have had time to learn a few rudiments of military discipline before he was discharged. He would meet men from other parts of Spain, and they all fought together against a common enemy, but their military experience promoted an underworld view toward life rather than a deep loyalty to the Spanish Crown. The army could promote cultural identity, but it was a two-edged sword that could help or hinder political authority.

Even though the Crown had to protect its citizens from the outrages of its soldiers, conflicts between soldiers and citizens could not destroy the mutually beneficial government-underworld partnership in the army. The underworld provided the Crown with the necessary manpower, and it helped nobles fill their military quotas. The local noble commissioned as a captain

27. Cuesta y Saavedra, folios 198 ff. AMS, Siglo XVII, Sección 4, Escribanías de Cabildo, Tomo 36, Nos. 37, 44.

to enlist soldiers looked upon gamblers, pimps, and petty thieves not as dangerous enemies so much as cannon fodder. The noble called to military service was often glad to pay an unemployed drifter to take his place in the army. On the other hand, underworld people welcomed military service as a livelihood and license to survive. They also found in it an hospitable breeding ground for their own culture.

CULTURAL RENEWAL OF THE UNDERWORLD

The underworld could not depend on biological propagation to replace its constantly moving members, nor on family socialization to preserve its culture, for it was hardly noted for its high birth rate or strong family structure. The army, however, was one of the institutions that served to transmit the culture of the underworld, for it promoted the qualities most characteristic of underworld people.

Idleness characterized both the soldier and the picaro. Soldiers for the most part were temporarily employed. Even when they were on active duty, there were long, boring hours of guard duty or idle periods on standby. Tradition permitted them to have gambling tables in their garrisons, and gambling became the most common way to fill idle hours.[28] Soldiers who had known nothing of the tricks of cards and games before they joined the army quickly learned from their comrades in arms. They also learned to survive the bloody quarrels that punctuated gambling sessions.

Military life fostered a collective identity that underworld people used to distinguish themselves from outsiders. Because soldiers were usually on the move with their company, they felt very separate from landholders or city residents. Encouraged by the tradition of a separate military justice, they considered themselves outside the formal laws and informal sanctions of the villages and cities they passed through. Soldiers also felt the hostility of civilians who had to board and feed them. When conflict erupted between a soldier and a civilian, other soldiers invariably ran to the defense of their comrade. Soldiers from the

28. Deleito y Piñuela, *Mala*, p. 225.

ships that came to port in Seville sometimes rushed into the city carrying flags from their ships and causing all kinds of "inconvenience," as the city council complained.[29]

City chronicles report many cases of soldiers acting together against the residents of Seville. When ships' soldiers caused trouble in the city in 1525, the city council asked the king to help restore order and control the crews of his ships. The rough soldiers, it pointed out, were a bad example to the rest of the toughs in the city. The city's complaint was repeated some seventy years later when the council passed a resolution referring to the "insults, aggravations, murders, robberies, scandals, and disrespect that the soldiers of the galleys cause in this city."[30]

Strong group identification among soldiers is evident in one account of a city-military conflict in 1595. Eleven ships had anchored in Seville at one time, and their crews had put gambling tables out on the river banks. When a violent quarrel erupted among the gambling soldiers, the sheriff of Triana intervened to make an arrest. A crowd formed, and people of Triana and the soldiers began to throw rocks at one another. The sheriff had to retreat without his prisoner. The next day the scene was repeated, but several sheriffs rushed a soldier and took him prisoner. Soldiers poured into the Plaza de San Francisco and everyone, including city officials, fled behind closed doors. The soldiers wanted to break into the prison to rescue their comrade, but their commanding officer negotiated with city officials, who agreed to release him if all soldiers returned to their ships. That night the head of the city council posted many guards on the city streets, locked the city gates, and hanged the imprisoned soldier in the Royal Prison. When a small group of his comrades came for him in the morning, they found his corpse.[31]

Although the king agreed in 1618 that galleys needing provision in Seville should be anchored farther from the city, uproars continued between soldiers and city residents. In one ruckus a

29. AMS, Siglo XVII, Sección 4, Escribanías de Cabildo, Tomo 5, No. 22.

30. AMS, Papeles Importantes, Siglo XVI, Tomo 12, No. 25. Also quoted in Guichot y Parody, 2:118.

31. Ariño, pp. 30–31. Guichot y Parody, 2:116–117. Pedro de León, appendix 1 to Part II, Case 208.

sheriff of the city was killed, one soldier was hanged in the windows of the audiencia, and two others were hanged in the windows of the city council chambers. The commander of the fleet came marching into the city with his soldiers and artillery ready to defend his men. The archbishop went out to meet him and pacify him before he confronted city officials. He convinced the commander to return his men to the ships, but the quarrels continued and more townspeople and soldiers died, "as always happens when ships arrive in Seville."[32]

Military life encouraged violence and justified the use of weapons. Weapons manufacture in Seville increased as the city was directed to send arms to defend Cadiz and the ships patrolling the Atlantic coast. Sevillian sword-making had been wellknown for centuries, and in ancient times the Calle Sierpes had been called the street of the sword-makers. By the sixteenth century, arquebus-makers also had shops on this street. One reason for Crown interest in rebuilding the gunpowder factory after its explosions in 1579, 1613, and 1667, was its concern for providing the artillery to defend Cadiz and the fleets of New Spain. City residents scrambled wildly for arms when the English appeared off Cadiz in 1596. Some 400 rusty arquebuses were found in the armory, but few other weapons were available to send to Cadiz. No one responded to a call for arms in 1619, so the city council repeated the public announcement calling for bids to provide 600 sets of complete armor, 2100 iron pikes, 660 arquebuses, 2100 powder flasks, 260 halberds, 1400 helmets, 67 bucklers, and 900 forked spears. In 1626 Philip IV directed Seville to maintain an armory to manufacture and store arms and ammunition. The city council named a warden to keep careful records of the people who checked out arms from the city armory.[33]

32. "Desde el año de 1616 asta el de 1634," Papeles varios, BC, 85-4-11. AMS, Efemérides, "Noticias y casos," cuaderno 1.

33. AMS, Siglo XVI, Sección 3, Escribanías de Cabildo, Tomo 3, Nos. 6, 7. José Gestoso y Perez, *Curiosidades antiguas sevillanas; estudios arqueológicos* (Sevilla, 1885), pp. 68-71. Ariño, pp. 33-34. AMS, Archivo General, Sección 1, Carpeta 9, No. 157. AMS, Siglo XVII, Sección 4, Escribanías de Cabildo, Tomo 5, No. 36.

Despite the care of city officials to control the distribution of weapons, all kinds of ruffians received arms and a lesson in violence when they enlisted in the army. The right to carry arms, in fact, was one privilege that distinguished soldiers from lesser civilians. Three hundred years later a national military force would stamp out the very qualities of swaggerer and bully in Spain that the military seemed to encourage in the early modern period.[34] The tightly disciplined *Guardia Civil* was not possible in this period, for the central government could not control the raggle-taggle thugs whom it had licensed to use violence and arms.

Ironically, military life encouraged mutiny more effectively than discipline. One soldier described a common pattern of mutiny in the Spanish armies of the seventeenth century:

> These mutinies usually take place on campaign, and the men get the name of the 'squadron of the disaffected.' Their first concern is to occupy some stronghold from which they can roam the surrounding countryside, the which, to avoid worse trouble, agrees to pay them tribute. And then they elect a leader, whom they call the *electo*, who has several counsellors. The infantry is commanded by a *sargento mayor* and the cavalry by a *gobernador*. Offices are bestowed and decisions taken by a show of hands. The quarters of the *electo* overlook the square, and from a window he makes his proposals to the squadron. When they are fed up with him, they pass from words to bullets. For this reason the *electo* has always a sentinel to watch over him. He cannot receive or transmit correspondence without notifying the squadron which in all respects maintains strict military discipline, for they impale on their pikes or shoot down anyone who commits an offence. Most of their rules are savage, therefore, though some are just and legitimate.[35]

Soldiers often deserted from an army of such "popular" discipline. The chaplain Pedro de León attended one deserter before he was executed in Seville in 1585 for highway robbery. Twelve

34. Caro Baroja in Peristiany, ed., pp. 110–111, 116–117.
35. Quoted in Domínguez Ortiz, *Golden Age*, p. 319, note 6.

years later he attended three other soldiers who were hanged in Seville for desertion, theft, murder, and rape.[36]

Parasitism thrived in the army. With a provisioning system that was no more formal than a daily allowance and an order to civilians to feed and shelter soldiers, the men of the army usually had to fend for themselves. They often lived off the land, learning to survive by their wits. When they actually spent their food allowance on food, they used other tricks to make money in the villages. One of the dogs in Cervantes' story, "The Dogs' Colloquy," joined a company of soldiers that was "full of ruffians and leadswingers who used to get up to some fine tricks in the villages we went through." His master presented him as "the Wise Dog" and charged a fee from everyone in the village who came to see his "marvellous tricks and accomplishments."[37] In underworld jargon, a *golondrero* (wandering parasite) was a thief who made himself into a soldier so he could steal more securely, protected by uniform, weapon, mobility, and a special legal status.[38]

The army was a fertile ground for underworld culture not only among soldiers, but also among all the many nonmilitary people associated with it. An army in this period included servants, boatmen, stable boys, and any women and children who could tag along for a while. In his study of the Spanish army in Flanders, Geoffrey Parker estimated that the 5300 Spanish veterans who left the Netherlands in 1577 were accompanied by 2000 lackeys.[39] These people also learned the parasitical, violent, distinctive life-style of the soldier. Many of them, to be sure, had already become acquainted with underworld ideology before they followed the army. Whether military service introduced people to underworld values or simply reinforced them, it was a powerful preserver and transmitter of underworld culture.

36. Pedro de León, appendix 1 to Part II, Cases 112, 235, 239, 246.
37. Cervantes, "The Dogs' Colloquy," p. 225.
38. Hill, p. 115.
39. Parker, p. 176.

MOBILITY AND THE NEW WORLD

The mobility of military service promoted a constant renewal of the underworld. As a parasitical culture, the underworld depended upon both geographical and intercultural movement to provide it with a ready supply of exploitable hosts. It could not survive as a closed caste. When one host dried up or resisted exploitation, the underworld character had to find another. Through military service, he was able to move geographically and socially. The army was his bridge to other cities and people, professions and trades.

Emigration to the New World was one of the best escapes for men in early modern Spain, but the Crown had attempted to control it so that the New World would be settled and governed only by royal license. Captains of ships sailing for the New World were closely questioned about their passengers, and they were required to list them and their licenses.[40] Some nonlicensed people were able to bribe a ship's officer or otherwise escape royal scrutiny. For most, however, military service was the best means to emigrate. Continuing attacks by English, Dutch, and French corsairs increased the need for armed soldiers on the Spanish ships that sailed between Seville and the New World. That many of these soldiers brought an underworld culture with them is evident in the many proceedings against them found in the documents of the Casa de Contratación in the Archive of the Indies. One soldier, for example, was prosecuted and punished on board his ship, the *San Juan Dios*, for blasphemy and hitting another soldier in his face with his open hand. Another shipboard case involved a bloody quarrel of soldiers over a gambling game.[41]

40. Royal ordinances on the discovery and populating of New Spain are in *Collección de documentos ineditos . . . del Real Archivo de Indias* (Madrid, 1865), 8:486. AI, Indiferente General, Sección 5, Legajos 2003 and 2162, contains examples of captains' testimonies and passenger lists.

41. AI, Indiferente General, Sección 5, Legajo 2676, has evidence of extra soldiers hired to defend the Spanish fleet. The two criminal cases cited are in AI, Casa de Contratación, Sección 2, Legajo 58.

The great numbers of soldiers who came to the New World may help to explain why the crown received so many complaints about the people of *mal vivir* who came to the New World and abused the Indians. One observer in Potosí, Peru, wrote in 1595: "There are 3000 Europeans, including Spanish, Portuguese, and other nationalities, 2000 of them idle delinquents who have no other occupation than gambling, drinking, fornication, robbery and assassination."[42] Contemporaries frequently regarded the New World as a Babylon,

> the refuge and shelter of all desperate folk in Spain, the sanctuary of bankrupts, the safe-conduct of murderers, the protection and cover of those gamblers known by the experts in the craft as sharpers, the general decoy for loose women, where many go to be deceived, and few find a way out of their difficulties.[43]

Not all emigrants who went to the New World were soldiers or rogues of the underworld,[44] but conditions in the New World encouraged Spaniards there to use the methods and attitudes of the underworld. In the first place, most soldiers lived there on booty rather than salaries. They sought jewels, precious metals, and slaves, for these became a standard of exchange as well as the bases for large fortunes. Soldiers who took Indian slaves bartered them or gambled them away among one another. "When ships arrive from Spain," an observer wrote, "they barter these Indians for wine, flour, biscuit, and other requisite things. And even when some of the Indian women are pregnant by these same Spaniards, they sell them without any conscience."[45] Transporting captured slaves to ports involved more brutality:

42. Quoted in Lynch, 2:218–219. *Colección . . . Indias*, Tomo 19, pp. 123–124. The picaresque life of Spanish soldiers in the New World described in Girolamo Benzoni, *History of the New World*, 1565, trans. W.H. Smyth, (New York, 1857).

43. Cervantes, *Exemplary Stories*, "The Jealous Extremaduran," p. 147.

44. James Lockhart, in *The Men of Cajamarca: A Social and Biographical Study of the First Conquerors of Peru*, (Austin and London, 1972), develops this point very clearly; see esp. pp. 17–22.

45. Benzoni, pp. 11–12.

And when some of them could not walk, the Spaniards, to prevent their remaining behind to make war, killed them by burying their swords in their sides or their breasts. It was really a most distressing thing to see the way in which these wretched creatures, naked, tired, and lame were treated; exhausted with hunger, sick, and despairing. The unfortunate mothers, with two or three children on their shoulders or clinging around their necks, overwhelmed with tears and grief, all tied with cords or with iron chains around their necks or their arms, or their hands. Nor was there a girl but had been violated by the depredators, wherefore, from too much indulgence, many Spaniards entirely lost their health.[46]

The search for treasure also encouraged brutality. Some Indians described the Spaniards' religion by holding up a piece of gold:

This is the God of the Christians; for this they have come from Castile to our countries, and have subjugated us, tormented us, and sold us as slaves, besides doing us many other injuries. For this they make war and kill each other; for this it is that they are never at rest; that they gamble, swear, tell lies, quarrel, rob, tear the women from each other; and finally, for this they commit every sort of wickedness.[47]

If Spanish soldiers were greedy for booty, it is also true that they faced severe hardships. These difficulties encouraged underworld methods. A Milanese soldier who joined a Spanish expedition to the New World in 1541 described the constant hunger that plagued these men and led to desertions. One night where there was no food, the Spanish governor issued orders for all the dogs to be killed and distributed among the men. "I, for my part, made a present of my share, for it was full of worms," he added. "I then went to [the governor] in the hope that he would provide me with something; but he told me to

46. Ibid., p. 8.
47. Ibid., p. 162.

go and eat of the roots of trees, whereat one of the Spaniards who heard him, said: 'Sir governor, since you will not share the good and the bad with us, go and make war by yourself.' "[48] The testimony of this foreigner was corroborated by a Spanish soldier, who wrote:

> The hardships which must be endured in these countries are so terrible, that the men who come to them, in order that they may not yield up their spirits, nor lose all their flesh, nor despair of the divine clemency, must not be over dainty, nor, to say truth, over wise; they must be hardy and vigorous, and not made of flesh and blood, but of iron and steel. O sinner that I am! to have come here to damage my conscience, waste my time, and lose my teeth. While one is seeking for riches, it is necessary to pass such an infernal life that, when they are attained, one has neither teeth to eat with, nor stomach to digest.[49]

Finally, the methods of exploiting the colonies of the New World encouraged the use of underworld methods. Mines especially depended on the slave labor of Indians, and the imposition of this system required the presence of armed soldiers. Spain had conquered the New World, but the imperial system required an effective occupation by people willing to use violence and brutality. In the army political authority and underworld met face to face and became unlikely partners.

48. Ibid., pp. 131–132.

49. Don Alonso Enriquez de Guzmán, *The Life and Acts of Don Alonso Enriquez de Guzmán, a Knight of Seville, of the Order of Santiago, A.D. 1518 to 1543*, Trans. Clements R. Markham (London, 1862), p. 119.

6

Holy Men and Rascals

PEDRO Fernandez de Esquibel, a clergyman in Seville, was arrested by secular authorities in 1581 for forging royal decrees. The magistrates, unwilling to release to the ecclesiastical courts a man accused of such a serious crime, consulted with Church leaders. The Church agreed to defrock him immediately so that he could remain in secular custody before hanging in the Plaza de San Francisco. Here is an example of the partnership between the Church and political authority, and clear evidence of the bonds between Church and crime.[1]

The Church in Seville had ties with both political authority and the underworld because the clergy included a variety of people from different classes. The poorest assistant to a parish priest belonged to the secular clergy, and so did the wealthy and notable officers of the Cathedral. The regular clergy, those who had accepted the regulation of a religious order, were various enough to include cloistered nuns from noble families and monks who wandered the countryside begging for bread. Some priests had experienced hunger and deprivation, and they blamed this injustice on the social order. A few sought redress through social action as well as prayer. One priest even became a popular leader in the Revolt of the *Pendon Verde* in 1652.[2] On the other hand, some were very unpopular, hated for their educated speech and their presumption that ordinary men could not deal with God without their intercession.

1. "Casos raros," Papeles varios, BC, 85–4–11.
2. Ortiz de Zuñiga, 4:744. See below, pp. 248–262.

Church relations with political authority and the underworld were further complicated because the Church was far more than a religious institution. During the early modern period the Church and the religious orders owned significant amounts of land. Some religious orders were producers; others invested in commerce. As creditors, they and the Church invested in government bonds (*juros*), mortgages on land (*censos*), and simple loans. In addition, the Church, as a political force, shaped legislation, bolstered the legitimacy of secular governments, and furnished men to act as ministers and diplomats. A social institution, the parish church was a focus for each neighborhood in the city. The Church was the major agency for education and charity. It sponsored most of the processions and fiestas of Seville, and it preserved the legends that helped to unify this diverse city.

Underworld people distinguished this complex institution, the Church, from religion, but other city residents believed that the two were symbolically fused. Most people of Seville looked on the Church and underworld as symbols of the holy and profane. More than opposites, the Church and underworld met in a curious confusion of antagonism and mutual exploitation. Their relationship is best demonstrated in three major roles that the Church played in early modern Seville: as intermediary, refuge, and caricature.

THE CHURCH AS INTERMEDIARY

In early modern Seville people usually looked to the Church as intermediary between them and God. From the pulpit they learned what God's laws were. In the confessional they learned how God expected them to translate His laws into everyday behavior. When they wanted to ask something of God, the traditional prayers and rituals of the Church helped them to present their petitions in the proper form and language. Latin, the language of the priest before the altar, was of course unintelligible to most people in the congregation, but they believed that the priest could use it to speak to God for them.

People often turned to the Church to explain disasters and to advise them what to do. A religious procession led by an image of our Lady of the Water in 1605 helped the people of Seville feel less impotent in time of drought. Later in that century, Church authorities explained an epidemic as divine punishment for loose morals, and they urged the city to prohibit all drama and comedies in order to avoid another plague.[3] These intermediaries offered the security of clear-cut answers in uncertain times. They promoted unity by offering a single interpretation of the causes of all ills and the best remedies for them. A community that looked to a priestly intercessor did not fall apart so readily into quarreling factions.

Underworld people awaiting execution in the city's prisons often turned from past cynicism and sinfulness to the monks and priests who could act as intermediaries. Pedro de León, the Jesuit chaplain of the Royal Prison in Seville between 1578 and 1616, described the prisoners' warm reception of his sermons and prayers. Many would kiss his hand and tell him with tears in their eyes how much his words meant to them.[4] There is no doubt that some lifelong thugs repented at the end and were sincerely grateful for the priests who walked and prayed with them and helped them to mount the steps to the scaffold, strengthened in spite of their quaking knees.

Not all condemned prisoners looked to the Church as intermediary. Pedro de León wrote that it was very difficult to pierce the tough exterior of some prisoners, and another firsthand account of the Royal Prison of Seville describes how the prisoners would mock priests, playing at saying Mass or performing as dramatic penitents. At night they would call for the penitential brotherhood of the prison, not out of devotion but for the

3. "Casos raros," Papeles varios, BC, 85-4-11. See also the discussion of this function of religion in William A. Christian, Jr., "De los Santos y María; Panorama de las devociones a santuarios españoles desde el principio de la Edad Media hasta nuestros días," in María Cátedra Tomás, et al., *Temas de antropologia española* (Madrid, 1976), pp. 86–87; and Keith Thomas, *Religion and the Decline of Magic* (New York, 1971), p. 152. AMS, Papeles del Conde de Aguila, Sección Especial, Tomo 62, en folio, No. 40; and Miguel de Mañara, "Motibo principal por que zesaron las comedias en Sevilla año de 1679," BC, 80-1-92.

4. Pedro de León, Part II, chapter 14, folio 151[v].

horrifying delight of watching them punish themselves.[5] To
these people the concept of the Church as intermediary was a
joke.

One reason for underworld cynicism was that the Church also
acted as intermediary between them and the secular law. People
of the underworld clearly recognized the close alliance between
the institutional Church and political authority. Prisoners often
tried to exploit this alliance, confessing to the prison chaplain
in such a way that the priest would be moved to intervene on
their behalf and get a last-minute reprieve. On the other hand,
secular authorities tried to persuade priests to force prisoners to
confess to crimes so that they could use their confessions as
evidence against them. They sometimes condemned a prisoner
to death without sufficient proof of his guilt, refused his appeals,
and then assigned a confessor who would insist that the prisoner
must confess to the crimes in order to "die a good Christian."[6]
Priests who helped condemned men go to their death as "good
Christians" undoubtedly provided comfort for many, but they
also helped to sanctify this ritualized act of violence by secular
justice against those accused of breaking its laws. One view of
the priest with a condemned man at the gallows is that he was
returning a stray sheep to the flock; another view is that he was
mesmerizing the sheep, so that the creature would accept its
fate as a sacrificial victim.

Churchmen frequently used underworld people to personify
evil to the people of Seville. The preacher who thundered against
immorality in the city warned of sins committed by the "gente
de mal vivir" (bad people), the "rufianes" (thugs), and the
"mujeres perdidas" (prostitutes). Because city residents saw these
underworld people on their own streets, they could understand
the priests' admonitions.

The secular government of Seville could use morality as a
pillar of its legitimacy, but it lacked enough sheriffs and judges

---

5. Ibid., Part II. C. Chaves, Part II. Rodríguez Marín, *La Cárcel*, p. 26.

6. This letter is quoted in AMS, Papeles del Conde de Aguila, Sección
Especial, Tomo 5, en folio, No. 11. See also Pedro de León, Part II, chapter
16, folio 156 [v].

to enforce its moral legislation without Church assistance. The parish priest railed against immorality from his pulpit, and he used the confessional to hear individual cases of immorality. The more formal courts of the Inquisition punished moral offenders as well as heretics. The Church was an open partner in upholding the moral order of the city oligarchy, and to many underworld cynics this partisanship belied its posture as disinterested intermediary.

Another reason for cynicism about the Church as intermediary was that some churchmen were more concerned with financial affairs than with matters of the spirit. The Archbishopric of Seville owned much of the land within the city walls, as well as large portions in the surrounding areas. Many religious groups administered extensive estates. In 1582 the Archbishop of Seville censured one of his bishops because he had virtually converted his residence into a manufacturing center and store. A great scandal erupted in 1642 when it was discovered that an administrator of the Jesuit School of San Hermenegildo in Seville had used the funds of his order for business speculations, buying and selling cargoes in the Indies and enriching many of his relatives while amassing a debt of 90,000 ducats against the Jesuits.[7]

Ecclesiastical privileges benefited many churchmen in commercial enterprises, and it also provided many opportunities for the white collar crimes of smuggling and counterfeiting. Clerics and Inquisition officials were exempt from import duties, and they transported goods and papers without customary inspection at city gates. Occasionally they were caught smuggling precious metals and merchandise.[8] Theoretically outside the jurisdiction of secular justice, religious houses could be used for undercover counterfeiting. In 1639 a clergyman was arrested for counterfeiting the stamped paper that was required for all legal and

7. Domínguez Ortiz, *Orto*, p. 43. "Los cargos que resultan de la residencia que se tomó por mando del R^rmo señor don Rodrigo de Castro Arçobispo de Sevilla . . . contra don Alonso Faxardo de Villalobos Obispo·de Esquilache Arcediano y Canónigo de Sevilla," BM 28358, folios 133–134; also cited in Pike, *Aristocrats*, pp. 71–72. Astrain, 5:40–47.

8. AI, Casa de Contratación, Sección 2, Legajo 58, folio 82.

commercial transactions in the seventeenth century, and thirteen years later secular authorities invaded a monastery to arrest some clergymen who were restamping money there.[9]

Ecclesiastical privilege permitted many people to escape the hand of secular justice that lay so heavily on people of the underworld. The numbers of *familiares*, lay servants to the Inquisition, increased dramatically as the Inquisition became more active during this period. Suspected of being secret informers, the familiares were also unpopular because they had the privilege of bearing arms and were exempt from certain prosecutions by secular authorities. The confusion resulting from the many new and unregistered appointments of familiares was very useful to those of the underworld, who would sometimes escape the secular law by claiming that they were familiares when they were arrested.[10]

Underworld people could also feel cynical about the Church when churchmen squabbled among themselves. The rivalry between Jesuits and Dominicans often degenerated into a power struggle involving the Inquisition, for it had been dominated by the Dominicans since Tomás de Torquemada of this order was appointed by Ferdinand and Isabella to head the Inquisition in 1483. Jesuits were denounced for heresy and for making political sermons. They insisted that they were responsible for their own members and would punish them for misbehavior, but the Inquisition asserted that these matters were subject to the Holy Office. In the case of Padre Barba, for example, a Jesuit accused of having "dishonest relations" with several women, the Society of Jesus argued that this was a matter for internal discipline within the Order, but the Inquisition successfully asserted jurisdiction.[11] The Dominican-Jesuit controversy was further complicated because some bishops, opposing the Inquisition as a

9. AMS, Efemérides, folio 33. Maldonado, BC, 84-7-21, folio 133[v].

10. Kamen, *Inquisition*, pp. 147-148. See also Morgado, pp. 189-190, for a description of numerous lay officials of the Inquisition in Seville.

11. Astrain, 2:94-98, 3:353-355, 503-504, 698, 723. José Deleito y Piñuela, *La vida religiosa española bajo el cuarto Felipe; Santos y pecadores* (Madrid, 1952), p. 47. AMS, Efemérides, "Noticias y casos," No. 1. Menéndez y Pelayo, pp. 99-102. Ortiz de Zuñiga, 4:517.

rival to their own powerful positions within the Spanish Church, encouraged the Jesuit-Dominican controversy in order to weaken the Inquisition.

Attempts to correct abuses and reform the clergy increased internal dissension within this group. When Cardinal Archbishop Rodrigo de Castro tried to reform the clergy in Seville in the last quarter of the sixteenth century, he ran into so much opposition that he asked the Crown to help him get support from Rome. He succeeded in making several reforms, but at the price of much dissension. Reformed monks attacked the unreformed secular clergy, a form of anticlericalism which one scholar has identified in the picaresque novel *Lazarillo de Tormes*.[12] In the midst of all the accusations and countercharges it is not surprising that one poor beggar of the city, Bartolomé Fuentes, declared that God would not lower Himself to the hands of undignified clergymen. This was too much for the Inquisition, which subjected him to public penance in an auto de fé on December 22, 1560.[13]

Clerical reform might "purify" the clergy, but it also served political purposes. Both Church and Crown were concerned with controlling ideology, and the Church was a strong competitor that showed disturbing tendencies to act independently. Recognizing that clerical reform could curb this competitor, Philip II readily came to the assistance of Cardinal Archbishop de Castro when he needed help reforming his clergy in Seville. Clerical dissension was a timely excuse for the Crown's imposition of restraint on the power, wealth, and independence of the Church. To many people clerical reform was simply an extension of central control over more members of the clergy, a device to ensure that the Church would be a tool of the secular government.

Cynicism about priests as intermediaries increased in the sixteenth and seventeenth centuries as Seville became a major center of an heretical sect, the Alumbrados. These religious mystics taught that direct union with God was possible without

12. Marcel Bataillon, *El sentido del Lazarillo Tormes* (Paris and Toulouse, 1954), pp. 8–10, 12–13, 22. See also Menéndez y Pelayo, pp. 201-2-3; and Deleito y Piñuela, *Religiosa*, p. 59. Ortiz de Zuñiga, 4:563–564, discussed the Cardinal Archbishop's reforms.

13. Menéndez y Pelayo, p. 115.

a priestly intermediary. The nuns, monks, and secular clergy who belonged to the sect acted as spiritual counselors rather than intermediaries. Mysticism was also an important part of the devotional exercises of Jesuits and followers of Saint Teresa of Avila and Saint John of the Cross, but these groups accepted the discipline of the Church and did not pose the serious Alumbrado challenge to priests. Churchmen like Pedro de León tried to distinguish the "false mysticism" of the Alumbrados from the "true mysticism" of loyal Christians, but their arguments seemed mere hair-splitting to many people.[14]

The Alumbrados also increased cynicism about priests because they provided such tantalizing stories about sexual irregularities accompanying religious ecstasies. Tongues wagged about the Alumbrado monk, Brother Juan de Jesús María, who convinced another monk and a young girl that he could communicate the spirit and love of God to them through his embraces and kisses. Asserting that they could not be guilty of sin because they were in a close state with God, he urged that the three make a spiritual union through the flesh. Francisco Mendez, an Alumbrado preacher, provided another juicy tale when the Inquisition charged him with dancing with a group of beatas after Mass and working them up into such a frenzy that they fell down with their legs uncovered. The Inquisition attempted to root out salacious heretics like these, but their prosecutions also helped to publicize the scandalous tales.[15]

Alumbrados held a special appeal for the women of Seville. Many noble women of the city were followers of Padre Mendez, who may be the Francisco Mendez mentioned above. He stayed at the Franciscan monastery in the city, and on some mornings more than thirty carriages waited there for women who had come to pray and consult with him. An anonymous letter from Seville in 1623 asserted that the greater part of the city was infected with the Alumbrado heresy, "and especially the women."

14. See the treatise originally written by Padre Rodrigo Alvarez as "Tratado se las discreciones de espiritus," and copied with additions by Pedro de León in 1576, in Dominguez Ortiz, "Vida," pp. 195–196.

15. AMS, Efemérides, contains an account of these clerics in a record of an auto de fé in 1624.

Though some of these women were nuns and beatas, many were the wives and daughters of respectable local aristocrats. It was reported that when the Church offered pardons to all who would denounce themselves as Alumbrados, so many women responded that twenty notaries and twenty inquisitors were not enough to handle all the confessions. More than 5000 pardons were issued in 1624 for this heresy in the Archbishopric of Seville.[16] The mass confession revealed not only the extent of the heresy but also the willingness of many to conform ideologically to the teachings of the institutional Church. It suggests that the ladies of Seville gained attention by indulging in a little mysticism and confession of heresy. Religious mysticism was one of the few ways they could protest the priestly and secular authorities who so rigidly controlled their lives. In addition, mystical experiments and confession of heresy offered the emotional intimacy and adventure so lacking in the lives of these women. Some well-born women in the city must have felt that they were regarded seriously as people only when they engaged in heresy. In this period of the Inquisition, heresy literally involved playing with fire. Facing this danger could reaffirm for many women a sense of self that was otherwise smothered in their sheltered lives.[17]

Folk practitioners posed another challenge to the priests' monopoly on the role of intermediary. Some priests specialized in exorcising the devil, but the people of Seville were as likely to call upon a lay expert in the occult arts to vanquish the devil by magic. Folk practitioners spoke a more appealing language than the priests. "The Evil Eye," for example, explained a misfortune more clearly than "God's will," the clergyman's explanation. The spells and charms of the neighborhood wise woman appeared more potent and concrete than a priest's plea to a God whose will seemed so capricious. A saludador (folk faith-healer) who applied his saliva to heal an infected arm performed a specific physical act, while the priest who prayed over the infected arm

16. Menéndez y Pelayo, pp. 236, 243. AMS, *Efemérides,* "Noticias y casos," No. 1.

17. Cf. Keith Thomas, "Women and the Civil War Sects," *Past and Present,* No. 13, April 1958.

seemed only to mutter.[18] Popular support protected many folk-practitioners from prosecution as sorcerers by the Inquisition. Underworld people favored folk-practitioners not only for their traditional wisdom, but also because the occult arts offered so many profitable opportunities for tricking unsuspecting believers.

Although they were challenged by folk-practitioners, attacked by heretics, and besmirched by internecine quarrels, monks and priests retained their role as intermediaries in Seville. This suited the purposes of a secular government which relied on these intermediaries to sanctify its rule. Secular officials were very much in evidence at the public autos de fé at which the Inquisition subjected some people to penance and handed others to the secular authorities for execution.[19] On the other hand, churchmen took a prominent role in the secular public executions. The partnership of Church and government bolstered the legitimacy of the secular order and assured the continuance of the Church as intermediary.

Another reason why the Church retained this role was that the people of the city needed religion as a verbal and symbolical language. Although the Church was a social, economic, and political institution, with worldly concerns far removed from matters of the spirit, it was also a religious institution. In Seville during this period the Church was the major interpreter and preserver of religious beliefs, for it had successfully stifled most popular religious groups and all contemporary religious challengers. Holding a monopoly on religion, it became a depository for the traditional metaphors and imagery by which people expressed ideas and attitudes about themselves, their city, indeed all of life. The populace explained public executions as the consequences of sin and believed that their city government was acting justifiably, as God did when he punished His erring children.

In addition, the rituals of the Church were a common language understood by all the people. Religious rites marked the significant

18. Saludadores are described in Pike, *Aristocrats*, p. 92.

19. For example, see Relacion de un auto de fée que se celebró en el, S[to] Oficio de la Inquisicion de la ciudad de Sevilla en el conv[to] de S[n] Pablo . . . el ultimo día del mes de febrero del año de 1627, BC, 64-7-118, folios 124[v]-125.

events in an individual's life, and all the community could recognize his birth, first communion, marriage, and death. Through religious processions and festivals, people of the city expressed collective unity, common fears, and aspirations. Everyone could participate in these familiar rituals, if only as a spectator observing this demonstration of community.

Ironically, the very dependence on religion as a language and on priests as spokesmen resulted in a form of anticlericalism that is apparent in underworld vocabulary. Just as common people of the city hated the lawyers and legal language on which they had to depend, they disliked the priestly intermediaries and religious language. Priests were hated for revealing the impotence and ignorance of less educated people, an attitude expressed in the underworld vocabluary that gave the religious title "bishop" to the cock.[20] Underworld people used the phrase *de San Martín el dormido* (of sleeping Saint Martin) to describe the crime of robbing or killing a sleeping victim. The poor box of a church was *Juan*, and a *Juanero* was a thief who specialized in robbing poor boxes. Underworld anticlericalism is implicit in their word for clergyman, *farfare*, a term suggesting thin skin or half-baked.[21]

The language of religion was useful to the underworld in a more serious sense also. For example, when the hero of one of their ballads was wounded, his friends gathered around him:

Some promised him Masses,
Others fingered their Rosaries;
Others lit candles
Others sang Psalms.[22]

In another ballad, a contrite young ruffian entered town and asked to talk things over with another he had wronged. The second ruffian conducted himself with dignity and bravado and casually threw out his "benediction" to the younger man.[23]

20. See the germanesca vocabulary at the end of Juan Hidalgo's ballads, printed in Hill, p. 118.

21. Ibid., pp. 107, 112, 113, 114, 116, 122.

22; Ibid., p. 90. The Spanish text is, "Vnos les prometen Missas,/otros rezalle Rosarios;/otros penella candelas/otros cantalle los Salmos."

23. Ibid., p. 92.

Religion provided not only the words but the procedures of some underworld characters.

A basic theological attitude is apparent in underworld words for God, man, and woman. Ballads often referred to a man as *coyme*, a word now used for gambling-house owner or keeper. Women in these ballads were *coymas*, usually meaning prostitutes. God was *el coyme del alto*, literally "the man from above."[24] The close similarity between the words for man, woman, and God suggests that these people sensed much less difference between God and themselves than conventionally religious people like the ancient Jews, who for a long time were forbidden to name God. Underworld people might have mocked the Church as intermediary because they felt more similarity with God and less need for an intermediary. They knew the words and procedures of religion, and they broke their holy spell by using them for their own purposes. The Church wanted to bolster its authority as the only agency capable of using the language of religion, but the underworld showed that anyone could use this language.

THE CHURCH AS REFUGE

Traditionally, the Church provided asylum for people whose lives were in danger, but after 1520 this role was limited. As more and more ruffians ran into churches to escape hotly pursuing sheriffs, the Church and secular authorities agreed that churches should not be allowed to become havens for unlawful thugs. The Count of Puñoenrostro took a hard line when he became head of the city government in 1597. He ordered his lawmen to enter churches and forcibly remove any fugitives.[25]

Though churches were no longer to be used for asylum from secular authorities, they were still considered sanctified buildings, places that should provide sanctuary from nonauthorized violence. One of the most shocking incidents in seventeenth-century Seville, for example, involved a murder in a church, committed by the gang called the "Esquiveles." A fight over a woman

24. Ibid., p. 114.
25. AMS, Archivo General, Sección 1, Carpeta 5, No. 70. Ariño, pp. 67–68, 80.

erupted between this gang and another man. Trying to escape, the man dashed into the Church of San Pedro and hid behind the priest. The gang killed him before the altar even though the priest tried to shield him with his chasuble. Leaving the dying man, a horrified priest, and the shocked congregation, the killers fled the city. The ecclesiastical chroniclers reported with some satisfaction that the killers soon died in other skirmishes, implying that Divine Justice had the last word.[26]

Although people could look less to the Church as an asylum during this period, they looked to it more as a refuge from need. The population of Seville grew rapidly in the sixteenth century, but many of the people who came to the famous port seeking their fortunes found only poverty. Monks and priests distributed food to the hungry and helped many homeless people find shelter. The Archbishopric provided charity from its own wealth and also administered many charitable bequests made by wealthy individuals. In addition, the Church encouraged less wealthy people to provide charity. One ecclesiastical report described a system by which people wanting indulgences from the Church went to a particular chapel in the Cathedral. There they left alms to buy bread for the poor, and in return they received the indulgences.[27]

As a refuge, the Church became a central meeting place for the down-and-out people of the city. Often the only buildings open to penniless vagrants were the churches and the houses of religious orders. In Quevedo's novel El Buscón, the picaresque hero and his roguish friends sought refuge in Seville's Cathedral, where they found some pretty prostitutes to keep them company.[28]

The monasteries and hermitages in the countryside around the city were even more likely to be used as refuges for nonreligious purposes. Because of their geographic isolation, they were remote

---

26. Memorias eclesiásticas, BC, 84-7-19, folio 204. Papeles varios, BC, 85-4-11.

27. Bernardo Luís de Castro Palacios, "Tratado de algunas ceremonias y cosas antiguas que se observasen en la Sta Iglesia Patriarcal, y Metropoliteria desta ciudad de Sevilla" (Sevilla, 1712), BC, 83-4-9, folios 24-25. For a more complete discussion of charity, see below, pp. 163-189.

28. Quevedo, p. 213.

from city lawmen and were sometimes poorly disciplined. In addition, the monks and priests who traveled the countryside from one monastery or hermitage to another resembled the vagabonds of the underworld. They depended on begging to get food and seemed to evade all legal jurisdiction. Underworld people recognized the close relationship and called highwaymen "hermits of the road" (*emitaño de camino*).[29] Murillo's painting of these traveling monks suggests their isolation and the ease with which they could escape the law. After a 1632 robbery in the Church of San Roque in Seville, a youth was hanged and his hand cut off, a girl accomplice was whipped, but the clergyman involved escaped as a traveling monk.[30]

Not surprisingly, hermits and monks found in the countryside were commonly suspected of crime. In one seventeenth-century picaresque novel, *La Garduña de Sevilla*, a monk acted as the front for a gang of robbers, who hid their loot in his hermitage and marked houses in the city where he got alms so that they would know the best places for robberies.[31] This fictional account of crime and remote religious houses is supported by many actual cases reported in histories and ecclesiastical records of Seville: the 1536 killing of an Augustinian provincial by four of his religious brothers; a 1597 scandal in a local convent that resulted in two maids whipped and one hanged; the 1639 murder of a Portuguese monk in his cell by two Augustinian brothers, who escaped; the 1640 discovery of the bones of a missing monk walled up in the monastery cell of a brother who had stolen the money that the victim had previously taken from his own order.[32]

One reason why monks and hermits were associated with crime is that the economic position of many religious orders deteriorated in the seventeenth century. Although the Archbishopric of Seville was reported to be very wealthy in the early

29. Hill, p. 113.

30. Papeles varios, BC, 85-4-11.

31. Alonso de Castillo Solórzano, *La Garduña de Sevilla y anzvelo de las bolsas*, 1642 (Madrid, 1922), pp. 172, 185.

32. Ortiz de Zuñiga, 4:295. "Casos raros," Papeles varios, BC, 85-4-11. Domínguez Ortiz, "Vida," p. 189. "Diferentes casos," *Memorias eclesiásticas*, BC, 84-7-19, folios 209ᵛ, and 211ᵛ-212ᵛ.

part of this century, many monasteries appeared to be far more wealthy than they actually were. Their huge art-filled churches were an expense rather than a source of income. Many new religious foundations had been funded by people eager for the esteem but unable to endow them adequately. As one commentator wrote,

> There is scarcely a pharmacist who has not been carried by his vanity to pass himself patron of a monastery and lord (señor) of its major chapel. And so, not having a strong endowment, if there is money for the building of the monastery, there is none for the officials of it; so that if they are nuns they eat from their dowries, and if they are monks they look for food from door to door.[33]

The proliferation of religious foundations meant that many more had to share in the generosity of religious supporters, and many supporters could give less as the cost of living continued to rise. Unable to feed all their members, religious orders turned them out to beg. In 1597 the Monastery of Santa María la Real in Seville wrote to the king that it could neither repair its buildings nor feed its members. The monastery had mortgaged its land in order to buy wheat and still could not feed its members on four days of each week. In a similar plea from the Jesuits of Seville in 1598, they declared that their economic position was falling rapidly with the continuing increase in the cost of living.[34] The Council of Castile recognized the gravity of this situation in a *consulta* of July 8, 1641, warning that poverty was pushing monks into scandal and crime.[35]

Squeezed by a shrinking economic base and a rise in the cost of living, religious foundations had to support a clerical population that continued to grow until the last half of the seventeenth century. A description of a religious procession in Seville in 1579

33. "Discurso sobre cierta razon de buen govierno," Biblioteca Nacional 17, 502, hojas 123–127, cited in Domínguez Ortiz, *Estamento*, p. 72.
34. Antonio Domínguez Ortiz, "Dos monasterios sevillanos en dificil situacion económica a fines del siglo XVI," *Archivo Hispalense*, Series 2, 54 (1971–72), 235–237.
35. Quoted in Domínguez Ortiz, *Estamento*, p. 212.

7 "Two Monks in a Landscape." Bartolomé Murillo.

asserted that 1500 clergymen participated; by 1635 more than 3000 religious were reported in Seville.[36] A list of religious foundations in Seville and its nearby countryside in 1650 included 48 monasteries, 28 convents, 23 *hospitales*, and 9 hermitages.[37] The growing clerical population led to economic strain, less effective discipline, and a decrease in moral and intellectual quality. A clerical association with crime, therefore, was not surprising.

Perhaps the most scandalous crime associated with monks and priests and isolated religious houses was *pecado nefando*, or sodomy. The Jesuit Pedro de León wrote that this was a serious problem among both religious and secular clergy. One Jesuit told him that women posed no problem for his brothers because they had many young male students and novices with whom they could sin. He mentioned one cleric who was penanced in a private auto de fé by the Inquisition for soliciting young boys in confession, but several other clergymen were "relaxed" (the euphemism for being handed over) to the secular authorities, who burned them for their crimes.[38]

The example of the Jeronomite Monastery of San Isidro del Campo suggests the problems of controlling a religious house. Located about two miles outside the city, this monastery had both spiritual and temporal jurisdiction over the village of Santiponce, site of the ancient Roman city of Italica. Noted in the sixteenth century for its rich endowment, the monastery had several powerful nobles as patrons. When the Duke of Medina Sidonia died in 1558, his body was taken there. When Philip II visited Seville in 1570, he stayed there.[39]

Despite its wealth and fame, the monastery was also known as a refuge for criminals and heretics. In the fifteenth century its patron, the Count of Niebla, wrote of cleaning out the monas-

36. "Relacion de la translacion de la imagen," Papeles varios, BC, 85-4-13, folio 156. Gordillo, reported in Domíngues Ortiz, *Estamento*, p. 10.

37. Joseph Maldonado Davila y Saavedra, "Que oy paren en la liberia de D^n Diego Ortiz de Zuñiga su sobrino," Memorias eclesiásticas, BC, 85-7-19, folios 106^V-180^V.

38. Pedro de León, Part II, chapter 26, folios 201-203.

39. Morgado, pp. 411-415. Ortiz de Zuñiga, 4:520, 723-724. Guichot y Parody, 2:73.

tery: "well, the cave of thieves has been turned into a house of prayer, in which our Lord is now served."[40] In the sixteenth century the monastery became the refuge for a group of Protestants. Its prior and several members, as well as several nuns of the nearby Jeronomite convent of Santa Paula, were secure in this monastery until the late 1550's, when they had to flee the Inquisition. The Inquisition found that the monastery was one of the major centers of Spanish Protestantism, and that it had been used as one of the depositories for New Testaments printed in the Castillian language and smuggled into the country by Protestants.[41] In 1567 Philip II ordered the reduction of this monastery and six others. "The causes that moved the king to this decision (which time has borne out)," wrote one chronicler, "were the small amount of conformity in the superiors of these houses that disrupted in them the religious observance."[42] One year later the hermit monks of San Jerónimo, who had occupied the monastery, were incorporated into the larger Order of the Monks of San Jerónimo by order of the Crown, undoubtedly a move to bring the monastery under stricter control.

The Crown wanted to curb the monastery of San Isidro del Campo because its wealth and fame and physical separation from Seville were increasing its independence. Philip II seemed less interested in the scriptural hair-splitting of heresy than in the political threat of a religious group who questioned the religious conformity buttressing his throne. He welcomed monasteries in his kingdom, but only if they supported this conformity. In Hapsburg Spain the Church could continue as a refuge only for people who did not threaten the teachings of the Church or the power of the secular order.

THE CHURCH AS CARICATURE

Underworld people used the Church as a butt for jokes and tricks. Tipsy prisoners dressed up as priests and held raucous

40. José de Sigüenza, *Historia de la orden de San Jerónimo* (Madrid, 1907), 1:328.

41. Kamen, *Inquisition*, p. 83. Menéndez y Pelayo, pp. 104–105.

42. Ortiz de Zuñiga, 4:529; Morgado, pp. 413–414.

religious "services." Ruffians broke into city brothels and hooted as priests preached and tried to convert prostitutes there. False beggars posed as monks collecting money to buy oil for church lamps. Street children hid their stolen loot behind altar pieces. Criminals masqueraded as priests and escaped prison in pious dignity.[43] What is the significance of these jokes and tricks at the expense of the Church?

Much underworld humor can be regarded as a strategy for survival. The false beggar posing as an alms-gathering monk took hard-earned maravedís from a pious widow in order to have money for food, drink, and gambling. He also played this trick in order to laugh at the absurdity and misery of the world around him. If he could not occasionally laugh at some poor wretch, he would probably disintegrate under the burdens of his own miseries. His joke got bread for him, and it also preserved his mental health.

Underworld jokes were often expressions of bravado. Prisoners who presented a religious "service" in the prison were making fun of the priest's performance before an altar, but they were also crying out against impotence. Tomorrow the priest might be able to lead them as lambs to the gallows, but tonight they could show how ridiculous he was as he bowed and chanted and mouthed words that he might not understand. Ridiculing the Church helped these prisoners to feel less impotent in the clutches of authority.

Bravado can bluster away fears. Prisoners who dressed up in white penitential robes to accompany two condemned highwaymen to the gallows turned this religious ritual into a blasphemous carnival. They put on false moustaches, squabbled over rosaries, and proudly preened themselves to the dismay of the prison chaplain.[44] Their parody of religion was very entertaining, and it also helped them feel less terror about their own approaching executions.

43. AMS, Papeles del Conde de Aguila, Sección Especial, Tomo 7 en folio, No. 20. Quevedo, p. 198, describes some irreverent ruses of false beggars. M. Chaves, pp. 80–81. C. Chaves, Parts I, II.
44. C. Chaves, Part II.

Humor as an expression of bravado can make a statement about power positions when no other statement is possible. The powerful Church in Seville was allied with the secular government, able to call on the powers of that government to restrain its enemies. It was a large landholder and had ties with a fearsome agency, the Inquisition, which was empowered to arrest, imprision, torture, and punish people. It could confiscate property, and it also seemed to hold the power of eternal damnation. A street thief who shouted from the Plaza de San Francisco that the Church was too powerful would probably get no farther than the gallows, but he would find an appreciative audience in a nearby tavern if he told them the hilarious tale of how he had escaped prison masquerading as a pious priest. To ridicule the Church and its clergy was a popular and practical way to make them seem less awesome and powerful.

When underworld people called a rooster "bishop," they may have exerted a form of informal social control on the Church.[45] Underworld burlesques of the clergy may have brought erring members into line in a manner similar to nicknames, popular ballads, and the *vito*, a form of *charivari* or "rough music." Church leaders undoubtedly saw the need to correct abuses within the Church without underworld assistance, but underworld burlesques helped to keep the Church open to popular scrutiny.

As burlesque, underworld humor could be considered a form of social criticism, but this should be distinguished from political protest. Underworld people were so busy exploiting the existing system that they had no interest in proposing a new system. They liked the bread and soup they got from the monks, and they wanted to use the prison chaplains as intermediaries to their own advantages. They also liked to ridicule this powerful institution. Underworld people could be considered cynics and protesters, but never revolutionaries.

Humor helped to defuse the social tensions that grew between the increasingly populous underworld and the powerful Church.

45. Hill, p. 118. Pitt-Rivers, "Honour and Social Status," in Peristiany, pp. 47–48, describes informal social controls in Spain.

As priests began to insist that they would give charity only to the "honorable poor," ruffians might have reacted with an outraged thrust of the dagger into a well-fed cassock. Instead, underworld people made fun of priests and charity. Ruffians hid in the shadows while their women posed as honorable wives whose husbands were in the Indies. Hoodwinking the priests into giving them charity not only avoided a violent confrontation; it also enabled the underworld to use the existing system. Thugs didn't hesitate to use violence, but they became better parasites when they could exploit and ridicule at the same time.

The obverse side of the Church's using the underworld to personify evil was that the underworld used the Church as a caricature. All around them the people of the streets of Seville saw an order that was not just or good or rational. Like the modern philosophers, they, too, looked into the abyss. The response of underworld people, however, was not despair, but jokes. They burlesqued the Church because it exemplified so much that was ridiculous: the wealthy ecclesiastical landholder in a city of paupers, the hypocritical preacher asserting that only the honorable poor should have bread, the pious monk urging the prisoner to confess and go meekly to his execution as a lamb to the slaughter. Such absurdity was not to be changed, but to be laughed at and used.

Inadvertently, however, underworld burlesques of the Church helped to debunk the old religious myths and prepare the way for the rational and secular myths of the modern period. Poking fun at a priest showed that he was human like other people. Stealing the crown and star from a Virgin and Child in the Cathedral demonstrated that these images had no supernatural powers and little value aside from their jewels and precious metals.[46] Wearing a rosary made from witches' teeth combined the profane with the holy in such a way that the holy would never appear quite the same.[47] In the modern period secular governments substituted national myths for old religious myths, and they replaced traditional religious rituals with modern

46. AMS, Efemérides, "Noticias y casos," No. 1.
47. Quevedo, p. 85.

secular rites. The interaction of Church and underworld in early modern Seville suggests some reasons for increasing secularization: the Church had been an unpopular intermediary; it had been exploited as a refuge for both the holy and profane; and it had been the object of raucous, cynical laughter.

7

Actors and Victims

HORTLY before Philip II died in 1598, he acceded to the pleas of Archbishop Vaca y Castro of Seville to prohibit comedies throughout his realm. Drama had become "scandalous" in Seville, as in many other cities, and it was often performed by ribald actors before crowds of raucous, jostling people.[1] But drama was also an integral part of religious ceremony, and many public entertainments were staid enough to support both God and political authority. In 1600 Philip III invited a group of theologians to determine the standards for dramatic performances. The problem was not to prohibit them but how to control them.

Both religious and political concerns affected public entertainments in the seventeenth century. The Counter Reformation had called for the separation of the holy from the profane, and churchmen urged authorities to curtail most drama and secular entertainment that had traditionally accompanied religious feast days. City officials generally cooperated, for they, too, were concerned that many feast days seemed to be degenerating into unrestrained license. The happy coincidence of interests strengthened the alliance of secular and Church authorities and increased their success in controlling popular entertainments. It also delineated even more sharply the lines between authority and underworld.

1. José Sánchez-Arjone, *Noticias referentes á los anales del teatro en Sevilla desde Lope de Rueda hasta fines del siglo XVII* (Sevilla, 1898), pp. 99–102.

Tensions arising from the struggle to control popular entertainments show that they were far more than mere spectacle or amusement. They were social rituals that unified the community and sanctified the social order, combining religion and theater to support the city oligarchy. On the other hand, some entertainments differed from the rituals favored by city fathers. These were "popular," presenting traditional folk culture and thinly veiled social criticism of authority. Popular entertainments were good business, creating commercial opportunities for artisans, street hawkers, and day laborers. In addition, entertainment fees supported both an itinerant entertainers' group and welfare programs of the city.

SOCIAL RITUAL

As social rituals, popular entertainments presented community events in traditional forms familiar to most people of the city. Public executions, for example, followed a well-known script. City and Church officials accompanied the condemned person in a procession to the Plaza de San Francisco. There law officers, executioner, victim, and clergy enacted a ceremony recognized by the spectators: presentation of the victim, the executioner's request for pardon from the victim, and the elevation of a crucifix to the condemned person's lips. The players rarely deviated from prescribed form.

Public executions were performed frequently and usually for a mass audience. Scarcely a week went by without a public execution in the heart of the city. By some estimates as many as 20,000 people would gather to watch an execution.[2] One contemporary described a scene in 1624 when the Plaza was so filled "with a world of people in the streets, plazas, and windows" that not a foot of space was unoccupied, and two companies of soldiers of the city militia marched in to keep order in the crowd.[3] Public executions attracted thousands of people because

2. Pedro Herrera Puga, *Sociedad y delincuencia en el Siglo de Oro* (Maddrid, 1974), p. 104. M. Chaves, pp. 108–111.

3. AMS, Papeles del Conde de Aguila, Sección Especial, Tomo 64, en folio, No. 3.

they offered the relief of a ritual purging of evil. Spectators could identify together against the condemned criminal, reaffirm their social solidarity, and feel relief when he was executed.[4]

Those in the streets were not passive spectators at these executions, however; they frequently participated in vilifying the victim as he marched in procession to the gallows. The chaplain Pedro de León reported that people eagerly awaited the execution procession of Juan de Madrid so that they could shout insults at this famous criminal who had helped the authorities catch other thugs before he, himself, fell out of grace. The chaplain also described the uproarious procession of Francisco García, popularly called *Manotas* or "The Paws," who was the target of insults and pranks as he walked to the gallows.[5]

Executions could be as gruesome and scandalous as the crimes that had been committed. In 1565 the Plaza was filled with people who wanted to see the execution of an innkeeper's wife and her lover. By ancient law, the wronged husband was permitted to execute his wife and her lover. Despite the pleas of monks to pardon the guilty couple, the husband remained adamant. He walked up to where they stood bound and repeatedly stabbed them with a knife. Finishing them off with his sword, he threw down his hat and said, "So much for the horns."[6]

Public punishment for sexual crimes had been a titillating event for years, a spectacle even when it didn't involve death. An engraving of Seville in a sixteenth-century book shows the public humiliation of an adulterous woman and her cuckolded husband. The horns of the cuckold were symbols of shame bestowed on a man who could not control his wife. He became a community joke and could regain his prestige only by demanding satisfaction as a wronged husband. The innkeeper who publicly stabbed his wife and her lover in 1565 was asserting his right to regain his

---

4. Victor Turner, *Schism and Continuity in an African Society; A Study of Ndembu Village Life* (Manchester, 1957), discusses this aspect of ritual. See esp. pp. 128, 298.

5. Pedro de León, appendix 1 to Part II, Cases 70, 285.

6. "Serie historical," Memorias eclesiásticas, BC, 84–7–19, folios 46[v]–47.

8   The public chastisement of an adulteress and her cuckolded husband. A woodcut from Georgius Braun, *Civitates Orbis Terrarum,* Cologne, 1574.

the community, but other wronged husbands were less cruel. In 1624 an adulterous woman and her lover were brought to the Plaza to be executed publicly by her husband. She had not been bound and ran to throw herself at her husband, kissing his feet and begging him to forgive them. He refused to listen and was "like a tiger, full of rage." After an hour of this pleading, however, he pardoned them and they were released in "great contrition for their sins."[7] The public spectacle of the begging woman and angry husband had been enough to reestablish his honor and her subordinate position.

The burning of people convicted of sodomy attracted many spectators, particularly as attitudes about young men became more puritanical in the late sixteenth and seventeenth centuries. In 1585 city authorities decided to make an example of a Negro who had been accused of sodomy and procuring young boys. They painted his face, dressed him in a large lace ruff, placed a huge curled wig on his head, and marched him through the city with two other dressed-up youths.[8]

Moralists decried the idleness and depravity of the sons of nobles. Juan de Mora described these young men as "poison of the cities, mutiny of the villages, iniquity of the citizens, suited to all sensuality and torpidity, greedy for all advantages belonging to others."[9] Another preacher railed against "men converted into women" and "effeminate soldiers, full of airs, long locks, and plumes."[10] In 1639 the city published a "Proclamation that His Majesty orders, because the abuse of long hair and hair pieces with which some men walk about, and the curls with which they set their hair, has come to be scandalous in

7. AMS, Papeles del Conde de Aguila, Sección Especial, Tomo 64, en folio, No. 3; the engraving is in Georgius Braun, *Civitates Orbis Terrarum* (Cologne, 1574).

8. Pedro de León, appendix 1 to Part II, Case 122.

9. Juan de Mora, *Discursos morales* (Madrid, 1598), quoted in Viñas y Mey, *Problema*, p. 47.

10. Francisco de León, 1635 sermon quoted in Viñas y Mey, *Problema*, p. 47.

these kingdoms, no man can wear long hair nor hair pieces."[11]

Mass burnings and cases involving young boys attracted large crowds. In 1597 the burning of Alonso Telles Giron was a major event. Giron, called *el gran tío* (the great uncle) because he was related to every noble in the province, had been convicted of killing his wife. The king ordered that this noble be strangled privately rather than endure public execution. However, Giron confessed to so many acts of sodomy that he was resentenced to burn publicly with one of his male partners. He was driven through the streets on a mule to the bonfire site in the Plaza.[12]

Blood and gore attracted many to the public executions, for authorities routinely mutilated the bodies of victims whom they wanted to make special examples. Gonzalo Xenis, the famous highwayman, was finally arrested and sentenced to death in 1596. When he was hanged, his body was quartered and his head cut off and placed in a niche in the tower beside the port called the *Barqueta*, a favorite gathering place of highwaymen. Royal treason was another reason for mutilation. A judicial officer of Seville, Francisco Mondexano, was condemned to death for conspiracy to support the "false" king of Portugal, Sebastian. He was dragged to the gallows and after he was hanged, his hands and head were cut off and displayed in the customs house and at the gallows, gruesome reminders of the power of the city and royal governments to carry out violence against those who challenged their authority.[13]

Religious symbolism in executions reinforced political authority because it sanctified the government's power to define crime and punish offenders. A chronicler of the late sixteenth century, emphasizing the role of religion in public executions, wrote that

11. Quoted in Herrera Puga, pp. 315–316.

12. "Algunas cosas," Memorias eclesiásticas, BC, 84-7-19, folio 102. Pedro de León, appendix 1 to Part II, Cases 7, 8. AMS, Efemérides, "Noticias y casos," No. 1. "Casos raros," Papeles varios, BC, 85-4-11.

13. Ariño, pp. 39–40. Francisco Pacheco, *Libro de descripción de verdaderos retratos, de ilustres y memorables varones* (Sevilla, 1599).

condemned people were taken in a procession to their execution, led by the *Niños de la Doctrina* carrying a cross and singing litanies. Clerics, monks, and priests of the Society of Jesus walked at the side of the condemned person; and at the place of execution they helped him go to a "good death." [14] An execution without a crucifix was as unlikely as an execution without a victim.

City residents saw a spectacular example of the sanctification of public executions in 1625 when a Moor was converted to Christianity in prison while awaiting his execution. On the day of his execution, he was dressed in sumptuous clothing and taken in solemn procession to his baptism. Juan Gutierrez Tello, an important noble and member of the Order of Santiago, acted as his godfather. Then, in procession with richly vested clergymen and solemn nobles, with six sheriffs on horseback to part the crowds, he was taken to the Plaza de San Francisco and hanged. Afterward his body was carried to the sacristy of the *Caridad*, where all the nobles attended a service for his soul. [15]

Not all Moriscos showed such cooperation with city and Church officials. In 1585 a Morisco sentenced to hang for silver robbery scandalized the crowd at his execution. When he was asked if he had anything to say before he was hanged, he replied that he had nothing more to say except that a tavern in Triana owed him a half-measure of wine. When the hangman asked him for forgiveness, according to custom, he answered impudently. As the noose was placed around his neck, people in the crowd said they heard him call out for Mohammed. Incensed, a group of boys stoned his body as it swung from the gallows. The crowd seized his body, dragged it away, and set it on fire. [16]

Religion and secular authority also mingled in religious festivals, another form of popular entertainment. During this period, Corpus Christi in late May or June was the most popular. City officials marched in the procession of Corpus, together with

14. Morgado, p. 194.
15. "1616–1634," Papeless varios, BC, 85-4-11. AMS, Papeles del Conde de Aguila, Sección Especial, Tomo 64 en folio, No. 4.
16. Pedro de León, appendix 1 to Part II, Case 116.

Church officials, regular clergy, and religious fraternities. Thousands lined the city streets to see the floats, dancers, musicians, players, and sumptuously dressed clergymen and officials with jeweled crosses and color-coordinated candles. Corpus celebrations included both secular and Church officials, participants who sometimes quarreled over the proper way to celebrate. The city council usually paid the acting companies that performed in the festival, awarding the leader of the company with *la joya* (the jewel), which was an object of gold, and a money payment.[17]

Fewer disputes arose over the religious processions that were prompted by floods, drought, famine, war, and epidemics. In the face of disaster, secular and clerical authorities marched together with religious images and lighted candles. These processions symbolized the unity of the community as well as the virtue of secular officials who used the rituals of the Church to seek relief for the city. Moreover, processions prompted by disasters welcomed all participants. Where Corpus processions were limited to clerical and secular authorities, religious fraternities and entertainers with the floats, processions of supplication included penitents of all kinds. Participants probably felt the social unity and sanctity of these events even more keenly than spectators.[18]

The single event in early modern Seville which best dramatized the marriage of religion and secular authority was the inauguration of the new Royal Chapel in the Cathedral in 1579. A long and colorful procession followed the same route as the Corpus processions, to carry the standards, images, and royal bodies that were to be placed in the newly constructed Chapel. One of the bodies was that of Ferdinand III, the "liberator" of Seville

17. Sanchez Gordillo, "Religiosas estaciones que frecuenta la devoción sevillana," in Memorial de historia eclesiástica de la cuidad de Sevilla, BC, 82-6-19, folios 92-92[V]. Ortiz de Zuñiga, 4:493. "Serie historical," Memorias eclesiásticas, BC, 84-7-19, folios 37[V]-38. Sánchez-Arjona, p. 96. Santiago Montoto de Sedas, "El teatro, el baile, y la danza en Sevilla," *Archivo Hispalense,* Series 2, 32-33 (1960), 372.

18. Processions of supplication are described in Ortiz de Zuñiga, 3:325-327, 4:523, 707-710; and in Christian, *Person,* p. 70.

in 1248, who had been canonized a saint. The procession included thirty religious fraternities, all the religious orders, the
military orders of Alcantara and Calatrava and Santiago, the
clergy and cross from each parish of the city, the council of the
Cathedral, the Archbishop, the Holy Tribunal of the Inquisition,
the faculty of the College of Santa María de Jesús, the consulate
and members of the Cargadores á Indias (shippers to the Indies),
the Tribunal of the Casa de Contratación, members of the city
council, and the chief justice and judges of the audiencia.[19]

Religious processions enhanced the positions of both Church
and secular officials and demonstrated their generosity, for
bread and wine and clothing and money were traditionally distributed to the poor spectators at the end. When Philip III
ascended the throne in 1598, a religious-political procession
raised the royal standard in Seville in his honor, and the Marquis
of Algava threw out handfuls of silver coins to people looking on.
The coins, which had been especially prepared for this occasion,
bore the likeness of Philip III on one side and a popular religious
symbol, the *Esperanza* (Virgin of Hope), on the other.[20]

An alliance of political and religious authorities was also apparent in the many autos de fé that were held during the sixteenth
and seventeenth centuries. When these ceremonies were public,
they became mass public expressions of penance and faith.
Everyone who attended an auto de fé was granted an indulgence
for forty days. Psychologically this ceremony was very impressive; a solemn religious mood permeated its procession and ritual.
Spectators saw the awesome power of religious authorities who
here publicly pronounced sentence on their enemies. Secular
authorities in places of honor solemnly witnessed the ceremonies,
sometimes seeing people of their own class subjected to public

19. "Casos raros," Papeles varios, BC, 85-4-11.
20. Sanchez Gordillo, folio 175. See also Victor Turner, "Ritual Aspects
of Conflict Control in African Micropolitics," in Marc J. Swartz, Victor W.
Turner, and Arthur Tuden, eds., *Political Anthropology* (Chicago, 1966),
p. 246. "La forma que se tuvó en levantar el estandarte real en la ciudad de
Sevilla por la Mag. del Rey don Phelipe Tercero," Poesías, BC, 82-3-26,
folios 188-189.

penance. The widow of a veinticuatro, for example, was penanced at the auto de fé of December 22, 1560.[21]

Autos de fé had their less solemn aspects, too. An example is the auto of 1627 at which Joan de Villapando and Catalina de Jesús were penanced. This couple had been accused of the Alumbrado heresy, but their great attraction was that they were also accused of engaging in sexual misconduct during their mystical experiences. The public delighted in the Inquisition's ability to dig up evidence of that exciting combination of religious heresy and sexual impropriety. For its part, the Inquisition found sexual impropriety a convenient way to discredit enemies. On the night before Villapando and Catalina were to be taken in procession to a convent for their auto, people began lining the streets at midnight. By the time the penitents were marched from their prison at 7:00 A.M. so many people crowded the streets that Inquisition officials could hardly move their procession to the convent. People stayed in their places on the streets all day, hoping to catch another glimpse of the famous couple as they left the convent.[22]

Thousands thronged the streets to watch Holy Week processions because these events also combined religion with less solemn and spiritual concerns. Although many spectators and participants found deep religious significance in the floats and processions of penitents, many others were attracted by the scenes of gore and violence. The suffering Jesus was depicted in bloody realism with nail holes, a gaping pierced side, and forehead torn by thorns. Only the scores of penitents whipping themselves with leather thongs could rival the scenes of the dying Jesus as demonstrations of sanctified, ritualized, authorized violence.

The parallel between Holy Week spectacles and public executions is striking. On Holy Saturday figures of Judas were erected in the streets and burned and vilified in the most horrible ways, scenes reminiscent of the hanging and burning of the uncooperative Moor in 1585. In both cases, people came to see the ritual

21. Kamen, *Inquisition,* pp. 183–185. Menéndez y Pelayo, 5:114–115.
22. Auto de fée, BC, 64-7-118, folios 124[v]–125.

of authorized violence carried out against one who symbolized evil. Continuous repetition of these familiar dramas deepened a collective feeling of unity and acceptance of the authority that was permitted to identify victims and carry out ritual violence.

Usually Church and city officials managed to maintain these ceremonies as popular events even while imposing censorship over them. The students of the Colegio de Maestro Rodrigo of the University of Seville had traditionally celebrated Saint Nicholas' Day with a fiesta and procession led by one of the students elected to be "bishop" for the day. In 1641 the son of a very rich Genoese was elected bishop, and students marched the city streets carrying forbidden weapons and shouting blasphemies. The fiesta degenerated into a brawl between some sixty students and many townspeople. The royal court in Seville fined the father of the bishop and forbade the students from ever again having a bishop in their celebration.[23] The combination of rowdy student behavior, forbidden weapons, and the son of a rich foreign merchant was too much for the nobles and churchmen of Seville, who wanted to use religious celebrations for their own purposes.

Even before this incident Church and city officials had tried to prevent religious celebrations from degenerating into popular secular holidays. In the 1570's the city council demanded that sheriffs patrol the streets on fiesta days to see that people went to Mass and did not spend their time idly visiting and playing in the streets. In 1643 the Pope reduced the numbers of religious feast days, and people of Seville lost nineteen of the fiestas traditionally celebrated in the city. While Church officials argued that this reduction was a solution to the problem of poor workers who could not afford so many days off for religious festivals, they could have added that reduction

23. "Diferentes casos," Memorias eclesiásticas, BC, 84-7-19, folios 218ᵛ-219. For a general Counter Reformation concern with controlling festivals and lay participation in the Church, see John Bossy, "The Counter Reformation and the People of Catholic Europe," *Past and Present*, No. 47 (May 1970), 51-70.

in festivals also prevented many from becoming popular holidays uncontrolled by Church or city officials.[24]

Corridas, the tournaments and bullfights of Spanish nobles, remained under the control of city authorities because they were public events limited to noble participants. Manuscripts describing a corrida in 1620 reported that the event opened with a procession of officers of the city council and audiencia, accompanied with trumpets, symbols, and drums. The sheriffs had dressed so magnificently that they looked like veinticuatros, the leading citizens of the city. Each man rode a handsome horse that was richly ornamented, accompanied by colorfully costumed lackeys, including some mulattos and a Chinese. Forty-eight nobles took part in the games of the tournament; they were of "illustrious blood, almost all related to one another."[25]

Even though the corridas were limited to noble participants, they were popular city events. They were often held in honor of a religious feast day or significant royal event. In Seville corridas were usually held in the Plaza de San Francisco or the plaza of the town palace of the Duke of Medina Celi. The streets leading to the plaza were closed off and special seats were placed so that honored dignitaries could watch in safety the brave men and bulls. Noble ladies filled the windows and balconies around the plaza. Lesser people of the city crowded into the other places, eager spectators if not participants in this ritual. Here they saw local nobles play the games of tradition, acting out legends of bravery as they faced the bulls or the long jousting sticks of their opponents. The strict separation of participant and spectator in these rituals reinforced the social structure of

24. AMS, Siglo XVI, Sección 3, Escribanías de Cabildo, Tomo 11, no. 77. "Diferentes casos," Memorias eclesiásticas, BC, 84-7-19, folios 227–228[v].

25. "Relación de las fiestas reales de toros y cañas que se hicieron en Sevilla a 2 de octubre del 1620 años hecha por don Francisco Morbeli y Puebla, cavallero de ella," and "Segunda relación de las cañas y toros que los cavalleros de Sevilla hizieron en 2 en octubre de 1620, por junta de sus altezas los principes herederos de España," Papeles varios, BC, 83-7-14, folios 279-287. These manuscripts are also presented in *Archivo Hispalense,* Series 1, Vol. 3 (1887).

the city. Many city fathers believed that these spectacles were more advantageous than sermons on feast days, for they diverted some people from idleness and "less honest occupations," such as the gang fights that the young men of the city held so often on Sundays and holidays.[26]

Underworld people played many roles in popular entertainments. They were often the victims in public executions, but sometimes they were cynical onlookers. An example is the case of the highwaymen who came to the Plaza de San Francisco to watch the hanging of four Moors convicted for the robberies that the highwaymen themselves had committed. "Well," said one of the highwaymen, "if they are thieves, hang them from the gallows."[27]

Underworld people were also spectators in religious festivals and corridas, although it is doubtful that they were merely passive. Brawls and knife fights broke out in many of these public events. An account of the inauguration of the Royal Chapel of the Cathedral in 1579 reported in surprise that this festival, unlike most in the city, was peaceful and free from scandal. There had been no quarrels or bad words among the people waiting to see the procession on the streets. There were usually forty or fifty people imprisoned each festival day, but there were none on this occasion.[28]

In contrast, the religious processions of Holy Week in 1642 erupted in a great uproar on the steps of the Cathedral. Several knife fights broke out, and when one badly wounded man entered the Cathedral, a rumor ran through the crowd that the Portuguese in the city had revolted. Women ran screaming into the chapels and choir of the Cathedral, and the men came running after them, swords in hand, to defend the Cathedral.

26. Turner, *Schism*, p. 297. "Relación de las fiestas" contains the observation on the advantages of corridas over sermons. See the "Relación de las fiestas" in *Archivo Hispalense*, Series 1, Vol. 3, p. 130. Gang fights were described by Pedro de León in his Compendio and are discussed in Domínguez Ortiz, "Vida," pp. 165–166.

27. Pedro de León, Part II, chapter 27, folio 204.

28. "Relación de la translacion de las imagen," Papeles varios, BC, 85-4-13, folios 177–177v.

Religious fraternities milled around tilting their floats in great confusion. Hysteria reigned inside the Cathedral until the city council sent a guard of soldiers to impose order.[29] As quarrelsome spectators, underworld people provided churchmen and city fathers with a reason for extending their control over public entertainments.

SOCIAL CRITICISM

Although city and Church authorities tried to control popular entertainments, they were never wholly successful. In her study of youth celebrations of "misrule" in sixteenth-century France, Natalie Davis found that these rowdy rituals were tolerated not only because they drained off excess youthful energy that might otherwise erupt more rebelliously, but also because they imposed informal social controls on people who had transgressed local codes of behavior.[30] City fathers of Seville must have tolerated student celebrations and nocturnal street-singing with a similar resignation. Let youth expend itself in noisy songs and raucous play that ridiculed the misbehavior of others. In the case of the Saint Nicholas Day celebration and student "bishop" of 1641, however, Church and city authorities came down hard against such misrule, for the charade had ridiculed authorities in the city far more than it had criticized some temporary lapses in the community's moral code.

Authorities also suspected social criticism in the entertainments of musicians and acting groups who traveled from city to city, easily escaping prosecution for blasphemy or libel. Always outsiders, these traveling musicians and players were commonly suspected of theft and prostitution. In addition, they often relied on unwritten lines and impromptu exchanges with the audience, difficult evidence for prosecutors attempting to prove blasphemy. Augustín de Rojas Villandrando, who traveled through

29. "Diferentes casos," Memorias eclesiásticas, BC, 84-7-19, folios 219ᵛ.-220.

30. Natalie Zemon Davis, "The Reasons of Misrule: Youth Groups and Charivaris in Sixteenth-Century France," *Past and Present*, No. 50, (1971), 41-75. This essay is chapter 4 in Davis, *Society*.

Spain with a group of traveling actors in the early seventeenth century, acknowledged the poor social reputation of acting groups in his rather breezy description of them. Frequently poor, these groups would perform for "a loaf of bread, a bunch of grapes, a cabbage stew . . . and anything else that happens along (not refusing the most worthless gift)."[31] These travelers resembled the vagabonds that city officials distrusted so intensely, except that actors were very clever in getting people to run to listen to them and watch them perform. They delighted their street audiences with ribald imitations of nobles and churchmen. Their bawdy songs poked fun at authority and at those who had money. Townspeople might consider them immoral, but they always gathered as an eager, happy audience for their unauthorized street performances.

Drama, music, and dance were usually performed by traveling companies, but all three were also an integral part of religious liturgy. The mixture of theater and religion reached its zenith with the founding of the Jesuits' houses in Seville. Many Jesuits used theater and drama to teach virtue and dramatize the life of Jesus and the saints. Students who were taught in the Jesuits' schools became stars in the acting companies in sixteenth and early seventeenth-century Spain.[32]

The festivals of Corpus Christi were famous for combining theater and religion. Singers, dancers, and actors accompanied the floats in the Corpus processions and performed periodically in the streets, as well as in the Cathedral. One dance, the *Seises*, is still performed before the high altar of the Cathedral in Seville on the feasts of Corpus Christi and the Immaculate Conception. Another dance, the *zarabanda*, was a traditional part of the Corpus celebration that became notorious. It was so provocative, the Jesuit priest Mariana warned, that it inflamed "even very honest people."[33] Like the *escarramán*, the *zarabanda* was a dance that represented the "abortions of Hell."[34] Its frenzied

31. Villandrando, *Viage entretenido*, quoted in Rennert, pp. 132–140.
32. Sánchez-Arjona, pp. 28–29. Montoto de Sedas, p. 371.
33. Quoted in Sánchez-Arjona, p. 85; see also Montoto de Sedas, p. 381.
34. Montoto de Sedas, p. 383.

rhythms and violent movements were more contagious than awe-inspiring, however, and spectators frequently joined in the dancing.

Dance was also a secular entertainment. Great dancers, such as the Marquis of Valencia and Antonio de Burgos, taught at famous dancing schools here in the seventeenth century. Many other dance teachers were "little masters" who accompanied themselves with a guitar as they gave lessons in small bars, taverns, and the city's plazas. Despite the fame of a few dance schools, dance was not an elite art. Many dance forms originated in the countryside, in rural pilgrimmages (romerías), and small taverns and local festivals. They were passed then from taverns and bars to the theater and salons of Seville.[35]

Although drama was presented on the streets and in the plazas of Seville, the city also had three famous theaters in the early modern period. The Corral de Doña Elvira, which was built in the sixteenth century, was a patio for performances, covered and surrounded by theater boxes and a gallery in back. The city council decided to build the Coliseo in the early seventeenth century so that it could control the performances and profits of the theater. The first Coliseo, finished in 1607, was a modest wooden building. It was replaced by a second Coliseo that was built much more lavishly in 1614. Rich marble and paintings by Diego de Esquivel and Gonzalez de Campos decorated the theater, and a handsome crest of the city council dominated the entry. This Coliseo burned in 1620 and was rebuilt in greater splendor in 1641. After fire destroyed the Coliseo once more in 1659, the city council lacked funds to rebuild it. It agreed to permit Laura de Herrera and her company to use the Coliseo rent-free for the next forty years in exchange for her financing the reconstruction of the theater.[36]

In 1626 the city built the theater of La Montería for the visit of Philip IV to Seville. Constructed in the shape of an oval, this theater had three floors and much more space than the Corral de Doña Elvira. La Montería and the Coliseo replaced

35. Ibid., pp. 382–383, 385.
36. Ibid., pp. 374–376. Sánchez-Arjona, pp. 64–65.

the old Corral, which was converted by stages into a tavern, gambling rooms, a center for thieves and vagabonds, and, finally, a refuge for poor, old, and disabled priests.[37]

The city council's attempt to control drama by owning the theaters failed to convert this popular entertainment into an activity limited to the social elite. One reason was that people continued to go to the theater without paying admission charges. In 1632 one company failed to collect enough money at the door of the Coliseo to pay for its expenses in Seville. Leases for using the theater of La Montería included a provision that two sheriffs had to be stationed at the door, but even these officials could not prevent the brawls at the door and the clever people who sneaked into the theater.[38]

The audience seemed to be as responsible for the scandalous reputation of the theater as the actors were, and the city government's efforts to control the audience failed. Custom dictated that men and women be separated in theaters, but separation had not been enforced. In 1627 a city council member declared that permitting women to sit with men in city theaters had resulted in many "offenses to God." He proposed that the city government require men and women not only to sit in separate sections in the theaters, but also to enter through different doors.[39] These regulations only promoted more scandals, like the uproar in 1654 when one man sneaked into the women's section in La Montería and lifted skirts and "touched legs."[40] Although he was imprisoned and then exiled from the city for two years, the women's gallery (called the *cazuela*, or stewing pan) remained one of the rowdiest sections of the theaters.

People came to the theater for fun and celebration. Customarily they brought fruit and cucumbers, and they pelted the actors who displeased them. They also used rattles, whistles, and metal keys to register their approval and disapproval as noisily

37. Montoto de Sedas, pp. 375–376. Sánchez-Arjona, pp. 257–258.

38. Rennert, p. 281. Sánchez-Arjona, p. 251.

39. Sánchez-Arjona, pp. 255–256. AMS, Papeles del Conde de Aguila, Sección Especial, Tomo 7 en folio, No. 134.

40. Sánchez-Arjona, p. 408.

as possible. In 1643 an audience in La Montería was outraged when the comedy they had come to see was censored by the Inquisition and replaced by a less offensive comedy. The city chronicler who reported the incident said that "lower and popular" people filled the audience on this feast day. Shouting in protest, they jumped up and began breaking the chairs and benches. They threw the pieces around the theater and tore up all the costumes and scenery they could find. The actors, according to the chronicle, fled from "the rabble."[41]

Students and young people who went to the theaters routinely protested against authority. Most of the incidents began with a refusal to pay the entry fee. In February 1633, for example, five or six young men who appeared to be students tried to force their way into the theater without paying. They got past the first sheriff, but when the second sheriff demanded that they pay, they drew their swords. In the ensuing brawl, the sheriff was wounded and the young men fled. Another uproar occurred in 1639 when a clergyman and a student cheered for the wrong person in the play and got into a shouting match with another man in the audience. Knives and swords flashed, and in the fracas the student was mortally wounded.[42]

City fathers were particularly concerned about youthful challenges to their authority. Young men came from many parts of Castile, the Canary Islands, and Andalucía to study at the University of Seville. Far from home, they lived in the city without parental restraints. Many had to live on meager allowances, and they felt separate from the wealthy residents of Seville who tried to impose restraints on them.[43]

In contrast, some young men of Seville did not even pretend to study. In the tradition of la Garduña, the picaresque heroine of a novel by Castillo Solórzano, these young people grew up

41. Rennert, pp. 117–120; "Diferentes casos," Memorias eclesiásticas BC, 84-7-19, folio 225.

42; Sánchez-Arjona, pp. 283, 334–335.

43. Richard L. Kagan, "Universities in Castile 1500–1700," Past and Present, No. 49 (1970), 50. For a more complete discussion of students in Spain at this time, see Richard Kagan, Students and Society in Early Modern Spain, (Baltimore, 1974).

with little parental control, free to roam the streets.[44] City residents recognized them as *mozos de barrio* (young people of the neighborhood) and *virotes* (young blades).[45] They usually had some money and delighted in trying forbidden games. They also liked to force their way into theaters and start fights in the rowdy theater sections.

Increasingly rigid moral attitudes reflected the increasingly rigid determination of Church and secular officials to maintain authority in the face of growing problems. By 1598 Philip II agreed to the repeated pleas of Archbishop Vaca y Castro of Seville to prohibit all dramatic performances. In 1600 the Crown called a meeting of theologians, who determined that dramas should be presented only under these conditions: they were not to deal with lascivious material, nor include lascivious dances, "wagging of the tail," melodies, or poems; they would be performed by only four licensed companies; no women would be permitted in these companies, and boys who represented them in plays would do so "honestly" and properly; comedies would not be presented in Lent or on certain other feast days, and no company could stay in one place for more than a month out of the year, nor perform more than three days in the same week, nor perform in the same place with another company; drama performed in churches and convents should be purely devotional. The Royal Council agreed to these conditions, except that it declared that women could continue in acting companies so long as they were in the company of their husbands or fathers. They also increased the number of licensed companies from four to twelve in 1615.[46]

The controls imposed by churchmen and Crown did not satisfy the city fathers, however. Between 1615 and 1648 Seville had suffered disastrous floods and droughts and a severe reduction in trade with the Indies. Repeated devaluations of *vellon* money had hurt most of the people of the city. Seville had had to send all available men and a large amount in taxes to help

44. Castillo Solórzano, *La Garduña*, pp. 23–24.
45. Rodríguez Marín, *Miscelánea*, p. 19.
46. Sánchez-Arjona, pp. 100–101, 166–169.

the Crown put down the revolts in Catalonia and Portugal. Maintaining political power was increasingly difficult in a city suffering so many misfortunes, and city fathers tried to buttress their positions by strengthening moral regulations. In 1629 the city prohibited charivaris or other songs or "dirty" or dishonest words in the streets or roads. Nineteen years later the custom of calling out requests for dances or songs in the theater was forbidden by law.[47] Moral restrictions such as these unified the community by identifying the evil practices that it would not tolerate. They also muffled criticism of authorities that had been expressed in the popular entertainments of drama and music.

In the 1670's local churchmen made several more attempts to control the theater. Seville had suffered a terrible epidemic in 1649, and several epidemics later threatened to spread to the city from other parts of Spain. Preachers declared that the city could avoid the evils of plague and hunger only by purging itself of things of the devil, such as drama. In 1679 the city council agreed with a letter written by a pious churchman who declared that drama had offended God and that prohibiting it would please God and lessen the sufferings from hunger, poverty, and pestilence within the city. The city council passed the prohibition, observing that these were "calamitous" times of "general distress," requiring special concern for idleness.[48]

Other forms of entertainment that were also social criticism were those involving the occult. The sorcerer, witch, fortune-teller, and *sabia* (wise woman) threatened the power position of priests and secular officials who posed as the only legitimate intermediaries between the people and God or secular authority. Magic, which is closely associated with religion, was not in itself repugnant to the Church so long as it was controlled by the Church. Religious custom even used such magical agencies as holy water and the sign of the cross. However, the neighborhood sabia competed with the priest when she performed magical

47. Guichot y Parody, 2:208–209. Sánchez-Arjona, p. 381.

48. Mañera, "Motibo," BC, 80-1-92. "Teatros de comedias en Sevilla," Memorias eclesiásticas, BC, 84-7-19, folios 241^V-242^V. AMS, Papeles del Conde de Aguila, Sección Especial, Tomo 62 en folio, No. 40.

rites or called on supernatural powers.[49] Implicit in her popularity was a form of anticlericalism, an insistence that common people could perform the rites that priests had sought to monopolize.

Priests and secular authorities tried to counteract popular seers and magicians by pointing to the numbers of charlatans who cheated other people under the guise of magic. Underworld people were not above using a trick or two, and they delighted in finding gullible people who would pay them for magic potions and hexes. "Seeing" the future was particularly easy for those who were constantly moving and could not be held to their predictions. The shadowy line between underworld and the occult permitted officials to discredit many sabias.

Through the Inquisition, the Church charged popular magicians and seers with being sorcerers and heretics. Although Inquisition tribunals did not prosecute witches as vigorously as secular courts, the Inquisition accepted responsibility for prosecuting "bad Christians" who took demons as familiars or made pacts with them and invoked superstitions.[50] They also prosecuted those who claimed to foresee the future. Heresy was a broad umbrella that could cover many forms of folk medicine, popular religion, and occult entertainments. It could discredit any popular movement that threatened to break away from official control.

Underworld people did not monopolize the practice of the occult or the traveling groups of players and musicians, but they must have found it easy to pass into these groups. The appeal of travel and visiting many cities was great for people who tended a little crime on the side. Moreover, little money was required to become a traveling player or palm-reader. Young boys were in great demand to play women's parts, and many must have gladly joined a traveling troupe to escape hardships and the law. These people had no formal program of social criticism to present through music and drama, but their very ribaldry and popularity suggest that public entertainments could ridicule and snipe at political authority as well as bolster it.

49. Pitt-Rivers, *People*, pp. 189–194.
50. AMS, Papeles del Conde de Aguila, Sección Especial, Tomo 4 en folio, No. 43.

COMMERCIAL OPPORTUNITIES

Public entertainments offered both licit and illicit commercial opportunities. Legitimate local industries, such as candlemaking, flourished with the demands of frequent religious processions. The 1579 procession inaugurating the Royal Chapel of the Cathedral, for example, consumed 25,000 pounds of wax candles.[51] Candlemakers thrived when the Inquisition held an auto in Seville, and so did carpenters, weavers, lawyers, guards, and day-laborers. Expenses for two autos held in the city included these items:

Auto of January 30, 1624

General expenses	28,076 maravedís
Benches, carpets, etc.	36,552
Cloth for *sanbenitos*	17,136
Candles	23,366
Advocates for criminals	26,520
Building scaffold	264,724
	396,374 maravedís

Auto of March 29, 1648

General expenses	84,184 maravedís
Painting effigies, clothing	37,400
Militia	10,200
Building scaffold	351,560
Meals for soldiers and effigy bearers	21,148
Candles, shawls, hats	82,416
Transporting accused from Cordova	68,000
Meals	156,680
	811,588 maravedís[52]

Street-hawkers who sold food always looked for a good business day when a public execution drew a huge crowd to the Plaza de San Francisco, or a corrida attracted people to the city from near and far. Selling seats or positions at a window also

51. AMS, Efemérides, Cuadra 2. "Casos raros," Papeles varios, BC, 85-4-11.

52. Kamen, *Inquisition*, pp. 195-196.

became big business for a special corrida or procession. According to one chronicler, seats cost 50 reales for the corrida held in October 1620, and they couldn't be found "for a treasure" within eight days of the event. A place on an ordinary balcony overlooking the plaza of the corrida cost 500 or 600 reales, and some places on a nearby street cost 150 reales even though they offered only a rear view of the entrance of the nobles' procession.[53]

Entertainment fees were used by the city to finance some of its welfare programs. When streets were closed off for a corrida, places in them were sold for a small amount that was given to the poor prisoners of the royal prison.[54] From the admission fee of each person who attended the theater in Seville, the city collected eight maravedís and gave this money to the poor in prison or in hospitales. City officials complained in 1611 that they were not getting their share of theater proceeds, and they sent inspectors to stand at theater doors to collect the eight-maravedí charity fee. From their careful records, they found that 526 plays were performed in the Coliseo and Corral de Doña Elvira between April 1611 and April 1614. Of the 53,346 reales brought in by these performances, 854 went to the leaders of the acting companies, and 716 went to the administrators.[55]

However, entertainment receipts also helped to support the traveling actors' groups that many city fathers feared and hated. In 1609 the director of one acting company declared that the city had taken so much from theater receipts that he was not even able to pay for expenses. He petitioned the city council to direct the administrator of funds for poor prisoners to reimburse his expenses from the amount he had taken from the theater for welfare.[56] The city's desire to control the entertainment of Corpus processions also meant that it had to pay participating actors and musicians. The head of an Italian acting company

53. "Segunda relación de las cañas y toros," Papeles varios, BC, 83-7-14.

54. Ariño, p. 95.

55. Sánches-Arjona, p. 147. AMS, Papeles del Conde de Aguila, Sección Especial, Tomo 62 en folio, No. 39.

56. AMS, Siglo XVII, Sección 4, Escribanías de Cabildo, Tomo 5, No. 69.

petitioned the city council to pay him a fee for appearing in Corpus, adding wistfully that he had had great expenses in making this appearance and his company was eager to continue on their travels.[57]

Gambling is a good example of the many opportunities for illicit profit in public entertainment. Certain games were officially banned, but they were played in the most luxurious casinos as well as at the meanest little street table. Gambling was a lucrative business for the owners of royal-licensed casinos, and it also brought in quick profits for some small local innkeepers who set up a gaming table in a rear room. There were games like *lansquet*, a card game that originated with mercenaries in the Middle Ages, and *taba*, a game played by throwing the knuckle bone of a sheep. Gambling attracted many onlookers as well as players, for it was customary for winners to distribute some of their winnings among the spectators.[58] Pedro de León, who talked with many gamblers during his ministry to the poor and prisoners of Seville, described a spirit of comradeship among gamblers. A player down on his luck could find food or a small handout from his luckier companions. Gamblers made a lot of money, according to this priest, and they cared about nothing except eating and playing.[59]

Crowds that gathered at public entertainments increased criminal opportunities. Whenever processions or public executions attracted big crowds, thieves found it very easy to lift valuables from onlookers or from empty houses. They also found it easy to resell stolen goods quickly among crowds. Old scores could be settled with a quick knife thrust hidden by the press of a crowd, and sheriffs were more easily evaded when they were diverted to carrying out their official roles in religious processions or public executions. Some traveling players specialized in holding street audiences enthralled while one of their members mingled with the crowd, stealthily relieving them of their

57. AMS, Siglo XVI, Sección 3, Escribanías de Cabildo, Tomo 6, No. 5.

58. Quevedo, pp. 138 and 146. Deleito y Piñuela, *Mala*, pp. 221–236. *Ordenamiento de la Tafurias*, quoted in Clifford Stevens Walton, *The Civil Law in Spain and Spanish-America* (Washington, 1900), p. 44.

59. Pedro de León, Part I, chapter 13, folio 32.

valuables. People enjoying a spectacle or amusement were the best kind of clients for much of the business of underworld people.

An account of the 1620 fire in the Coliseo described the underworld's talent for finding profitable opportunities. As the fire spread from the backdrop of the stage, the audience ran to the doors in panic. Thieves in the audience demanded that women give them their jewels, and these "poured out in a flood" as the terrified women gave up anything in order to run from the fire. Some of the thieves even ventured into the fire and picked up ornaments and clothing that had not burned.[60]

Public entertainments were profitable to both underworld people and city officials. If the fees charged for these events helped to support a subculture that ridiculed authority, they also supported the position of the city government as kindly benefactor of the poor in prisons and common houses. More important, these entertainments provided social rituals that buttressed the power of the ruling elite and symbolized the unity of the community.

60. AMS, Efemérides, "Enzendio del corral de comedias llamado El Coliseo de Sevilla año 1620," cuadro 2.

8

Beggars and Benefactors

IN 1639 the administrator of Seville's orphanage for girls petitioned the city council to prohibit voluntary mendicity. All poor people, he declared, should be required to register before city deputies so that the "truly poor" could be differentiated from those who could work but instead "go about in little bands, running through the city, and taking alms from the truly poor who cannot work."[1]

The problem of determining who should receive charity was not a new development in the seventeenth century, but it became more critical as the wealth of the city declined in this period. Benefactors who continued their traditional generosity were unable to satisfy all the demands for charity. The Crown took an active interest in new charitable programs, and the city government became a major benefactor. Charity continued as a response to human need, but increasingly it became a political tool. In early modern Seville, it ran headlong into the idle vagrants and false beggars of the underworld.

Charity in this city has been described in literature and written documents, but even more vividly in the paintings of Bartolomé Murillo. Born in Seville in 1617, he was orphaned by the time he was ten years old.[2] He left his apprenticeship with a local artist

1. AMS, Siglo XVII, Sección 4, Escribanías de Cabildo, Tomo 24, No. 26.
2. Murillo's life is discussed in Jacques Lassaigne, *Spanish Painting from Velasquez to Picasso*, trans. Stuart Gilbert (Geneva, 1952). A. L. Mayer, *The Work of Murillo* (New York, 1913). *Encyclopedia of World Art* (New York, London, and Toronto, 1965), Vol. 10. Jonathan Brown, *Murillo and His Drawings* (Princeton, 1976).

and went to work painting coarse, popular pictures to sell on the street of the Feria. Here among many other street-artists and street-hawkers, he saw the poorest people of the city. Murillo first became famous when the monks of the local Franciscan monastery commissioned eleven paintings. Later the wealthy Miguel de Mañara commissioned Murillo to paint eleven paintings for the church of the Hospital de Santa Caridad. By the middle of the century, he was wealthy and famous enough to marry a rich noble woman.

Murillo had seen his city on the streets of the Feria, in a wealthy monastery, in a gorgeously decorated charitable institution, and from the salons of the city's leading citizens. He saw charity as a noble, pious gesture, evident in his painting of Saint Elizabeth of Hungary. However, the diseased head of the small boy that she is healing in this painting is so realistic in detail that it is almost repulsive. If charity was noble and pious, it was also concerned with real people who suffered hideously. Murillo supported the social order in which he had won so much wealth and fame, but he was also aware of its imperfections. While he depicted charity as individual efforts to bring human society closer to God's perfection, he recognized that charity to many was simply a question of survival. His paintings, together with written archival sources, present memorable portraits of receivers, benefactors, and the uses of charity in early modern Seville.

RECEIVERS OF CHARITY

Several children crowd around the monk in Murillo's painting "La Sopa Boba." Orphans and abandoned children were by tradition the largest group who received charity. Unwanted infants often died, but others were taken to a house next to the Cathedral, where they could be received for care when they were placed anonymously in a revolving window. The Church established a perpetual fund to care for 140 foundlings each year. On the feast of the Annunciation, Cathedral clerics led a solemn procession of the foundlings carried by their nurses. Many found adoptive parents in this way, but some orphaned babies

9 "St. Elizabeth of Hungary Healing the Sick." Bartolomé Murillo.

were not adopted and were sent to the city orphanages sheltering older children.[3]

The brotherhood of Santo Niño Perdido was founded in 1589 to care for older children abandoned in the city. Brothers walked through the streets at night and took any abandoned children they found to their house where they gave them food and shelter. When they saw adults begging with children, they took the children away from them "so they wouldn't be beggars all their lives and could be placed with masters."[4] Some children were sent out to beg by the parents, and others were used by professional beggars, who found that ragged or sickly appearing children greatly improved their pitch. Sometimes these small beggars were completely on their own. In 1593 the city council heard that city streets and plazas were "full of small boys who wander about lost and begging and dying of hunger and sleep in doorways and on stone benches by the walls, poorly dressed, almost nude, and exposed to many dangers . . . and others have died of freezing by dawn."[5] Whether abandoned, orphaned, or in the care of a professional beggar or thief, the plight of these children was pitiful.

By 1580 city archives recorded pleas for charity from many adults. These grew in the seventeenth century as Seville suffered from a decline in trade, a devastating epidemic, and repeated monetary devaluations.[6] Old people who had no income and no one to care for them were another large group of people dependent on the "sopa boba." Some were cared for in hospitales, but

3. Morgado, pp. 319–320, 372. He even cites one day in which 70 babies were adopted. For a more complete discussion of orphans, abandoned children, and the underworld, see below, pp. 190–211. See also Ortiz de Zuñiga, 4:499.

4. Quoted in M. Chaves, pp. 78–79.

5. AMS, Siglo XVI, Sección 3, Escribanías de Cabildo, Tomo 12, No. 6.

6. For economic dislocations, see Anes Alvarez, pp. 194–195. Domínguez Ortiz, *Golden Age*, p. 186. Domínguez Ortiz, *Orto*, pp. 34–36, 84. Viñas y Mey, *Problema*, pp. 14, 16–29, 113–116, discusses agricultural distress. Monetary restamping and revaluation in Seville are reported in "Otros sucesos singulares," Memorias de diferentes cosas, BC, 84-7-21 esp. folios 192, 196[V], 228[V], 240, 253, 260[V], 264. Pleas for help in the 1580's are in AMS, Siglo XVI, Sección 3, Escribanías de Cabildo, Tomo 5, No. 17, and in Tomo 11, No. 43.

10 "San Diego of Alcalá Feeding the Poor," also called "La Sopa Boba."
Bartolomé Murillo.

many others turned to begging. A registry of people licensed to beg in Seville in 1675 shows that 69 percent were sixty years old or older, and 84 percent were fifty years or older. The age distribution in Figure 11 suggests that licensed begging in Seville was an old-age occupation.[7]

Disabled people of all ages formed another group who received charity. The registry of 231 people licensed to beg in 1675 includes a description of the afflictions of most of these people. Some of the descriptions are too general to be helpful, but the registry does suggest the most common problems:

Affliction	Number
Crippled	74
Blindness	42
Urinary illness	13
Gout	9
Asthma	6
Palsy	5

Mental illness seldom brought with it a license to beg. Mentally retarded adults were treated as dependent children, some of them free to support themselves as beggars and others confined and cared for in the common houses that were popularly known as *casas de locos*. Mentally ill people were less likely to receive charity. Even though a few seventeenth-century thinkers argued that mental disorders should be treated as illness, many regarded deranged people as cursed. The madman whose family could not care for him was often run out of town, an outcast, whose exile strengthened a sense of solidarity in the community and also relieved it from supporting him through charity.[8]

7. AMS, Siglo XVII, Sección 4, Escribanías de Cabildo, Tomo 29, No. 9. Note that of the 231 names entered in this registry, ages are given for only 213. Percentages are based on the numbers for which ages were given. Also note that these ages may be approximate and represent the age the beggar or the registrar believed the beggar to be. The only beggar registered who was under twenty years of age was sixteen-year-old Luís de Carbes of Málaga, who had a hole in the left side of his mouth, presumably a birth defect.

8. Michel Foucault, *Madness and Civilization: A History of Insanity in the Age of Reason* (New York, 1965), pp. 7, 10. For seventeenth-century

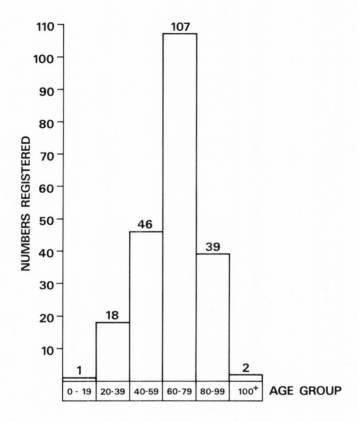

11 Age distribution of people licensed to beg in Seville. Based on a registry
    of beggars in 1675, reported in Archivo Municipal de Sevilla, Siglo
    XVII, Sección 4, *Escribanías de Cabildo,* Tomo 29, No. 9.

Women without husbands frequently received charity. A 1667 survey of the poor in Seville listed 261 female household heads and only thirteen male household heads in the parish of the Cathedral.[9] Typical of the male heads was Pedro de Campo, who had a wife and seven children still at home, and was so ill that he had been unable to work. Many of the female household heads were listed as widows, and many others were listed as having husbands who were "captive," "in the Indies," or simply "absent." Noticeably absent from "La Sopa Boba" were young, able-bodied men.

The 1667 survey suggests that the women considered deserving of charity came from respectable families as well as poor ones. The list for the parish of the Cathedral, for example, includes the sister of a former admiral, "noble and very poor." Women in the survey were frequently listed as *gente principal* (people of note). They appeared on the lists because they were poor, had no means of support, and shared an intangible quality that placed them among the "honorable poor." One term used very frequently in the lists is *pobre de solenidad*, a suggestion that these people lived seriously and soberly. Compare this term with the marginal comment that one priest wrote after he crossed off the name of Laura de Esquibel and her household *no sirben a Dios* (they don't serve God).

Prisoners were considered worthy of charity, not because they were honorable, but because they were often poor and helpless. The 1667 survey for the parish of Triana listed María Josepha, who had been forced to sell everything, even her husband's sickbed, in order to pay off the debt for which he had

---

opinions of madness, see Richard Hunter and Ida Macalpine, *Three-Hundred Years of Psychiatry 1535–1860* (London, 1964), pp. 94–97.

9. Memoria de todas las parroquias de Sevilla y de las necesidades y pobres que habia en ellas; que pedia, el V^es D. Miguel Mañara para tener cuidado de socorrer las como lo hijo, y mientras recibo los remedios como por estas memorias parece, 1667, manuscript in HSC, Estante 4, Legajo 18. The survey does not cover all parishes, but it is remarkably detailed for those included. Taken by parish priests who were directed by Miguel de Mañara, these lists are of people whom the priests considered "honorable poor."

been imprisoned. Lucky prisoners received money to buy food or pay off the debts that had sent them to prison. The unlucky ones got a burial ground directly under a gallows, their corpses protected from dogs and scavengers by members of a pious fraternity, the *Hermandad de Santa Caridad*.

Many people who received charity in Seville were transients or immigrants. Of the 231 entries in the 1675 registry of beggars, 137 came from outside the province of Seville. A sixteenth-century chronicler of the city explained that there were many charitable houses in Seville because of "the excessive number of poor who enter the city each day, almost from every part of the world."[10] Another contemporary grumbled that two thirds of the people who were supported by charity in Seville were foreigners who didn't want to spend the money they had earned in Spain.[11] Soldiers and sailors in the royal service demanded preference over other people seeking help from city charity, and galley slaves who were sick or hungry or in spiritual need also received charity when they landed in Seville.[12]

Benefactors tried to distinguish deserving recipients from dishonorable rogues, but the line between underworld and legitimate charity was neither sharp nor stationary. City fathers identified the deserving poor as those unable to work, as opposed to those unwilling to do so. Priests who took the 1667 survey added a distinction between those who were willing to go to Mass and those who were not. Poor people sometimes defined themselves as the victims of underworld thieves who went through their neighborhoods stripping poor houses even of their mean pallets.[13] Underworld people undoubtedly identified themselves as those clever enough to exploit the best deal in town, whether a soup line or a street theft. Belonging to the underworld subculture was not always a fulltime occupation, however, and it could be com-

10. Peraza, pp. 1147.

11. Anes Alvarez, pp. 166–167.

12. AMS, Papeles Importantes, Siglo XVII, Tomo 4, No. 14. Pedro de León, Part I, chapter 9, folios 22–23.

13. For an example see the survey of the parish of the Cathedral (Santa Iglesia), which listed María de Santillan, who was robbed even of her bed, which was a poor uncovered mattress, in Parroquias, HSC.

bined with legitimate occupations, such as street-hawking and unloading ships. City fathers tried to use the underworld as a foil
against which to define the *deserving* poor, but underworld
people were too mobile and crafty to be placed in a single cate-
gory where they could not feed on their host.

BENEFACTORS

The Church, religious groups, pious individuals, and the city
government had traditionally acted as charitable benefactors in
Seville. As the need for charity increased in the sixteenth and
seventeenth centuries, these benefactors found their traditional
forms inappropriate or ineffective. Indiscriminate handouts to all
beggars were no longer possible as their numbers increased. Small
hospitales for fifteen or twenty poor supported by the begging of
a few monks became less effective in meeting the city's growing
need for charity. As benefactors tried to limit their charity to the
deserving poor, they also changed their strategies for giving.

The hospital, a common house providing charity, underwent
several changes in the late sixteenth century. When Fernando III
first conquered Seville from the Moors in 1248, he had directed
each parish of the city to establish a hospital to care for its poor,
sick, abandoned, and disabled people. By 1586 the city had outgrown this parish system of charity and boasted more than 100
hospitales. Most were very small and specialized, such as the
Hospital del Rey, which was founded to care for twelve old
people who were poor but of noble status.[14] The financial base
for most of these small institutions dwindled in the sixteenth
century at the same time that demands for charity increased.
Dependent upon the alms that their inmates or a few monks
begged in the streets, the hospitales took in fewer people and
provided less care as the numbers of beggars increased. Underworld people recognized the declining quality of hospitales,
sardonically using the same word *coto* for both a hospital and a
cemetery.[15]

14. Morgado, p. 356. His estimate may be conservative, since Ortiz de
Zuñiga, 4:567–568, reports 76 hospitales in the parish of San Pedro alone.
15. Salillas, p. 280.

One solution to the proliferation of inadequately endowed hospitales was to consolidate them into a few larger institutions that could be more effectively and efficiently administered. When the Church and Cardinal Archbishop Rodrigo de Castro proposed consolidation, Philip II supported them against local opposition. Residents of one street opposed the plan because it would bring all contagiously ill people to the Hospital de los Desamparados in their neighborhood. Other opponents pointed out that when one hospital, the Hermita de Santas Justina y Rufina, had complied with reduction orders, it had been rented out as a tavern "where much dishonesty has occurred."[16] Despite these arguments, the Cardinal Archbishop reported in March 1587 a list of 77 hospitales that he had, complying with the king's direction, reduced to two. Hospitales again mushroomed, but they were never again as many as there had been in the mid-sixteenth century. One list reported 24 hospitales in Seville in 1673.[17] Hospital consolidation changed charity into a centrally controlled, more efficiently administered strategy for confining the poor.

Accompanying the changing pattern of hospitales was a change in charitable bequests. Before the end of the sixteenth century, the wills of many wealthy people contributed to charity by endowing a small hospital or paying money to monasteries and churches for singing designated Masses. Giving alms to the poor at the funeral fulfilled pious requirements for charity and also ensured a large crowd at the funeral procession. It reflected a rather primitive belief that giving a gift could ward off the threat of death or damnation, as well as the traditional Catholic belief that good works could purchase the repose of a dead person's soul.[18]

16. AMS, Siglo XVI, Sección 3, Escribanías de Cabildo, Tomo 10, Nos. 5. 18, 19. Memorias eclesiásticas BC, 84–7–19, folio 52.

17. AMS, Papeles del Conde de Aguila, Sección Especial, Tomo 5 en folio, No. 8. AMS, Siglo XVII, Sección 4, Escribanías de Cabildo, Tomo 11, No. 18. The two hospitals remaining in 1587 were renamed Espiritu Santo and Amor de Dios.

18. Thomas, *Religion*, p. 601, discusses the primitive aspects of this practice.

A comparison of the charitable bequests of two of the wealthiest men of the city suggests the changing patterns of giving between the early sixteenth and late seventeenth century. Don Fadrique Enriquez de Ribera, Marquis of Tarifa, died in 1539. Among other things, his will provided for 2278 different Masses to be sung in 27 parish churches, eight monasteries, three convents, one hermitage, and one hospital. Directing a payment of between two and seven reales for each Mass, his will distributed thousands of reales to many different religious foundations in the city.[19]

When Miguel de Mañara died in 1679, his will expressly forbade spending money on a pompous funeral because he wanted to leave his money to the poor.[20] He left all his wealth, except for small amounts given to long-time servants, to the Hospital de la Santa Caridad, a very large charitable institution that he had built for the city. The chapel of this hospital was a treasury of paintings, frescos, and sculpture by some of Seville's most famous artists. It was a fitting monument to a citizen who was as famous for his charity as for his wealth. Instead of distributing smaller amounts to paupers at his funeral or to many churches and religious orders as payment for Masses, Mañara concentrated his bequest on one large institution that has continued to preserve a treasury of art and to confine and care for many poor people up to the present day.

Michel Vovelle, who recently completed a monumental study of the attitudes toward death that were revealed in some 19,000

---

19. Francisco Collantes de Teran, *Memorias históricas de los establecimientos de caridad de Sevilla y descripción artística de los mismos* (Seville, 1884), pp. 138–139, 241–272. See also Antonio de la Banda y Vargas, "El Barrio de la Macarena," *Archivo Hispalense*, Series 2, 44–45 (1966), pp. 44, 48.

20. Juan de Cárdenas, *Breve relación de la muerte, vida, y virtudes del venerable caballero Don Miguel Mañara Vicentelo de Leca y Caballero del Orden de Calatrava, Hermano Mayor de la Santa Caridad*, 1679 (Seville, 1903), pp. 144–151. Rafael Sanchez Arráiz, "Hospital de la Santa Caridad," in *Quién no vió a Sevilla*, (n.d., Sevilla). At the present time the Hospital de la Santa Caridad cares for approximately 300 old men who have no family or income.

wills, found a similar pattern of change in eighteenth-century Provence.[21] Wills progressively called for fewer Masses, less ostentatious funerals, and charity given only to the poor confined in hospitales. He concluded that these changes were part of a larger pattern of secularization in the eighteenth century.

Miguel de Mañara, whose will demanded a simple funeral and restricted all charity to the Hospital de la Santa Caridad, might seem to be a seventeenth-century forerunner of modern secularization. However, he was a very devout man who certainly did not consciously promote secularization. His desire for a simple funeral stemmed from his great feeling of unworthiness before God. He directed that a verse be written over the place where he was buried in the floor of the church: "Here lie the remains of the worst man that has ever lived. Pray to God for him."[22] He restricted charity to one institution because he believed that charity was best administered through large, well-controlled institutions for confining the poor. His will suggests that the changing patterns of charity in the seventeenth century still wore the garb of piety and effected changes in wills even before eighteenth-century secularization.

Religious orders and fraternities continued to channel money to charity. The Counter Reformation reforms tried to curb the proliferation of inadequately endowed religious groups, but the numbers of *cofradías* (religious fraternities) increased in this period. Unlike the *scuole grandi* of Renaissance Venice, these fraternities unually did not distribute charity among their own members.[23] Instead, they were small groups that gave to less fortunate people—a useful way to establish position as notables of the city.

It is cynical to suggest, however, that the numbers of religious fraternities increased simply because socially ambitious merchants needed ladders for social climbing. Some religious

21. Michel Vovelle, *Piété baroque et dechristianisation en Provence au XVIIIe siècles; Les attitudes devant la mort d'après des clauses des testaments* (Paris, 1973).

22. Cárdenas, p. 147.

23. Brian Pullan, *Rich and Poor in Renaissance Venice: The Social Institutions of a Catholic State, to 1620* (Cambridge, 1971), p. 86.

fraternities had been founded by pious men who performed genuine acts of humility and compassion, such as burying the bodies of executed criminals. Some had been established to preserve and venerate religious images, and their rites of devotion included charity.

While charity continued to be a concern of some religious fraternities, social identification appeared to be the primary interest of many others. The Negroes who had been Christianized formed a religious fraternity that was noted for its devotion to the Holy Virgin. Rather poor, they each contributed what they could to a fiesta honoring the Immaculate Conception in 1653. When they fell 200 ducats short of the necessary amount, one free Negro pawned his liberty to raise the money. Some twenty years later this same fraternity presented a mummery that was recorded as the most "deserving" of the celebrations honoring the majority of Carlos II.[24]

Some religious fraternities founded in the early modern period were social extensions of occupational groups. Although royal policies deliberately opposed a strong guild system and expressly prohibited guilds from having religious fraternities, cofradías seemed to rise informally among some occupational groups. The report of a religious festival in 1579, for example, described two cofradías from Triana that were composed of "people of the sea."[25] Social functions undoubtedly received more emphasis than charity in these religious fraternities.

By tradition, the Church had been a major benefactor in Seville. The Archbishopric of Seville was wealthy enough to feed many of the hungry, and it distributed food to them in the surrounding countryside as well. During a famine in 1636 it distributed 1000 reales in bread each day for 100 days.[26] Nevertheless, it could not sustain all the charity needed in Seville. In the late sixteenth century the administrator of the Hospital del Cardenal petitioned the city council for wheat and said the only

---

24. Ortiz de Zuñiga, 4:753. Guichot y Parody, 2:293.

25. Ortiz de Zuñiga, 4:753. Guichot y Parody, 2:293. Anes Alvarez, p. 23. De Siguenza, Papeles varios, BC, 85-4-13.

26. Memorias eclesiásticas, BC, 84-7-19.

other alternative was to discharge the poor from the hospital and close its doors. The city government became patron to several hospitales; it contributed 96,201 marvedís annually to the Hospital del Rey.[27]

The city council was undoubtedly responding to the greater need for charity when it increased its contributions, but it was also responding to a royal interest in charity. Realizing that charity was so vital to political order that it could not be left to the caprice of local communities, the Crown ordered the city government to give 20,000 maravedís to relieve the financial plight of the Hospital del Amor de Dios in 1542.[28] From the Crown came directives about controlling and sheltering beggars, providing food for the poor in time of dearth, establishing schools and orphanages, and confining diseased people in hospitales. Philip II's interference in the controversy over hospital reduction in Seville was not an isolated case of meddling in local affairs, but part of a larger pattern of royal concern with charity.

Schools and orphanages increased in relative importance as charitable institutions in the sixteenth century. This reflected not only the increased number of abandoned children, but also a Humanist belief that a good society depended upon educating all children to be useful, upright citizens. In the Patio de los Naranjos outside the Cathedral a school taught writing and reading to acolytes and other poor boys of the parish. A religious fraternity paid the salary for the teacher of this school, and a local bookseller offered to provide primers so that poor children could attend.[29]

The city government became a significant contributor to

27. AMS, Siglo XVI, Sección 3, Escribanías de Cabildo, Tomo 10, No. 14. de Sigüenza, p. 306. AMS, Papeles Importantes, Siglo XVI, Tomo 9, No. 6.

28. AMS, Siglo XVI, Sección 3, Escribanías de Cabildo, Tomo 10, No. 11.

29. Juan Luís Vives, *Del socorro de los pobres o de las necesidades humanes*, 1526, in *Biblioteca de Autores Españoles*, Vol. 65 (Madrid, 1922), pp. 283–284. Astrain, 2:588, 3:201. de Castro Palacios, folio 7. Guichot y Parody, 2:314.

charity schools as expenses rose above the contributions of Church, religious groups, and individual benefactors. In 1545 the city was asked to pay the salaries for two teachers and provide a house for a charity school. Soon after it began paying teachers' salaries, the city government insisted that it should license teachers. In 1561 the jurados of the city council pointed out the importance of licensing teachers who were competent and "of good life and custom."[30] As the city council became patron to several charitable schools, it gradually extended its control over them.[31]

City government, Church, religious fraternities, and pious individuals gave large sums for charity, but they were never able to satisfy all the demands. What happened to the poor people who were not considered deserving of charity? Who cared for homeless old people who could find no room in a hospital? How did the hundreds of street children survive when orphanages could not feed them? One answer is that the underworld devised its own charitable strategies.

Juvenile begging was one of the most common of these methods for survival. Since children were able to escape the prohibitions against unlicensed begging, they were sent out to beg by surrogate parents who provided them with food and shelter and some supervision in return for the alms they took in. Most children were successful beggars only in their younger years, for people gave more to the smallest ragged urchin holding out a dirty hand.

Criminal apprenticeship, another underworld device, afforded practical training and socialization into the underworld organizations. Aimed primarily at older unattached children, it also used little boys who could slip through small openings and open doors from the inside for the thieves known as *fulidores*.[32] Young girls were usually trained in the art and commerce of prostitu-

30. Guichot y Parody, 2:311–313.

31. AMS, Siglo XVI, Sección 3, Escribanías de Cabildo, Tomo 12, No. 2; Tomo 5, No. 39; Tomo 8, No. 28. Also AMS, Archivo General, Sección 1, Carpeta 27, No. 376.

32. Salillas, pp. 113–114.

tion. In Quevedo's *El Buscón*, the picaro described how his landlady taught girls to be prostitutes, "how to pluck a man and what sort of things to say to him. She taught them how to get jewels . . . She showed them how to ask for cash and how to get necklaces and rings."[33]

Underworld people used children to "run errands." This often provided opportunities for thefts or casing likely houses for thefts. Girls went out on the streets "on errands" to procure customers for older prostitutes. An adminstrator of a girls' orphanage in the seventeenth century requested the city to prohibit young girls from being sent out on errands because this was the major cause of "lost women" (prostitutes).[34] Lost or not, a young girl learning prostitution brought in money for her underworld confederates. To these people, prostitution made far more practical sense than paying a dowry to young girls.

Finally, the underworld helped to care for elderly people. Cervantes' Monipodio had recognized the usefulness of older people in performing certain jobs for his criminal organization. Called "hornets," these older men cased houses by day to determine the ones that could be most easily broken into by night. They also followed people who withdrew money from the *Contractión* (businessmen's exchange) or mint so they would know where they were keeping the money.[35] The division of labor in underworld organizations could easily capitalize on the expertise of old thieves who were perhaps slower in their reflexes but wise in the ways of crime.

Underworld charity, then, was as selective in its own way as the charity of the city. While city benefactors helped only the deserving poor, underworld charity helped only the exploitable poor. The underworld created alternatives to city charity and helped to complement it, but it intentionally provided very little for people who were so disabled or weak that they could play no useful role in underworld occupations.

33. Quevedo, p. 195.

34. AMS, Siglo XVII, Sección 4, Escribanías de Cabildo, Tomo 24, No. 28.

35. Cervantes, "Rinconete," p. 108.

THE USES OF CHARITY

There is no doubt that much of the charity of Seville was motivated by a deep compassion and sincere religious feeling, such as that depicted in Murillo's painting of Saint Thomas of Villanueva healing a cripple. Many people gave to charity hoping to purchase a heavenly reward for their own souls. Others performed charitable deeds as penance or as an act of devotion. Charity continued in the early modern period as a gesture of human compassion and spiritual concern, but it also increasingly became a very practical tool for both the dominant culture of the city and the underworld subculture.

The city oligarchy used charity as a defensive strategy. It used hospitales to enclose and separate the poor and disabled who, in a crowd, seemed very threatening. Hospitales helped to remove from the public eye those unfortunates who could dismay upright citizens and provoke embarrassing questions. Enclosure and removal was an effective way to neutralize the potentially subversive idea that something must be wrong with the existing system if it produced so many people wandering about with neither job nor family. It also served to isolate the infection of poverty and disability.

City officials used charity as a defensive strategy against uncontrolled and unschooled children. Stubborn juveniles who refused the shelter and masters provided by the *Cofradía del Santisimo Niño Perdido* were forced by the authority of the asistente to accept this charity. City fathers feared that homeless children grew up to be criminals, and they asserted that there were fewer thieves when schools were available for them.[36]

Fearful of the flood of vagrants in sixteenth-century Seville, the city government had decided to license beggars in 1597. Public announcers called out all over the city that the poor and unemployed should go to the field next to the Hospital de la

---

36. Morgado, pp. 372–373. AMS, Siglo XVI, Sección 3, Escribanías de Cabildo, Tomo 12, No. 3. See also the 1639 petition of Alonso Ruiz, administrator of the girls' orphanage, in Siglo XVII, Sección 4, Escribanías de Cabildo, Tomo 24, No. 26.

12 "St. Thomas of Villanueva Healing a Cripple." Bartolomé Murillo.

Sangre.[37] More than 2,000 people filled the field, a hubbub of old people, cripples, healthy vagrants, men, women, and children. A procession of city council members, royal justices and the asistente, medical doctors, and scribes arrived. They entered a room in the hospital and then directed the poor to enter to be examined, one by one. The incurably ill were ordered to a hospital, the able-bodied were ordered to go to work, and the disabled and very old were given a license to beg, a small placard with white ribbons. People without these placards were prohibited from begging and would be whipped and exiled if they were caught. Licensed begging continued in Seville throughout the early modern period with periodic examinations and registration.

The city oligarchy found many advantages in licensing beggars. They were better able to control vagrancy and ensure public order. They could force able-bodied people to work, providing a larger pool of labor that could keep wages low. Periodic inspections helped the city to control epidemics and confine ill people in hospitales. At the same time, this procedure took a middle position in the controversy over whether poor people should be confined or be free to beg for their bread. Finally, it emphasized the power and the authority of the city oligarchy to determine who should receive charity—literally, a matter of life and death to many people.

Dowries were a defensive strategy against uncontrolled youth. According to the Spanish code of law, one reason for marriage was "to avoid quarrels, homicides, insolence, violence, and many other wrongful acts that would take place on account of women if marriage did not exist."[38] This view of marriage as social control reflected the commonly held belief that social order depended upon subjecting women to the authority of husbands. It also reflected a belief that young girls who had reached puberty were especially dangerous to social order. A seventeenth-century medical writer warned,

37. Ariño, pp. 45–47. For the earlier laws on vagrancy, see Guichot y Parody, 1:374.
38. Fourth Partida, Titulo II, discussed in Scott, p. 886.

It is of the same significance in these animals when they conceive eggs, as it is in young women when their uterus grows hot, their menses flow, and their bosoms swell—in a word, when they become marriageable; and who, if they continue too long unwedded, are seized with serious symptoms—hysterics, furor uterinus, etc., or fall into a cachetic state, and distemperatures of various kinds. All animals indeed, grow savage when in heat, and unless they are suffered to enjoy one another, become changed in disposition. In like manner women occasionally become insane through ungratified desire, and to such a height does the malady reach in some, that they are believed to be poisoned, or moonstruck, or possessed by a devil.[39]

Marriage or the convent seemed to be the best means to control such a potentially dangerous group. The archbishopric provided dowries so that poor young girls could enter convents, and several cofradías and wealthy individuals contributed dowries so that poor girls could marry. Between 1666 and 1670, for example, the philanthropist Miguel de Mañara provided marriage dowries for 95 poor girls.[40] When the priests surveyed the poor of the city in 1667, they made a point of listing girls of marriageable age (*doncellas*) so that dowries could be given to girls like María Andrea, an orphan in Triana "so poor that she cannot marry." Murillo's paintings of young girls on the streets of Seville show them as pretty and robust, cheerful and calm—hardly the dangerous creatures described in the medical treatise. He also recognized, however, that earning a livelihood was a major problem for most of them. His painting "Fruit-Sellers Counting Money" emphasizes their economic vulnerability by

---

39. William Harvey, *Exercitationes de generatione animalium,* quoted in Hunter and Macalpine, p. 131.

40. Dottes que pago N[ro] Venerable herm[o] May[or], el Sr D. Miguel Mañara en los años desde el de 1666 hasta el de 1670 a diferentes pobres para que se casasen, in HSC, Legajo 18, Estante 4. An example of dowries provided by the Archbishopric is in the survey for the parish of the Cathedral (Santa Iglesia) in Parroquias, HSC. Morgado discusses charitable dowries on p. 321.

13   "The Dice-Players." Bartolomé Murillo.

the great concentration with which the young girls study the money they have earned.

If the city oligarchy used charity as a defensive strategy, it also used it as a tool for cultural promotion. Schools for poor children were one means to impose control on them, and they also served to socialize the young into the dominant culture. Proponents of charity schools argued for the need to rescue children, like those in Murillo's painting "The Dice-Players," from lives of idleness and crime. They said that these children should be brought off the streets and placed under the discipline of an education in "all good customs." This would increase not only the spiritual health of the city, but also its temporal prosperity.[41]

Charity helped to provide the kinds of laborers that the city needed. Orphanages and foster parents taught children practical skills so that they could be useful artisans, teamsters, sailors, and domestic servants. Licensed begging forced able-bodied vagrants into the labor pool, a strategy to keep wages lower and obtain workers for the fields that had been abandoned by small producers.

The public processions that accompanied charitable events clearly demonstrated the strength of charity as a pillar of the social order. Fray Diego Calchorran, for example, thanked the city council for its support of the girls' orphanage in 1595 and promised that the girls would march in a procession from their house to the Cathedral so that everyone would know the good work of the city.[42] Poor girls who received dowries from religious fraternities also marched in a special public procession, each girl dressed in a white gown and flanked by two brothers of the cofradía.[43]

These public displays of charity reinforced the values and good reputation of the dominant culture in the city. They

41. AMS, Siglo XVI, Sección 3, Escribanías de Cabildo, Tomo 11, No. 52.

42. AMS, Siglo XVI, Sección 3, Escribanías de Cabildo, Tomo 8, No. 21.

43. Morgado, p. 321.

14　"Fruit-Sellers with Money." Bartolomé Murillo.

demonstrated the power of the city oligarchy to define and support the deserving poor, while confining and punishing others. Public displays of charity also fostered among the city's poor a feeling of security that the dominant culture would take care of them. Seville's charitable system carefully distinguished between the givers and the receivers; it did not permit them to mix together, as they did in the scuole grandi of Venice. Thus charity in Seville enhanced the position of the benefactors, a lesson quickly learned by the city government as it became a more active benefactor in the early modern period.

Above all, charity was used to preserve the existing system. The Crown and city government might occasionally differ on the proper way to regulate beggars, and the orphanage administrator might disagree with clergymen about the best way to handle children. Nevertheless, all of these benefactors agreed that charity had a fundamentally conservative function. It should neither try to redistribute wealth nor change positions of power in the ruling oligarchy.[44]

Underworld people also recognized charity as a tool to protect and promote the existing system. In addition, however, they used it as a tool to exploit that system. Licensed begging, for example, ended the opportunities for some false beggars, but it merely encouraged others to use herbs, chemicals, and cleverly applied tourniquets to simulate aging and physical disabilities. Surveys of "deserving poor" prevented some underworld people from receiving charity, but others found many ways to masquerade as the honorable poor. How was a priest to know that the reformed prostitute who appeared to him as a penitent Mary Magdalene by day often returned to her former occupation by night? Which priests could distinguish women truly destitute from those who had an exploiting man in the shadows and some small children borrowed to beg alms?

Children learned how to exploit charity. Clergy of the Church of San Salvador complained that after they had given food and shelter to abandoned boys in their house, these small thieves hid

44. Pullan, pp. 8, 229, points out a similar usefulness for the scuole grandi in Venice.

their sacks of stolen loot behind the altar pieces of the church.[45] Using charitable homes and schools to socialize abandoned children could help to make them into good citizens, but it also provided a fine opportunity for these children to socialize one another into the society of the streets. Henry Mayhew later recognized this problem in the English Ragged Schools when he wrote, "however well intentioned such institutions may be, they are, and must be from the mere fact of bringing so many boys of vicious propensities together, productive of far more injury than benefit to the community."[46]

Even marriage dowries could misfire. Underworld men had few qualms about accepting a charitable dowry, going through a marriage ceremony, and then quietly disappearing. In 1574 two young girls of the city tried another ruse. One dressed up like a man so that they could appear as a couple entitled to the charitable dowry of 100 ducats. Unfortunately, they were discovered and sentenced to public humiliation, including 100 lashes.[47]

Underworld charity was based on the principle of exploitation. If a child were not pathetic enough to be a good beggar or quick enough to be a good thief, he received no food or shelter from underworld people. The elderly were given jobs in the underworld, but only so long as they were useful. To provide for a senile old lady out of respect for age was completely foreign to underworld charity.

Charity provided the underworld with a vehicle for cultural continuity. Young children were trained in the skills of crime and initiated into the values of the underworld by juvenile begging and criminal apprenticeship. While the Spanish Humanists called for all citizens to be given a practical, useful education, the underworld quietly and efficiently carried on its own vocational training program.

Charity was useful to both city government and underworld, but it was also an arena of conflict. City fathers often viewed

45. City commission report of 1593, quoted in M. Chaves, pp. 80–81.
46. Quoted in Tobias, p. 176.
47. AMS, Efemérides, No. 1.

the underworld as a threat, and they stiffened their resolve not to support this evil culture with their alms. They used the underworld as a foil against which they struggled to define the deserving poor. Underworld people, on the other hand, frequently regarded the city oligarchy as an antagonist to be tricked and exploited. Seeing that this antagonist could extend its power through charity, the underworld resisted city efforts to swallow it up in charity schools and confine it in institutions. Underworld resistance stopped short of trying to overturn the social order, however, for the underworld saw that charity was many things. It was a gesture of piety, a touch of compassion, an agency for control, a tool of coercion, but also a first-rate opportunity.

9

Children of the Streets

ITIZENS of Seville gave alms to the orphans and abandoned children of their city, hoping to keep these young people from lives of crime. Childhood, they believed, should be a time of holy innocence, beautifully illustrated in Murillo's painting, "Saint Michael the Archangel." Children might look questioningly at their elders, as the child is doing in this painting, but they listened dutifully. Angels directed their tiny feet and shielded them from evil.

Despite their preference for sweet and trusting cherubs, city residents kept bumping into swarms of tough little thieves on the streets. These rag-tag urchins, so wise in the ways of the world, alarmed officials, who repeatedly warned that "masterless children" would grow up to be adult criminals. Yet the evidence suggests that the city oligarchy found street children very useful in performing essential tasks for the city economy.

To discuss the living conditions, means of survival, socialization, and youth of these children is to describe a lively, juvenile street culture. In addition it demonstrates how crime feeds both itself, as an underworld subculture, and the concerns of those in political power.

LIVING CONDITIONS

One of the best descriptions of the living conditions of street children is the unpublished parish-by-parish survey that priests made of the honorable poor of Seville in 1667.[1] According to

1. Parroquias, HSC, parish of Santa Iglesia (the Cathedral).

15 "St. Michael the Archangel." Bartolomé Murillo.

this survey, the poor lived collectively. Many lived in *corrales*, or courtyards surrounded by several low buildings. For example, in one courtyard near the Cathedral 22 children under the age of 10 years lived with two widows and one other husbandless woman. Another form of collective housing for poor adult females and children was the *hacera*, a row of houses sharing walls along one side of a street. Typically, the houses of the poor were very crowded, providing little space or privacy, often lacking beds or other furniture. One priest reported in the 1667 survey a house with the following furniture: one small mattress, two mats made of rushes, three little seats made of straw, and one small box. Adults in households so crowded with people and so lacking in physical comforts must have constantly shooed the children outside to fend for themselves in the plazas and alleyways of the city.

Living conditions did not remain the same throughout the early modern period. The population of the city grew very rapidly in the sixteenth century; as houses bulged inside the city walls, more were built just outside.[2] Once a refuge for criminals and the site of rickety little hovels of prostitution, the land along the river in the last part of the sixteenth century was slowly transformed by new houses, shops, and public buildings. All this activity suggests that rents increased while the poor of the city lived more and more collectively in the houses they could afford. It also helps to explain why underworld people frequently lived in cheap inns or in makeshift hovels pushed up along the city walls and rubbish heaps, and why abandoned children often had no house at all.

With a falling birth rate, two serious epidemics, and more emigration to the New World than immigration into the city, Seville's population declined in the seventeenth century. The limited data available on births do not describe a birth pattern in the underworld; it is unlikely that underworld births were recorded in parish registers. Nevertheless, the sharp increase in the numbers of births in the sixteenth century and decline in

2. Jaime Vicens Vives, *An Economic History of Spain*, trans. Frances M. López-Morillas (Princeton, 1969), p. 333. Domínguez Ortiz, *Golden Age*, p. 134. Domínguez Ortiz, *Orto*, p. 45.

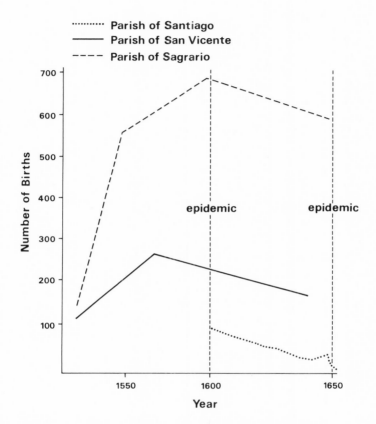

16 Numbers of births in three parishes of Seville 1530–1650. From Antonio Domínguez Ortiz, *Orto y ocaso de Sevilla,* Sevilla, 1946.

the following century, punctuated by two major epidemics, suggest that children in seventeenth-century Seville grew up with fewer children in their courtyards and row houses. They may have lived in less crowded houses, and they may have been able to live rent-free in abandoned buildings. A 1679 survey of the silk merchants' quarter, for example, revealed that 40 percent of the buildings were vacant.[3]

Although street children often lived in the poorest houses along the city walls or in abandoned buildings in areas of city decay, it is misleading to conclude that they grew up together in small ghettos within the city. Seville was large enough to have some class patterns of residence, but it was small enough geographically to retain many collective activities for all city residents. Public executions in the central plaza were within easy walking distance for residents of Triana and all other parishes of the city. The same is true of the Coliseo, the city's theater near the Cathedral. Even within their courtyards, the poor of Seville did not live in isolation. The survey of 1667 showed that of the fourteen courtyards reported in the parish of Santa Cruz, all of the residents were listed as needy in only one courtyard. At least 30 percent of the householders in other courtyards were either not poor or honorable enough to be listed.

Legal status is another reason to believe that street children did not grow up in isolation, for secular law included them in the larger community. Children of prostitutes and unknown fathers had a legal identity, and all children were entitled to support by their parents or other members of the community. The law also provided some protection against ill treatment by parents, as one seventeenth-century resident learned when he was exiled from the city for drowning his three-year-old son.[4]

3. Antonio Domínguez Ortiz, "La Alcaiceria de la Seda, de Sevilla, en 1679," *Archivo Hispalense*, Series 2, 44–45 (1966), 262–268.
4. Scott, Fourth Partida, Titles XV, XIX, XX, esp. pp. 952, 955–976. Memorias eclesiásticas, BC, 84-7-19, folio 103.

Since no law prohibited adults from beating their children, street children probably found that their best defense was a pair of fast legs and a clever hiding place.

These street children grew up in contact with a larger community, but their living conditions fostered a distinctive juvenile subculture. Crowded by collective living patterns, they easily found many young companions in the freer streets and alleyways outside. Their meanly furnished homes, teeming with scolding women and flocks of children, would never be a symbol of stability and security to them. As soon as they had outgrown their swaddling bands, children were pushed out of the house to learn to care for themselves in a larger community. Their living conditions promoted a childhood that was relatively free from adult interference, but they also imposed the early necessity of learning to survive.

MEANS OF SURVIVAL

Murillo's painting "The Fruit-Eaters" depicts street children who are ragged but happy and well fed. Undoubtedly these children had to get their own food, for there is no hint of adult benevolence or support in this painting. From their posture they appear independent and self-sufficient. They can recognize their own hunger, and they know how to fend for themselves and fill their stomachs. To Murillo's street children of the rounded arms and rosy cheeks, survival was hardly a problem.

But the painting idealizes them. It ignores their dependence on the economy of the city, which faltered as well as flourished. The painting also masks the striking similarity between adult crime and the ways these children got their bread. Finally, it glosses over the ideology fostered by the particular ways that children survived. In this ideology survival was not only a central problem, it was the highest value.

Children unable to depend on adults for food had several ways to get bread. The very young turned mostly to begging, particularly for leftovers at the doorways of inns and wealthier homes. They hung around the markets, where they begged the leftover bread or partly spoiled produce that wouldn't keep

17 "The Fruit-Eaters." Bartolomé Murillo.

for the next day. It is doubtful that they drank much milk or ate many eggs. Fish was less expensive than meat, and fish scraps were probably more available. Since rice, potatoes, and corn were rare in Seville, the basic food of the children had to be bread.

A typical pattern was for a child to begin begging when he was two or three years old with the guidance of an adult who told him where to beg and how to make the best pitch. He was supposed to turn over all the money he took in, but he must have learned very quickly how to convert his cash into food that could fill his stomach. If he was clever enough, the child soon threw off his adult mentor so that he could keep all his earnings for himself.[5]

As these children grew older and could perform useful tasks, they often became servants. They carried water, ran errands, swept floors, and accompanied fine ladies as they rode about the city in their sedan chairs. Many became servants to adult criminals. The boy who was called a gate-watch in underworld vocabulary was a look-out for ruffians. The news-mongerer gathered information through gossip and street chatter which suggested good criminal opportunities.[6]

Basket-boys helped to move merchandise within the city, a task that grew with the population of Seville and the activity of its port. Stevedores were in great demand to load and unload ships and could not possibly provide all the transportation of goods required by merchants within the city. The problem became more acute when the city periodically banned carts on rain-damaged   streets. Using children as basket-boys was one answer to a labor shortage.

Juvenile street hawkers helped to solve another problem, namely the lack of established markets in the newer areas of the city. Street hawkers brought bread and produce, charcoal, firewood, clothing, and bedding to these neighborhoods. During festivals they brought sweets and drink to the people crowding the streets. A child who acted as a street hawker had to be able

5. Herrera Puga, p. 68. Quevedo, pp. 198–199.
6. Salillas, p. 89.

to handle money, and he had to be strong enough to carry his goods. He also had to be wise to the ways of wholesalers trying to exploit him.

As children grew up in the streets of Seville, they learned to make a living as gamblers and prostitutes. The law provided that a young girl could begin work in a city brothel if she could prove to a judge that she was older than twelve years, had lost her virginity, was an orphan, and was not a noble woman.[7] Most young girls probably became prostitutes more informally, however. A procurer might put her to work, or she might catch the eye of a more respectable citizen. A *germanesca* poem suggests the ease with which a constable could seduce a young girl of the streets:

> And nearby a fresh
> Young girl told me
> That, being pretty and young,
> She ground her mill.
> Yesterday she earned six ducats,
> And a constable loaned me
> Three times a *real* and a half
> In order to pay the inn.[8]

Obviously, the mill-grinding in this poem refers to sexual activity, but the two references to money suggest that this mill-grinding was as commercial as that of the miller.

Prostitution also offered a livelihood for boys. Some became pimps for their sisters or girl friends, but others became prostitutes themselves. A prison chaplain in Seville described a sheriff who owned "a house of play" in which he kept young boys, painted and elegant, for sodomy and male love-making. Some

---

7. Deleito y Piñuela, *Mala*, p. 36.

8. Juan Hidalgo, *Romances de germanía de varios autores con el vocabularios por la orden del a.b.c. para declaracion de sus términos y lengua* (Madrid, 1779), p. 149. The Spanish text is, "Y á mi dió por vecina/una muchacha reciente,/que por ser bella y muchacha/solo su molino muele./Ayer ganó seis Ducados,/y á mi me prestó un chorchete/ para pagar la posada/real y medio en tres veces."

boys involved in homosexual acts in Seville were as young as eight years, but it is likely that the younger boys were victims rather than working prostitutes.[9]

Children growing up in the streets learned the tricks of gambling very early. Like the rascal in Quevedo's picaresque novel *El Buscon*, they learned to mark cards with pin pricks, scratches, and watermarks. They had decks with broad cards and narrow ones, which they could easily identify. Survival was not such a weighty problem when these young gamblers had mastered the finer points of their art, like loading and palming dice.[10]

A child's success in winning his bread through these occupations depended to some extent on his cleverness, but it also depended on the economic fortunes of the city. As Seville grew into a world trade center in the sixteenth century, young prostitutes and gamblers found more people willing to spend money on various forms of amusements. Merchants were more open-handed in hiring basket boys and errand boys, and young street hawkers found no shortage of customers. However, the wealth of the city also attracted many people who were willing to perform the lowliest jobs, and these people sometimes competed with youthful street hawkers and basket boys.

These young bread-winners were especially vulnerable in times of famine, extreme weather, and epidemics. Drought was responsible for the high prices of wheat and meat in 1561, but the poor harvest for 1599–1600 may have reflected the major epidemic of that year. The price of wheat again rose in 1605, because of a bad harvest and a scourge of locusts. Children in the streets found that the money they could earn bought less food, and they also found that monasteries and churches were unable to distribute as much free bread in times of scarcity.[11]

9. Pedro de León, appendix 1 to Part II, Cases 7, 8, 180, 181.

10. Quevedo, p. 210.

11. The 1561 drought is described in Memorias eclesiásticas, BC, 84-7-19, folios 39ᵛ–40. A letter from the archbishop in 1599 reporting the Church's inability to distribute more wheat is in AMS, Siglo XVI, Sección 3, Escribanías de Cabildo, Tomo 3, No. 24. The 1605 dearth is reported in Memorias eclesiásticas, BC, 84-7-19, folio 102ᵛ, and in Guichot y Parody, 2:159–160.

Periodically, health became a critical problem for street children. Their susceptibility to disease increased when food scarcity reduced their diet to bread alone. Living in very crowded houses and working in narrow streets, they came into contact with all the diseases that were present in the city. Some of these were no more serious than the frequent scourge of ringworm, but others were lethal plagues. Floods like that of 1618 also brought more disease to the children who often lived in houses along the river banks and frequented the inns and garbage heaps near the river. Since they lacked warm clothing and shoes, they died from exposure in severe winter weather. It snowed twice in the city during 1624–1626, an exciting novelty to many residents but a fearful time for barefoot children. Actual numbers are unknown for children who died of disease, starvation, and cold. One study of deaths in the parish of San Bernardo, a poorer district just outside the city walls, shows that 27 percent of the burials between 1617 and 1653 were of children sixteen years or younger, and that was not an unusual rate of juvenile mortality in the early modern period.[12]

Survival must have been extremely difficult for underworld children born in 1640. When they were two years old, they had to survive the hardship, disease, and economic dislocation of a major flood. Five years later they shivered in a freezing rain that killed much of the wheat crop and greatly increased food prices. When they were nine years old a terrible epidemic struck their city. The children who did not die from the three kinds of plague running through Seville probably died of hunger. One merchant left a horrifying report of orphaned and abandoned

12. See Guichot y Parody, 2:174, for a description of the flood of 1618. Domínguez Ortiz, *Golden Age*, p. 326, reports the snowfalls. Poorly dressed children covered with grime and ringworm are described in Herrera Puga, p. 68. Juan Carriazo, "Negros, esclavos y extranjeros en el barrio sevillano de San Bernardo (1617–1629)," *Archivo Hispalense*, Series 2, Vol. 20, (1954), suggests that disease ran through crowded households, killing several members at the same time. City concern with the hazards in public health posed by the garbage heap and the low areas holding stagnant water between the city walls and the river is reported in Navarro García, "Puerto," p. 146. The study of burials is in Carriazo, pp. 130–132.

children wandering the streets. They slept in public doorways, and many died from exposure and hunger. Afraid to take them in because of the danger of infection, city residents put bread outside their windows or on the streets for the hungry children.[13]

Problems of survival increased as the city's economic fortunes declined in the seventeenth century. Displaced by Cadiz as the major port for trade with the New World, and reeling from the economic dislocations of two serious epidemics in 1600 and 1649, Seville had much less wealth to sustain small beggars and young servants. Fewer people now came into the city to compete with its youthful prostitutes and street hawkers, but this also meant that there were fewer customers.

The ways that children of the streets earned their bread were strikingly similar to adult occupations in the underworld. Both juvenile and adult occupations were mobile, disdaining the fetters to a loom or shop for the greater freedom of the streets and inns. Antipathy to physical confinement in one place may have grown out of the mean housing conditions of the children, but it was certainly reinforced in adulthood by the conviction that rules and authorities were more easily evaded by physically mobile people. Underworld people used the word *calle*, which usually means street, to mean liberty, and children very early learned to associate streets with freedom.[14]

Following the example of adult counterparts, underworld children learned to combine their occupations with theft. The basket boy who snitched flour from his master was only a smaller image of the adult retail bandit who sold watered-down wine. The small beggar who stole coins from the poor box at the church and the young prostitute who took what she could find in the pockets of her groggy client reflected the adult

13. The 1642 flood is reported in AMS, Sección Especial, Papeles del Conde de Aguila, Tomo 10 en folio. No. 30. The 1649 epidemic is described in Ortiz de Zuñiga, 4:711–712, and Domínguez Ortiz, *Orto*, p. 88. A remarkable firsthand account of this epidemic is in Memorias de diferentes cosas sucedidas en esta muy noble y mui leal ciudad de Sevilla copiaronse en Sevilla año de 1696, BC, 84-7-21. The merchant's description is on folio 99^v.

14. Hill, p. 110.

underworld tendency to combine theft with other occupations. These children were also learning skills that they would use as adults.

Juvenile occupations fostered the ideology of the adult underworld. Survival was the highest value for the small beggar, the young basket boy, and the youthful prostitute; and these children quickly learned that this end justified most means. They learned in the streets that survival depended upon quickness to exploit. They learned the wisdom of the parasite, that survival depends upon preserving a healthy host. In *El Buscon*, Quevedo suggested that his young rogue learned this ideology at the knee of his surrogate father, who told him, "Look, lad, being a thief isn't just a job; it's a liberal profession."[15] Such father-son chats may have taken place in the underworld, but it seems far more likely that children of the streets learned an underworld ideology from their own attempts to earn bread.

Survival, then, was not simply a physical matter for them. It was also a question of cultural survival, and this fact greatly alarmed city fathers. They were glad to use the children for their own amusement or for economically useful tasks, and they were relieved to be spared the cost of feeding them in schools and orphanages. Nevertheless, the ways that the children survived served to socialize them into an underworld culture that seemed threatening to city fathers. As the Humanist Juan Vives warned, "The small sons of the needy are educated very perversely."[16] To children of the streets, the basic problem was survival; to city fathers, the central problem was socialization.

SOCIALIZATION

"Socialization" can be defined as the process by which a child becomes a member of a larger community. He learns the values of this community, and he learns skills so that he can assume a role in his community. He learns to accept restrictions on his behavior, and he learns the verbal and symbolic languages through which he can communicate with other people in his community.

15. Quevedo, p. 86.
16. Vives, p. 280.

Traditionally, the family or household plays a major role in the socialization of children, but this pattern was modified in the case of Seville's street children, who often did not live with their biological parents.[17] Other adults might act as their sociological parents, but underworld children lacked a stable, continuous relationship with either a biological or a sociological father. Even in those cases where they lived with both parents, they could not depend upon them as their source for food. A hungry child who must go out to beg or steal bread on the streets has a very different relationship with the adults around him than the child who sits down to eat with his parents the food they have obtained and prepared for him.

To a certain extent, surrogate parents and criminal organizations played the traditional socializing roles of the family in the underworld. Cervantes described the criminal chief Monipodio in "Rinconete and Cortadillo," as the "father, master, and protector of thieves."[18] The pícaro Lazarillo de Tormes entered the larger world apprenticed to a cruel, blind beggar.[19] Underworld prostitutes often called their pimps and procuresses *madre* and *padre*, although these terms may not describe parental roles so much as a concept of parents as grasping and exploiting.[20] To surrogate parents of the underworld, the first principle of parenthood was to exploit their children.

Children socialized themselves to a greater extent in the underworld than they did in traditional society. Their very living conditions placed them in close physical proximity to one another, pushed them out into the streets, and encouraged them to teach one another as youthful surrogate parents. Dependent upon their own efforts for food, they also learned through their

17. For socializing roles of traditional families, see Arnold Gesell and Frances L. Ilg, *Infant and Child in the Culture of Today; The Guidance of Development in Home and Nursery School* (New York, Evanston, and London, 1943), p. 4; and William J. Goode, *The Family* (Englewood Cliffs, 1964), p. 2.

18. Cervantes, "Rinconete," p. 94.

19. Bataillon, p. 19.

20. Salillas, pp. 90, 99.

work to become members of a larger community. They learned the attitudes, values, and skills that were essential for survival—lessons that prepared them for adult roles and also helped to transmit an underworld ideology.

Play has long been recognized as a key in the socialization of children. Seville's street children were busy getting food, but they also had time for fun. Since they generally played free from any adult supervision, their games and pastimes demonstrate how the members of a juvenile subculture socialized one another. Several contemporary reports from early modern Seville as well as a study of children's games and amusements in sixteenth-century Spain provide evidence of their play. Though the latter is based largely on literary sources, the games and ditties required little education or equipment or adult supervision. It is very likely that underworld children played similar games. The concepts of two modern experts on child development, Jean Piaget and Erik Erikson, can be applied to this evidence in order to explore the ways that children socialized one another through their play.

Erikson has suggested that play permits a child "to try out some role pretensions within what he gradually learns is his society's version of reality."[21] The sixteenth-century boys who played matador in Seville's slaughterhouse had fun simply daring one another to more dangerous tricks, but they were also trying out the adult roles they had observed in the city's tournaments. That bullfighters in real-life tournaments were nobles mounted on fine horses did not deter their play, for they were imitating adults who appeared very grand and heroic. They used the same graceful, quick movements to evade the rushing horns. As the cattle rushed the boys, however, they often bashed into the pillars supporting the roof. This infuriated city fathers who demanded that the city council prohibit the boys from teasing the cattle and damaging the city-owned slaughterhouse.[22]

21. Erik H. Erikson, "Play and Actuality," in Maria W. Piers, ed., *Play and Development* (New York, 1972), p. 152.

22. AMS, Siglo XVI, Sección 3, Escribanías de Cabildo, Tomo 11, No. 75.

Public executions must have been impressive spectacles for children. Early in the seventeenth century a group of boys staged their own hanging. Imitating the adults they had observed in the main plaza, they constructed a makeshift gallows and hanged a six-year-old boy who had been chosen to play the victim. This imitative game was too successful, for the young victim died.[23]

Play was also a way for children to imitate or try out adult attitudes. In his study of children's games in the sixteenth century, Francisco Rodríguez Marín suggested that some ditties reflected the adults' prejudice against converted Jews and Moors. For example,

I, a sinner,
confess to Andero,
to Pedro Botija
and Anton Perulero.[24]

Since a *botija* can mean a huge wooden cask used for transporting wine and oil at this time, Rodríguez Marín believed the name Pedro Botija was used to burlesque the Moors' custom of praying with their faces to the wall. Another ditty suggests antisemitic attitudes:

Blessed
fried bacon;
I praise
roasted bacon.[25]

It is easy to imagine street children chanting this rhyme with its allusions to the Jewish prohibition of pork as they tagged along after a Christianized Jew in the city. They were learning not only to identify those groups that the adult world despised, but also to use ridicule as a means of social control.

23. Papeles varios, BC, 85-4-11.
24. Francisco Rodríguez Marín, *Pasatiempo folklorico; Varios juegos infantiles de siglo XVI* (Madrid, 1932). The Spanish text is, "Yo pecandero/ me confieso a Andero,/a Pedro Botija/y Antón Perulero."
25. Ibid.; the Spanish text is, "Benedito/tocino frito;/alabao/tocino asao . . ."

Erikson's concept of play as a way for children to try out the
boundaries and possibilities of the adult world is evident in
another rhyme:

Churchurumbé,
little goddess of honey;
stale bread;
and you're back on your tail.[26]

This ditty, which was probably chanted as a line game or game
similar to "One Potato, Two Potato," implies that plenty (the
goddess of honey) is possible, but so is dearth (stale bread).
Children chanting its lines may have been adjusting to an adult
world in which people had to grasp for the honey but would
likely end up on their rears with nothing more than stale bread.

The problem with speculating about children's ditties is that
we do not really know what these lines meant to children in
early modern Seville. Many times children chant rhymes not for
the meaning of their words, but for the pure joy of repeating
familiar sounds. Like Mother Goose rhymes, these ditties may
have outlasted their original significance. Children may repeat
what is nonsense to them simply because nonsense is fun. Nonsense shared is even more fun. Since ditties are usually rhymes,
they are readily learned. Older children can easily teach them to
young children, and they become a collective rhetoric of humor
and nonsense.

Despite the risks, however, it is instructive to look at some of
the metaphors in the rhymes and games. Food figures very
largely in the symbolic language, as in the ditties about bacon
and stale bread. One explanation is that food is a basic everyday
item that all children know. In addition, food metaphors may
have appealed to street children who were very much concerned
with feeding themselves.

Religious metaphors are also evident in the games and ditties.
In one line game a dialogue is carried on with a player representing the monk "Fray Juan de las Cadenetas."[27] Another ditty deals
with heaven, the devil and divine judgment:

26. Ibid., p. 38. The Spanish text is, "Churchurumbé,/deaíta de miel;/
pan duro;/que te vuelvas de culo."
27. Ibid., p. 23.

He who gives and takes away,
He bears the devil.
He who gives, he who gives,
He will go to heaven.
He who gives and then takes away,
He will go to hell.[28]

Children have a strong sense of justice, and their play often involves the imposition of rules. Piaget has differentiated between practice games, symbolic games, and games with rules. He believes that children impose rules on their games as they become more socialized. Though some games with rules are shared by adults and children, others belong only to children and are handed down from one generation of children to another without adult interference.[29] In his study of games, Rodríguez Marín recognized the great importance that children placed on following the rules in their games. He found in their play a concept of rules so strict and serious that he described it as "the penal code of the children."[30]

Following an intricate set of rules is absolutely essential to the success (and fun) of a game such as "Fray Juan de las Cadanetas." Players stood in a line, holding hands, and the two at either end carried on the following dialogue:

Oh, Fray Juan de las Cadenetas!
What do you wish, sir?
How many loaves are there in the breadbasket?
Twenty-one, burned.
Who burned them?
That thief who is beside you.
Well, pass on the penalties that he never suffered.[31]

28. Ibid., p. 34. The Spanish verse is, "Quien da y quita/se lo lleva la perra maldita./Quien da, quien da,/a la gloria se va;/quien da y luego quita,/a la gloria maldita."
29. Jean Piaget, *Play, Dreams, and Imitation in Childhood* (New York, 1962), pp. 87, 112–113.
30. Rodríguez Marín, *Pasatiempo*, p. 6.
31. Ibid., pp. 23–24. The Spanish text is, "Ah, fray Juan de las Cadenetas!/¿Qué mandáis, señor?/¿Quántos panes hay en el arca?/Veinte y un quemados./¿Quién los quemó/Ese ladrón que está cabe vos./Pues, pase las penas que nunca pasó."

Led by the player at the foot of the line, all the players continued holding hands and passed under an arch formed by the
head of the line and the player next to him. These two players
remained with their arms crossed over their chests and returned
to the opposite side from the rest of the players. This was repeated until the last two players carried on the dialogue. Then
they pulled on the line of players opposite them until the line
broke in a clamor.

When the players followed the rules of a game like "Fray
Juan de las Cadenetas," they were learning to perform rituals
as well as to accept rules. Both of these lessons were essential
in the socialization of street children in Seville. As adults they
would participate in the informal rituals of the marketplace and
the port. They might become involved in more formal rituals
in the courtroom or church. They would be spectators of other
rituals, such as plays or processions or tournaments. Most important, they would need to know the collective symbolic
language that rituals provide for a society. A growing child finds
security and significance in rituals that prescribe patterns for
conduct and endow them with special meaning. He also learns a
way of symbolic thinking that is basic to his larger community.

Some ritualized play helps children learn to work out conflicts
and deal with violence. Gang fights may be considered too
serious for play, but they were certainly among the most popular
amusements in Seville at the end of the sixteenth century.
Each Sunday the boys and young men of rival gangs would
gather for battles just outside the gates of the city. They had
superimposed on their rivalries a time and place for battle, and
an agreement to use stones and sidearms as weapons.[32] It is not
difficult to imagine smaller-scale neighborhood gang fights
carried on by younger boys who ritualized their battle sites and
weapons.

Underworld children learned many skills from their play. In
ritualized games they learned to accept rules and think symbolically. Their rhymes taught them to communicate verbally and to
understand the social nuances of words like "bacon" in the

32. Domínguez Ortiz, "Vida," pp. 165–166.

antisemitic ditty. In tag they learned to move quickly, and in gang fights they learned to compensate with speed and cleverness for what they lacked in physical strength. Team games taught them the value of specialization and organization. Gambling games taught them some adult rituals as well as many tricks for cheating. Playing matador in the slaughterhouse taught them how to accept dares and how to challenge others.

Most important, play taught the street children how to survive. Free from adult supervision, these children had to learn to make and enforce their own rules. No protective, benevolent parent stood between a child and the penalties of his game. He had to learn to accept the outcome fatalistically, or he had to be stronger, faster, or more clever. The socialization of underworld children taught them that survival depended as much on wits as on bread.

YOUTH

When did childhood end for street children? When did they pass from their juvenile subculture into the adult underworld? Was there a "rite of passage" between childhood and adolescence and adulthood? What was the distinction between a child of the streets and a *mozito* (youth)?

There is no evidence of a formal initiation rite into adulthood in the underworld. Perhaps the legal age of criminal responsibility, fourteen, or the legal age for prostitution, twelve, divided children from adults. Some people may have considered poise and experience a better indication of adulthood. In Cervantes' story, Monipodio allowed the worldly-wise teenagers, Rinconete and Cortadillo, to enter his criminal organization without the usual apprenticeship period.[33]

One reason it is so difficult to find a dividing line between childhood and adulthood is that childhood was not a period of parental protection and guidance. The young street hawker had to be as adroit as the adult retail bandit in finding food for himself. On the other hand, the adult helper of a master thief

33. Cervantes, "Rinconete," pp. 100–101.

might be as exploited by his master as the young beggar who was apprenticed to a blind man. Dependency and exploitation knew no age limits.

The best way to distinguish between childhood and adulthood in the underworld may be to examine the attitudes of the larger community. To city fathers, children of the streets were a nuisance that they could sometimes use profitably; ragged and hungry, they were often to be pitied. As a child grew into adolescence, however, he grew as a threat. One sixteenth-century city father reported to the city council on the many "bad youths" who gathered on the steps of the Cathedral to plan robberies and meet other vagabonds.[34] He urged the city council to get information on these young men and control them. His own lack of success in controlling them, he explained, resulted from the ill will these boys had shown him since he had tried to correct them. Whether this man was reporting as an official or simply as a father, his alarm is apparent.

Several factors may help to explain why street youths appeared so threatening. In the first place, they had become accomplished in criminal skills. Most of them had survived a childhood of the streets. They were experienced in theft and cheating, and they had already learned an underworld attitude of cynical exploitation. In addition, they were more physically able to carry out violence. A child had less choice of violent weapons, and less strength to use them. He could be overwhelmed more easily than an older youth.

More basically, youth can challenge adult authority, for it presents a sexual rivalry. The merchant who brushed aside the small boys in the street felt a much greater irritation about the brash, idle young men who hung around the city brothels. What is more, he usually had to deal with these young toughs in groups, for youth loves to act collectively in breaking adult taboos.[35] On the other hand, adult hypocrites who, themselves, broke taboos were the targets for groups of gleeful young people.[36] The young toughs who swaggered down the streets of

34. AMS, Siglo XVI, Sección 3, Escribanías de Cabildo, Tomo 12, No. 44.
35. Christian, *Person*, p. 25.
36. Ibid., pp. 25–26. Davis, *Society*, chapter 4.

Seville moved together. They laughed uproariously at their own jokes, raucously insulted older citizens, and collectively bumped into adults whose position they were challenging, both literally and figuratively.

Finally, these idle young men tended not to fit into the mold that city fathers had prepared for them. They disdained the jobs that were available in the city, refusing to load and unload ships or even to train to become ships' pilots. They would not work as low-paid agricultural laborers, nor would they become well-mannered servants and lackeys for local aristocrats. These young people had become so jaded that churchmen and city officials could no longer hope to convert them into good citizens. Why waste time trying to train youths who were already hardcore thieves, dishonest and opportunistic cynics? These young hoods were more useful in killing one another off, filling military quotas, or justifying a hard line on law and order, a persuasive argument for stringent enforcement of curfew laws and regulations against carrying weapons.

In contrast, children of the streets appeared more vulnerable. They performed useful jobs in the city economy, and they provided vivid examples of the evil befalling people who lived outside the mores and customs of the city oligarchy. They were less able to challenge the city's adults or to carry out violence against them. One of the conditions of their survival was that they recognize their vulnerability, but this did not mean passive acquiescence. Perhaps their youth was more violent and explosive because they had stored up a childhood of anger at their own vulnerability. Perhaps city fathers most feared street children as youths because their swaggers proclaimed that they had survived without accepting the city oligarchy as their masters, that their underworld subculture persisted, refusing to be absorbed into the dominant culture. The young hoods who twirled their newly sprouted mustaches felt the heady exhilaration of having survived childhood in the streets. Strutting and crowing, they challenged city authorities. Here was new blood for the underworld and proof of its persistence.

10

"Lost Women"

CONCERNED with swaggering bullies and street urchins, churchmen and city leaders were also aware of the women in the underworld. They heard the raucous voices of the women who hawked wares in the streets. They saw the coarse manners of women who kept inns, and they watched the colorful actresses and singers. All of these women, they assumed, were prostitutes, or "lost women."

The euphemism that city fathers used suggests that the women were outcasts who had completely lost their way in the dominant culture of the city; but historical evidence shows that "lost women" were an integral part of their community, just as prostitutes are in present-day society. They supported themselves, their children, and a vast network of pimps, procuresses, and entrepreneurs. Pushed by the socioeconomic disruptions of the period, they easily crossed the invisible line between respectable society and the underworld. Their lives demonstrate how the underworld culture renewed and preserved itself in a city ruled by men who loudly proclaimed the evils of the underworld.

"Lost women" also demonstrate the political utility of the underworld. Concerned with maintaining order as the city rapidly grew and declined in the sixteenth and seventeenth centuries, city leaders consciously used legislation and existing institutions. They found in prostitution a commercial prop, an agency to reinforce lines of authority, and a symbol of evil. They pointed to prostitutes as diseased, disgusting, and parasitical. Prostitution became a symbol that united the community and justified the extension of governmental powers.

Evidence that is available from early modern Seville cannot answer all of our questions about women and the underworld. It does not tell how many women became prostitutes, nor does it detail the ages or social backgrounds of prostitutes in Seville. Despite these limitations, a study of "lost women" contributes to our understanding of how the underworld fit into the culture of this city. First, it suggests that the changes of this period disrupted traditional patterns and promoted prostitution as a livelihood. Second, it demonstrates that prostitution was not only acceptable in the society of this city; it even acted as a pillar of the moral system that buttressed the existing social order. Finally, it argues that prostitution thrived because it was politically useful to the ruling elite.

PROSTITUTION AS A LIVELIHOOD

For centuries women in Seville had found many ways to survive. As wives or nuns, many had depended for a livelihood on husbands or convents. Others worked in crafts and industry, street-hawking and retail, domestic service, folk medicine, inns and drama. Widows owned and operated the shops and dramatic companies that they had inherited. Some women were kept as concubines by the wealthier men of the community, and others earned a living as prostitutes on the streets or in the public brothels. In the early modern period, social and economic changes combined to disrupt the other traditional roles of women and promote prostitution as a livelihood.

Convents, for example, offered fewer women a livelihood. Fathers had traditionally placed their daughters in convents when they lacked enough money for a suitable marriage dowry. In his poem "La Devoción de la Cruz," Calderón called this the "crime of poverty":

Because a poor gentleman
In things such as these
Cannot equalize
His quality with wealth
For a marriageable daughter
Without discrediting his blood,

He places her in a convent,
Which is the crime of poverty.[1]

Most convents also required a dowry, although a smaller
amount, and they had to increase this amount as prices rose and
money declined in value. One convent reported in 1597 that
its building was in danger of collapse and its poverty was so
great that it could feed its members on only three days of the
week.[2] Nuns were particularly hurt by the devaluation of money
because they had few ways to augment their incomes. Unlike
monks, nuns could not earn fees for preaching, burying the
dead, or saying Masses. In addition, they were prohibited from
begging door to door for food.

The silk-weaving of some nuns had supported some convents
in Seville. By the late sixteenth century, however, the city's
silk industry had fallen behind French silk weavers, who were
able to produce in quantity the fashionable fabrics most in demand. Foreign competition pinched silk-producing convents so
severely that the Crown prohibited the sale of foreign-made
silks in 1621, declaring that foreign producers had caused many
convents to lose their livelihood. By the middle of the seventeenth century an official of the silk masters' guild reported that
of the city's 3,000 silk looms, only sixty were in use.[3]

Since convents offered fewer women a livelihood, many
became beatas, or holy women. Usually widows and young unmarried women who lacked a dowry for either marriage or convent, they lived together in "congregations," often in a house

1. Quoted in Deleito y Piñuela, *Religiosa*, p. 107. In Spanish the poem
reads, "Porque un caballero pobre/cuando, en cosas como éstas,/no puede
medir iguales/la calidad y la hacienda,/por no deslucir su sangre/con una
hija doncella,/hace sagrado un convento,/que es delito la pobreza."

2. Parroquias. Morgado, pp. 465–466. AMS, Siglo XVI, Sección 3,
Escribanías de Cabildo, Tomo 14, No. 7. Domínguez Ortiz, *Estamento*,
p. 118.

3. Memorial to the king from the head of the city's silk guild, quoted
in the Eighth Discourse of Martínez de Mata in Anes Alvarez, pp. 194–195.
See also Domínguez Ortiz: *Golden Age*, p. 186; *Orto*, pp. 34–36, 84; and
Estamento, p. 119.

next to the parish church. They supported themselves by the work of their hands and by income from any property they owned, but they were generally very poor. Although they often obeyed the parish priest as their director, they were suspected of being ungoverned and immoral. Churchmen who disapproved of this spontaneous form of religious community life tried to impose on beatas the control of the regular clergy.[4]

Marriage became less likely for women in the lower income groups as local industry and small-scale agriculture declined. In his Third Discourse, the contemporary economist Martínez de Mata recognized the problems resulting because marriage was discouraged for young men with no livelihood.[5] He blamed foreign competition for taking away the jobs of many Spaniards and causing small farmers, textile workers, and artisan producers to become vagabonds. The women who could have married them in better economic circumstances, he declared, remained single and perished from hunger.

Wives were frequently abandoned by underemployed and unemployed husbands who left to seek their fortunes in the cities, the army, or the Indies. Foreigners married women of Seville so they could enjoy certain economic and political privileges in the city, only to leave their wives and return to their homelands when they had earned enough money. Although statistics of abandoned women are not available, this appears to have been a general pattern throughout the early modern period. The Venetian ambassador to Spain reported in 1525 that so many men had left Seville for the New World that "the city was left in the hands of women,"[6] and 150 years later this same problem was noted in the 1667 survey of the poor.

Emigration, of course, was open to women as well as men, but it was regulated by the Crown. A royal letter of 1604 complained that more than 600 women had sailed from Seville for New Spain, although only fifty of them had been licensed.[7] Women

4. Domínguez Ortiz, *Estamento*, pp. 113–144.
5. Quoted in Anes Alvarez, p. 129.
6. Navagero, p. 57.
7. Jorge Nadal, *La población española, siglos XVI a XX* (Barcelona, 1966), p. 73.

who emigrated had to have recommendations for a royal license or enough money to buy passage as nonlicensed emigrants. They also had to have a certain venturesome spirit.

One emigrant in 1603 was *La Monja Alférez* (nun second lieutenant) Catalina de Crusa. A nun in Vizcaya, she had run away from her convent and arrived in Seville in 1603. Disguising herself as a young man, she went to the New World, where she worked for twenty years, using a string of mules in Vera Cruz to bring in merchandise carried by the Spanish fleet to Mexico. Acquaintances in New Spain knew her as a young man, too tall for a woman, but lacking the stature and bearing of an arrogant youth. Her face was neither ugly nor beautiful, distinguished by shiny black wide-open eyes and a little fuzz above her upper lip. She wore her hair short like a man's, and carried a sword very well. Her step was light and elegant. Only her hands appeared rather feminine.[8]

Catalina might have taken her secret to the grave, but in 1624 she was accused of killing a man. To save herself from the gallows, she declared that the court could not hang her because she was a woman and a nun. In great amazement, the local authorities sent her back to Spain, where the king gave her 500 ducats and the formal title of second lieutenant. She became a popular hero, treated as an awesome sensation. In 1630 she was licensed to dress as a man, and she was formally invested with this privilege in a ceremony in the Cathedral of Seville.[9]

Obviously, Catalina was an exception. For most women, emigration was available neither as a means of escape nor as a catapult to fame. Marriage was favored in this society not only as a means of livelihood, but also as an institution to impose authority over young girls and prevent them from "losing themselves."[10] Because marriage appeared so crucial to social order, many benefactors provided charitable dowries so that poor girls could marry

8. Ignacio de Góngora, reported in M. Chaves, pp. 174–176. Catalina was also referred to as "Catalina de Eranso."

9. AMS, Efemérides, "Noticias y casos," No. 1.

10. AMS, Siglo XVII, Sección 4, Escribanías de Cabildo, Tomo 24, No. 1. Morgado, pp. 373–374.

and become safely absorbed into a traditional authoritative and economic system. Marriage was not always a formal arrangement, however, and many people took partners with neither dowry nor occupation. Poor people accepted these temporary alliances with practical cynicism, an attitude apparent in the following verse from a germanesca ballad:

A husband by night
Is a well-known threat:
Don't believe any promises,
Trust only what you can touch.[11]

Women who were unable to depend upon a husband for bread and shelter found their own wages inadequate and irregular. When the fleet for New Spain prepared to sail, seamstresses and silk workers worked night and day trying to fill merchants' orders. After the fleet had sailed, however, demand fell off dramatically and little money came in. Widows and women without husbands lived together to cut expenses and support one another as they tried to augment their small incomes. A report on charitable works in the city during the 1670's described the great number of widows and single women who had no other income but what they could earn with the labor of their hands. It estimated that each woman could earn only one real a day; bread cost five reales.[12] Unemployment, underemployment, and inadequate wages pushed many women into prostitution, which for them could be a part-time occupation that would supplement their meager incomes.

The economic and social dislocations of early modern Seville encouraged the exploitation of every possible means to survive. Traditional informal social controls no longer restrained exploitation in neighborhoods teeming with newcomers who soon moved

11. Hill, p. 64. The Spanish text reads: "Ningun marido de noche,/ que es peligro conocido:/no te creas de promesas/lo seguro es lo granido."

12. "Consulta theologica en que se pregunta se será justo y conveniente que se apliquen las obras pias de esta ciudad al remedio de la necesidad publica que al presente ay en esta ciudad de Sevilla," Papeles varios, BC, 83-7-14, folio 109.

away. Thousands of children and youths without parents appeared in Seville, overwhelming the few institutions that could provide food and shelter. People took in orphans and used them to beg money or get customers for both male and female prostitutes. Young women fortunate enough to find a job were considered fair prey by their employers, a problem still prevalent among poor young working women.[13]

In his report on the Royal Prison of Seville, the lawyer Cristóbal de Chaves reported a case that probably described many young women servants.[14] Ana was seduced by Juan de Molina, the son of her master. He gave her lessons every day in how to be a successful prostitute, and he placed her in a brothel on the Calle del Agua. On the days that she did not take in much money, he beat her, for he wanted the money for gambling. He taught her how to call out and get clients, and he showed her many tricks for getting money from them.

Juan developed a system to prevent Ana from cheating on him. He watched from an alleyway outside the brothel and carefully counted her clients, placing a pebble in the hood of his cape for each one. Since he had made her agree to charge each client a set price, he could easily tell if she held back any of her earnings by counting the pebbles.

Ana finally talked with another prostitute about her problems, and Juan was soon arrested. Sentenced to the galleys for ten years, he tried to keep his hold over her. He wrote to her from prison, reminding her that she was his "thing." He drew a picture for her that showed him, the former master, now a galley slave in chains with a chain leading from him to the hands of a woman he entitled "Ana." Between the two figures he drew a heart pierced by two arrows. The heart, he wrote was Juan's, and the arrows were Ana's. Chaves did not indicate whether Ana saw the irony in the reversal of their roles.

Many people tried to maintain control over prostitutes who

13. AMS, Siglo XVII, Sección 4, Escribanías de Cabildo, Tomo 24, Nos. 26, 30; Oscar Lewis, *The Children of Sanchez: Autobiography of a Mexican Family* (New York, 1961), p. 306.
   14. C. Chaves, Part II.

provided them with money, but others simply pawned women to the city brothels for a single lump sum. Fathers, brothers, boy friends, or husbands sold women into brothels for ten or twenty ducats.[15] The 1621 city ordinance reforming the administration of city brothels expressly prohibited the pawning of a woman to a brothel by a person to whom she owed a debt, even though she might agree to this arrangement. No woman, it asserted, should be sold into the brothels nor kept there to pay off a debt.[16]

City regulations of this period encouraged prostitution because they made it difficult for women to earn a living in other occupations. Street-hawking, for example, was banned by city officials who suspected, with some justification, that it was a cover for prostitution and vagabonds. But their attempts to ban street selling cut off the livelihood of many people who then turned to prostitution in earnest. One woman agreed to leave prostitution in 1572 if she could regain her place for selling fruit, which a public official had taken from her.[17] Murillo painted street hawkers as quiet, rather serious young women trying to earn a living. City fathers, however, saw them as noisy, brazen price gougers who threatened the peace of the city.

The livelihood of another group of women was cut off by regulations on dramatic productions. Under pressure from clerics, Philip II prohibited all dramatic performances in 1598. Two years later the Crown directed a group of theologians to draw up conditions for dramatic performances in Spain. Among other conditions the theologians insisted that no woman should be permitted to act in dramatic productions because "such public activity especially provokes a woman to boldness . . ."[18] A royal council agreed to the conditions, except that it allowed women to continue in dramatic companies as long as they were

15. Dóminguez Ortiz, "Vida," p. 167.

16. AMS, Siglo XVII, Sección 4, Escribanías de Cabildo, Tomo 22, No. 14.

17. AMS, Siglo XVI, Sección 3, Escribanías de Cabildo, Tomo 11, No. 33. AMS, Archivo General, Sección 1, Carpeta 151, No. 238.

18. Sánchez Arjona, p. 100.

accompanied by husbands or fathers. These regulations came at the same time that the number of religious festivals was reduced.

Sumptuary laws were passed in the sixteenth and seventeenth centuries to prevent rich people from parading their wealth. Although they were aimed at the newly rich merchants and shippers who liked to dress and behave as nobles, the real victims of these laws were women workers. Prohibitions against silk and brocade fabrics reduced the jobs available for women in the silk industry and embroidery shops, while limitation of the numbers of domestic servants meant that fewer women could earn a living as servants.[19]

The Inquisition's campaign against heresy brought many folk practitioners and sorcerers to an unhappy end. The Holy Office was not so much opposed to superstition as desirous of controlling all uses of superstition. During the early modern period it prosecuted many women who challenged its monopoly. For example, a woman hanged in 1581 for practicing witchcraft and abortion was a Moor.[20] As a member of this rival religious group, she had challenged the Church's attempts to monopolize truth. In 1624 a twenty-two-year-old woman was burned in an auto de fé because she claimed to have the power of knowing the future.[21] She might have escaped notice by the Inquisition if she had been older and had quietly plied her occult gifts as a neighborhood sabia (wise woman). The Inquisition dealt very cautiously with madness, and it often treated people accused of witchcraft as lunatics or senile eccentrics who should be only mildly punished. Insanity could be used by the Church as a weapon to discredit its competitors, but it could also provide a protective shield for folk practitioners who continued their traditional profession as "María la loca" or "Ana la fantástica."

Official regulations extended to the practice of medicine during this period, and uneducated women practitioners suffered.

19. Domínguez Ortiz, *Orto*, p. 80. Stone, p. 28, presents a similar view of sumptuary laws as buttresses of the existing social order.

20. Pedro de León, appendix 1 to Part II, Case 59.

21. AMS, Efemérides, cuadro 2. See Thomas, *Religion*, pp. 49, 255–256, for a discussion of Church opposition to magic.

A royal decree of 1593 required all medical practitioners to be licensed, and it prohibited women from having or dispensing medicines. In 1629 the asistente of Seville formally required that all midwives, as well as all other people practicing medicine, be examined and licensed by him within fifteen days. Practitioners who did not comply were subject to a fine of 10,000 maravedís. Since most midwives and folk practitioners were older women their inability to obtain a license did not necessarily mean that they became prostitutes. However, it is very likely that they increasingly turned to the subsidiary occupations by becoming procuresses, street bawds, and false "abbesses" who kept houses of prostitution.[22]

Prostitution flourished in this city not only because it provided a livelihood for women who had few alternatives, but also because it was a commercial enterprise that supported pimps, procuresses, property owners, innkeepers, and renters of little rooms and secondhand clothing. Underworld people regarded prostitution as a business, referring to brothels as *aduanas* (customs houses) or *cambios* (exchanges). They called prostitutes *pelotas*, a word that usually means a ball or toy, but underworld people also used it for a bag of money.[23] Some women saw prostitution as their only means for survival, while others willingly entered prostitution as commercial enterpreneurs. Whether women became prostitutes under duress, unable to find another livelihood and shake themselves free of an exploiting "friend," or whether they voluntarily chose this profession as offering the best livelihood in the city, the socioeconomic changes in early modern Seville disrupted traditional roles for women and encouraged many to turn to prostitution.

PROSTITUTION AND MORALITY

One reason that Seville's social order survived the serious

22. AMS, Siglo XVI, Sección 3, Escribanías de Cabildo, Tomo 11, No. 78. Guichot y Parody, 2:213. Older women procuresses are described in AMS, Ordenanzas, "Titulo: De las mugeres barrangas y desonestas," folio 63.

23. Hill, pp. 106, 110, 119.

economic disruptions of this period was that city fathers used a widely accepted system of morality to preserve the hierarchy of authority. Prostitution was an integral part of the city's moral system. The connection between prostitution, morality, and social order is clearly evident in the three most popular female symbols of this period.

The Holy Virgin was elevated in the early seventeenth century through the doctrine of the Immaculate Conception and stylized into the beautiful image still carried in the Holy Week processions of present-day Seville. Forever girl-like, she became a grieving woman. With diamond teardrops on her cheeks and a dagger thrust into her breast, her head slightly bowed by the weight of a golden crown, she held out her hands for the cares and sorrows of the world.

The Virgin was a pillar of the moral order of the city. Young girls who were taught to emulate her example of chastity and modesty would be less likely to defy parental authority and run off with the wild young men of the streets. With their eyes on the Virgin, women who entered convents had a beautiful image of perfection through chastity and obedience. For married women, the Virgin also symbolized chastity and submission to authority; but in addition, she represented a curiously asexual and influential motherhood.[24] Women could thus feel elevated, content with their social roles, and inspired to obedience. They would be chaste and modest, restricting sex to marriage and never endangering the social order or the system of property inheritance.

Men were considered to be much more active sexually than women, and this required another female symbol, the Painted Prostitute. Women who emulated the Virgin were thought to be elevated above the weakness of the flesh, but men were naturally expected to succumb, to look for sex outside marriage. If men lacked prostitutes to absorb their lust, who knew what would happen to an innocent woman walking along the street on a proper errand? The problem was to distinguish respectable women from those who served men's baser needs.

24. Christian, *Person*, p. 100.

The Painted Prostitute represented depraved, sensual, commercial woman. Condemned for advertising herself in dress and manner, she was nevertheless required by law to wear a yellow hood so that she could be distinguished from the respectable women of the city. Unlike the well-kept courtesan or flirtatious matron, she was often hungry and ill-dressed. She usually walked the city streets, unable to afford a sedan chair or carriage.[25] She held out her hands like the Virgin, but she sought money rather than grieving hearts. She epitomized the unnatural, painting herself and publicizing her promiscuity. When syphilis appeared in Seville in the sixteenth century, she was blamed for spreading that disfiguring, often fatal disease. The Painted Prostitute was another pillar of the moral order, for she permitted the existence of a double standard for men and women and provided a clear example of how respectable women should not behave.

Occasionally, however the symbol of the Painted Prostitute was not entirely negative. Orphanage administrators and priests who tried to reform prostitutes understood that the examples set by experienced pimps and prostitutes were as infectious as any diseases they might carry. The Jesuits established a little house as a temporary haven for converted prostitutes, and they carefully separated those young women from the older "women of the world" who wanted to procure for them and make money from them.[26] The Jesuits' temporary home did not solve the problem, however, and city officials continued to worry that converted prostitutes could infect young girls, who would emulate them. One administrator of a girls' orphanage wrote to the city council complaining that the city's practice of placing converted prostitutes in his institution provided bad examples for young orphan girls.[27]

25. See the royal letter to the city council of Seville in 1500 printed in Guichot y Parody, 1:375–377. The problems of respectable women walking in the city was discussed in a January 1570 petition to the city council, reported ibid., 2:68–70.

26. Pedro de León, Part I, chapter 5, folios 14–15.

27. AMS, Siglo XVII, Sección 4, Escribanías de Cabildo, Tomo 22, No. 12.

Mary Magdalene, the converted prostitute in the stories of Jesus, was the third major female symbol of early modern Seville. Many clergymen taught that prostitution was an evil from which prostitutes and the entire city could be saved. They preached fervently to the prostitutes on the feast days of Mary Magdalene, and they gloried in counting their conversions. This symbol reinforced both their faith in converting sinners and their belief that extramarital, commercial sex was evil. In their view, unregulated sex threatened both social order and individual salvation.

A cult had grown up around the seductive figure of Mary Magdalene in the seventeenth century, perhaps a reaction to the puritanical tendencies of the sixteenth-century Counter Reformation. Mary Magdalene represented the titillating combination of sex and religion. Murillo painted her as a voluptuous young woman gazing heavenward. Her expression suggests the rapture of earthy sexual delights as well as spiritual transport. She avoids looking the observer boldly in the eye, for she is an appropriately modest, though sensual, "bride of Christ." One explanation for her popularity is that she represented the love goddess, Venus. Under the guise of pious devotion to a Church-approved saint, many people continued to venerate an ancient and traditional folk goddess who covered sex with a cloak of religion.

The symbols of Virgin, Prostitute, and Mary Magdalene were as useful to city fathers as they were popular with all city residents. Through these symbols churchmen and city officials demonstrated their authority to define good and evil. The image of the Holy Virgin sanctified political events and provided a single visible personification of good that was understood by the entire community. On the other hand, the Painted Prostitute personified sex outside marriage, sex without the responsibility of children and home, sex with the threat of disease. When unregulated sex threatened their society, they could point to the lessons of the Virgin, the Prostitute, and Mary Magdalene, which taught very clearly that women should be safely enveloped in a convent or marriage, obedient, chaste, and modestly accepting their places in the social hierarchy.

Some city fathers may have preferred to rely only on the

18 "Mary Magdalene." Bartolomé Murillo.

Virgin to support their moral order, but the Painted Prostitute and Mary Magdalene appeared to be necessary corollaries. A social order acknowledging sexuality in men could not survive if men had to treat all women as the Virgin. Elevating women through this symbol seemed to require that they also be degraded to the status of prostitute. Sexuality in women was permitted only if it were the acknowledged evil of prostitution or the converted religious ecstasy of Mary Magdalene. Ironically, this moral system depended as much on symbols of evil as on symbols of perfection.

Francisco Farfan, a sixteenth-century cleric of Spain, recognized that upside-down morality of prostitution. In his treatise on avoiding the sins of fornication, Farfan presented an argument for the moral practicality of prostitution. He declared that the brothel was necessary to a society just as a latrine was needed in a house:

> The brothel in the city, then, is like the stable or latrine for the house. Because just as the city keeps itself clean by providing a separate place where filth and dung are gathered, etc., so neither less nor more, assuming the dissolution of the flesh, acts the brothel: where the filth and ugliness of the flesh are gathered like the garbage and dung of the city.[28]

To Farfan, the prohibition of prostitution was a greater evil than prostitution itself, because a society without brothels encouraged homosexuality, incest, the propositioning of innocent women, and an increased number of people living together in sin. Farfan recognized the weakness of the flesh and believed that the only way to deal with it was to divert human behavior away from mortal sins. In order to avoid mortal sin, he

28. Francisco Farfan, *Tres libros contra de peccado de la simple fornicacion; donde se averigua, que la torpeza entre solteros es peccado mortal, segun ley divina, natural, y humana; y se responde a los engaños de los que dizen que no es peccado* (Salamanca, 1585), p. 730. I am indebted to William Christian, who found this book in the Biblioteca Nacional, Madrid, and permitted me to use his notes. This essay echoes an earlier argument by St. Augustine which described prostitution as a necessary evil.

argued, behavior must be controlled. Prostitution could support the moral order, but only if it were closely regulated.

PROSTITUTION AND REGULATION

City fathers had long tried to control prostitution in Seville, but many nonlicensed prostitutes pursued their trade outside the confines of city-regulated brothels. They gathered in several areas along the river bank, close to the port where many prospective clients entered the city. Prostitution also thrived in the poorer parts of the city that grew up along its margins and just outside its walls, such as the extramural parish of San Bernardo. Rents were undoubtedly lower in the marginal areas, and prostitutes could afford a room or a little shack. Since police power was less likely to invade the alleyways on the edges of town, innkeepers there were probably less conscientious about keeping prostitutes out of their rooms. The 1568 syphilis epidemic in the city was called *el contagio de San Gil* because it first broke out in San Gil, another parish bordering the city's walls. Hospitals for victims of this epidemic were set up outside the city walls in the parish of San Bernardo.[29]

Fear of disease is the major reason that the city government increased its efforts to regulate prostitution and limit it to the medically inspected, city-licensed brothels. Plagues passed from port to port in the early modern period and ravaged city populations. They posed a political threat as well as a very real physical danger, for the city in the throes of an epidemic was noted for neither law nor order. The machinery of local government frequently fell into paralysis, and many officials died or disappeared. On the other hand, rumors of an epidemic so frightened city residents that they were willing to accept greatly

29. Deleito y Piñuela, *Mala*, pp. 50–54. Domínguez Ortiz, "Vida," p. 168. Herrera Puga, pp. 55, 66. Rodríguez Marín, *Miscelánea*, p. 67. Ordinances prohibiting innkeepers from providing prostitutes with shelter or food are in AMS, Ordenanzas, "Titulo: De los tabernos y mesoneros," folio 89. Concern with disease is in José Velasquez y Sanchez, *Anales epidémicos; reseña histórica de las enfermedades contagiosas en Sevilla desde la reconquista cristiana hasta de presente* (Sevilla, 1866), p. 67.

expanded government regulations. These regulations were directed particularly against prostitutes, who were commonly suspected of passing on plagues. Clients of prostitutes, after all, often entered the city from a ship that had arrived in port, and prostitutes could easily contact any diseases they carried and pass them on into the city. Prostitutes were more susceptible to illness, too, if they were the poorer women who were undernourished and used secondhand clothing and bedding, both of which frequently carried disease in this period.

The epidemic of syphilis brought death and disfigurement to thousands, and frightened the city government into redoubling its efforts to regulate prostitution. The city council appointed medical inspectors to examine prostitutes and recommend action against the disease. One doctor warned that the city's health was endangered by the bad condition of lettuce and deer's tongue (a plant) that were being sold in the city brothels as remedies for syphilis. Another surgeon urged that the city not merely discharge sick prostitutes from brothels, but also confine them in hospitals to prevent them from continuing their trade. In the early seventeenth century, the administrator of city brothels countered clergymen's proposals to close the public brothels. He argued that this action would not end prostitution, but merely deregulate it and damage the health and well-being of the city. If prostitutes were not confined to city-licensed and medically inspected brothels, he said, they would scatter throughout the city, free to spread disease and provoke quarrels and murders.[30]

Seville, however, lacked the hospital space to confine all its syphilitic prostitutes. Several hospitals would not accept people with any contagious disease. In the last part of the sixteenth century the Hospital de San Cosme y San Damian was known as *las Bubas* because it was designated to treat syphilitics, or those with pustules (*bubas*) resulting from *la mal frances*. Unfortunately, this hospital had only forty beds, and only twelve were

30. AMS, Siglo XVI, Sección 3, Escribanías de Cabildo, Tomo 11, Nos. 62, 69; Siglo XVII, Sección 4, Escribanías de Cabildo, Tomo 22, Nos. 9, 17.

for infected women. Patients here were treated for thirty days with *agua del Palo*, a medicinal water.[31]

Most treatments for syphilis were, obviously, ineffective, and it became a sixteenth-century successor to leprosy, flourishing despite city attempts to detect and isolate infected people. When Pedro de León began working with the people in the city brothels in the late sixteenth century, he found many who were ill. He described the illness as "hideous," causing great pain, many pustules, and death.[32] The 1621 ordinances to reform the ancient regulations on prostitution in the city prohibited the city brothels from admitting boys under the age of fourteen, adding that many "boys of a tender age" had become infected in the brothels.[33] The infected prostitute released from city-licensed brothels could continue her trade as long as she was able to, but when her infection became so obvious that she could no longer get clients, she was as likely to die from starvation as from infection.

It is not surprising that the little houses of a brothel were sometimes called *boticas*, a word also used for pharmacies or little shops. Prostitutes were traditionally believed to use potions, herbs, ointments, and pessaries as contraceptives. In the sixteenth century they also began to use herbal preparations to treat syphilis infections, and it has been suggested that men first used contraceptive sheaths in brothels as a means to prevent venereal infection.[34] Prostitutes and procuresses knew many other forms of contraception. They prepared pessaries and ointments from herbs and dung. They made amulets, such as a seed of sorrel enclosed in a cloth bag, which was thought to prevent conception as long as it was carried on the left arm.

31. Morgado, pp. 365–366.
32. Pedro de León, Part I, chapter 4.
33. AMS, Siglo XVII, Sección 4, Escribanías de Cabildo, Tomo 22, No. 14.
34. John T. Noonan, *Contraception: A History of Its Treatment by the Catholic Theologians and Canonists* (Cambridge, 1966), p. 221. Norman E. Himes, *Medical History of Contraception* (New York, 1970), p. 187. An example of brothels referred to as "boticas" is in AMS, Siglo XVI, Sección 3, Escribanías de Cabildo, Tomo 11, No. 58.

They mixed alum and the yellow pulp of pomegranate to make vaginal pessaries, and they practiced some numerical magic, such as jumping backward seven or nine times after coitus. Prostitutes were closely associated with the practice of abortion, as well, and they and their older female companions also prepared aphrodisiacs.[35] The brothel as pharmacy represented the evil of illicit sex supported by an unlicensed folk medicine that bordered on magic. It challenged both the Church's claim to monopolize magic and the city's presumption to license doctors.

Concern with increasing public disorder also pushed city officials into more energetic regulation of prostitution. The ships sailing between Seville and the New World brought numbers of soldiers and sailors to the city. Fights over women often ended in big street brawls. Confining prostitutes to city-licensed brothels could prevent many quarrels, fights, and crimes. It could also get rid of the swarms of streetwalkers and the children or false beggars who acted as procurers.[36]

Closely related to the desire to keep public order was the necessity to protect property. When a captain wrote the city council to complain that ships in the port were being robbed and damaged, he asserted that men were robbing the ships in order to give money to the "bad women" who lived in little houses in the area of the port.[37] Other residents complained of property damaged in the brawls that began over women.

Confining prostitutes in licensed brothels prevented some property damage, and it also protected the interests of those who owned the property used as the city brothels. The historian Francisco Rodríguez Marín examined documents, which are no longer available in the city archives, and concluded that the property used as city-licensed brothels in the last part of the sixteenth century was owned by city officials and religious corporations, including the Cathedral council. These owners leased the property to private individuals, who then rented it to

35. Noonan, pp. 17, 201–202. Himes, pp. 153–154.

36. AMS, Siglo XVII, Sección 4, Escribanías de Cabildo, Tomo 16, No. 20, and Tomo 24, No. 27.

37. Ibid.

various prostitutes. In 1571 owners of the houses used by the city brothel included a veinticuatro, an official of the Santa Hermandad, and one of the twenty sheriffs with major law enforcement responsibilities. In 1604 the houses of the city brothel were rented by a sheriff who collected a daily rent of one and one-half reales from each prostitute.[38]

The property involved in the city-licensed brothels was low-lying and close to the river, so that it had little commercial or residential value. When the Bishop of Esquilache asked permission in 1575 to establish a monastery in place of the brothels, he pointed out that this area was "of such poor quality that it could not be purified." The city council appointed a commission to study the proposal, and it suggested compensating the owners of the property with houses on another street and moving the brothels to a section next to the city wall. The council rejected this proposal, however, concluding that the brothels should remain in their "ancient and proper place."[39] It might have added that this "proper" place was also highly profitable to members of the city government.

The city government's proprietary interest in the licensed brothels is evident in the time and money it spent administering, inspecting, and repairing them. The city council appointed *padres*, or administrators of the city-licensed brothels. In the last part of the sixteenth century, there were three padres, each the head of a separate house licensed by the city. The 1621 ordinances limited the number of padres to two and required that they swear to uphold the laws of the city. These ordinances also prohibited the padres from renting clothing or bedding to prostitutes and from accepting "pawned" women in the brothels,

38. Rodríguez Marín, *El loaysa*, and his critical edition of Cervantes' *Rinconete y Cortadillo* (Madrid, 1920). This material is also discussed in Joaquin Hazañas y la Rua, *Los rufianes de Cervantes: "El Rufian Dichoso" y "El Rufian Viudo" con un estudio preliminar y notas* (Sevilla, 1906), note 1 on p. 26; and in Pike, *Aristocrats*, p. 204.

39. AMS, Siglo XVI, Sección 3, Escribanías de Cabildo, Tomo 11, No. 1.

two prohibitions that were also contained in a set of 1570 royal ordinances.[40]

Brothel administrators often requested that the city repair walls and gates that seemed to crumble rapidly in the dampness of the river air and the harshness of their use. In 1590, for example, one padre reported to the city council that the gate for the brothel had been destroyed, allowing ruffians to mistreat the prostitutes, destroy the little houses of the brothel, and steal doors and other materials. Other padres invited the city council to send a deputation to visit the brothel and see for themselves that repairs were necessary.[41]

City officials inspected the brothels not only to maintain the value of their real estate, but also to preserve the value of the human property contained in their brothels. Three officials accompanied the canon of the Church of San Salvador on July 22, 1620, when he visited the brothels to preach to the prostitutes and try to convert them. Immediately after the visit, the officials announced that they would bring a doctor to examine the prostitutes. They fined one padre twelve reales for receiving an unlicensed prostitute into the brothel, and she was ordered to leave under penalty of 100 lashes. Another prostitute was ordered to leave the brothel because she appeared ill and could infect the others. A third prostitute was ordered to leave because of her age; she had been in the brothel too long. Evidently, city officials were as concerned to have attractive prostitutes as to prevent epidemics.[42]

Prostitution made sound business sense not only to the procurers and owners of brothels, but also to the charitable benefactors who were unable to provide every poor girl of the city with a dowry or a job. As demands for charity increased in the

40. The 1570 ordinances are in BM, Egerton 1873, "Tractatus varii, et collectanea," folios 155–156. See AMS, Siglo XVII, Sección 4, Escribanías de Cabildo, Tomo 22, No. 14, for the 1621 ordinances.

41. AMS, Siglo XVI, Sección 3, Escribanías de Cabildo, Tomo 11, Nos. 60, 63.

42. The account of this visit is in AMS, Colección del Conde de Aguila, Tomo 7, Letra A, No. 63. It is also presented in "Documentos relativos a la mancebía," *Archivo Hispalense*, Series 1, 3 (1887), 16–18.

last part of the sixteenth century, many city fathers concluded that practicality outweighed morality in the question of prostitution. They saw that it was an evil, but they agreed that it was better to accept it and regulate it than to forbid it and send converted prostitutes to seek a nonexistent livelihood. Even the optimistic and diligent Pedro de León, who worked so hard to convert women from prostitution, admitted the difficulty of finding husbands, parents, or jobs for converted prostitutes.[43] The 1667 survey of the poor in Seville is filled with the names of young women of marriageable age unable to marry because they were too poor, unable to find work, and doomed to die from starvation. City fathers who owned brothels could thus argue that these brothels benefited the entire community because they provided a livelihood for otherwise destitute women. It is not surprising, then, that the city council listened sympathetically to a padre of a brothel when he complained bitterly about "strange clergymen" and pious laymen called *congregados* who were driving women away from city-licensed brothels.[44] To most city fathers prostitution was not only thinkable; it was practical.

"Lost women" were not lost at all in early modern Seville. They lived within the specific social and economic conditions of their city, and prostitution was one response to these conditions. But if they were not lost, they *were* used. Prostitution was commercially profitable for city officials and churchmen as well as street people. It reinforced the authority of the ruling class over unmarried women, folk practitioners, sailors, youths, and quick-fisted dandies. Prostitution was even a form of public assistance, providing jobs for women who would otherwise starve. It strengthened the moral attitudes that supported the city's hierarchy of authority, and it permitted the city oligarchy to demonstrate its authority to define and confine evil. Under the guise of public health and public order, it extended the

43. Pedro de León, Part I, chapter 5, folios 14–15. See also Domínguez Ortiz, "Vida," p. 167.
44. AMS, Siglo XVII, Sección 4, Escribanías de Cabildo, Tomo 22, No. 11.

powers of city government. If prostitution was a symptom of social disease, it was also an example of social adaptation. In Seville prostitution helped to preserve the existing social order. It became a useful, practical political tool.

11

The Ill and the Hungry

THE underworld survived in early modern Seville. Abandoned children socialized one another into this criminal subculture, and women frequently entered through the profession of prostitution. Yet survival was difficult, for Seville, the city of sunshine and orange trees, was also the scene of many disasters. Dependent for food on good harvests, the city was particularly vulnerable to the natural disasters of climate and insects. The price of bread increased 1000 percent after poor harvests in 1520 and 1521. Neither price controls on wheat nor public granaries for storing excess food in years of plenty had been able to prevent this disaster. The frantic efforts of citizens who gathered up 120 bushels of locusts from one field near the city in 1547 could not save the harvest of that year from the insects. Drought, freezing, and floods also devastated harvests. City chronicles report dearth in 1520–21, 1547, 1570, 1580, 1626, 1636, 1642, 1647, 1649–52, and 1677–79.[1]

The river brought another danger. Disease frequently entered the city from the ships and boats that came into port. In some cases the sick men on board were quarantined, but in the winter of 1562–63 so many galley slaves were ill with influenza aboard seven ships in port that the Jesuits asked permission to take them

1. "Feria y Pendon Verde de Sevilla año MDXXI," Papeles varios, BC, 85-4-13. Ortiz de Zuñiga, 4:504. AMS, Siglo XVI, Sección 3, Escribanías de Cabildo, Tomo 19, No. 19. AMS, Archivo General, Sección 1, Carpeta 27, No. 379. Memorias eclesiásticas, BC, 84-7-19. Guichot y Parody, 2:294.

to a house near the port where they could be given better medical treatment. Too often quarantine measures could not prevent disease from spreading into the city. Chronicles record epidemics of influenza, bubonic plague, carbuncular plague, or typhus in 1520–22, 1562–63, 1581, 1588, 1599–1600, 1626, and 1649.[2]

Disasters attacked the poor of the city first, but no one remained untouched. Even the wealthiest citizens felt the dislocations in trade and marketing. When famine or disease hit the supply of labor, the entire economy of the city reeled. Disasters prompted extraordinary community measures, including religious processions and travel restrictions. Underworld people were not immune to city disasters. If they were not among those poor people who succumbed first, they were among the first who cleverly exploited misfortunes. They often ran headlong into emergency measures passed by city officials, and frequently they were identified as agents of misfortune.

The relationship of the underworld and the city oligarchy is best understood if it is examined in times of crisis as well as in periods of calm. Although epidemics and famines sometimes struck together, they can be discussed separately. People of Seville responded differently to each, and the differences are useful in considering ways that disasters affected the relationship between city government and the underworld. Epidemics and famines were usually regional, affecting both rural and urban people, but this discussion will focus on the responses of city government and underworld people. A comparison of two rebellions in 1521 and 1652 reveals the changes that occurred in Seville, and it demonstrates that the underworld played a political role that was essentially conservative.

2. Astrain, 2:528–530. AMS, Efemérides, "Noticias y casos," No. 1. AMS, Siglo XVI, Sección 3, Escribanías de Cabildo, Tomo 7, Nos. 16. 17. Memorias eclesiásticas, BC, 84-7-19. Diego Ignacio de Góngora, "Relacion del contagio que padeció esta ciudad de Sevilla el año de 1649," Memorias de diferentes cosas, BC, 84-7-21. Note that epidemics of "bubas" may have been syphilis rather than bubonic plague.

EPIDEMICS

Fear was the first response to an epidemic in the early modern period. Lacking antibiotics, people had ineffective treatments for typhus, bubonic plague, and influenza. One Portuguese entrepreneur asked the city council for permission to distribute his "medicinal water" in Seville as a defense against epidemics, but city council members refused, evidently wise to the empty promises of so many similar remedies.[3] City fathers recognized the importance of public health measures, like cleaning streets and isolating contagiously ill people. They directed citizens to burn the garments and bedding of sick people, and then to purify the air with rosemary and thyme.[4]

Despite these measures, the specter of an epidemic was fearsome. Descriptions of Seville in the midst of one read like scenes from Dante's Inferno. Flooding and freezing added to the city's suffering in 1626. So many people died that corpses were piled by the fifties in the Puerta del Perdon, the main gate in front of the Cathedral. Dogs and pigs ran through the city, eating at the corpses that completely blocked some streets. A chronicler of the 1649 epidemic estimated that at its height 300,000 people died, 500 or 600 each day.[5] The city lacked healthy people to bury the dead, and the bodies lay in heaps beside churches and cemeteries, some wrapped in a sheet or the cloak of a religious order, others naked with green limbs and swollen abdomens. One morning a bed appeared on the steps of the Cathedral and in it were four small children, all dead from the plague. Churchmen attributed these disasters to sin. Penitents joined religious processions through the streets, their whips and cries punctuating the somber chants of monks. Fear grew in the confusion of chanting monks, ranting preachers, piles of bodies, and bonfires of contaminated clothing.

3. AMS, Siglo XVI, Sección 3, Escribanías de Cabildo, Tomo 7, No. 8.

4. Nicolás Monardes, *Sevilla medicina, que trata el modo conservativo y curativo de los que habitan en la muy insigne ciudad de Sevilla, la cual sirve y aprovecha para cualquier otro lugar de estos reinos* (Sevilla, 1866), p. 42.

5. AMS, Efemérides, cuadro 2. Góngora, folios 86[V], 101[V].

When people heard of disease in a neighboring area, they closed the city gates. Travelers could enter Seville only with a health passport showing that they were free of disease and neither they nor anything they had with them had just come from a diseased area. The guards who were posted at the gates demanded to see the health certificates and arrested those who tried to enter without them. City council members had periodic reports on the health of surrounding areas. Some members even rode to other villages to check their residents.[6]

Health passports protected the city from some disease carriers, but Seville remained vulnerable to others. The priest of the parish of San Bernardo reminded the council in 1600 that his parish was outside the city walls and unprotected. In addition, the parish had a number of inns where people without health certificates gathered. He warned that his parish could become the center of "a great conflagration and general pestilence," and he pleaded that the city council extend its protection to San Bernardo.[7] Triana, the suburb across the river, as well as the entire port area were also outside the walls.

Once disease was discovered, the council took emergency measures. It ordered families to separate their healthy members from ill ones, and directed householders to clean their houses scrupulously and burn all clothing and bedding used by diseased people. Owners of cats and dogs were ordered to kill them. Schools were closed. All cases of illness were to be reported to the city government immediately, so that infected inns or entire parishes could be closed off. Hospitals were set up to isolate and care for the ill. In 1649 the city council appointed a health commission, composed of the chief justice, the president of the Contratación, the chief sheriff, and the head of the royal audiencia. Evidently these officials recognized that an epidemic threatened law, order, and commerce as well as public health.[8]

6. A sample letter to be used as a health passport is in AMS, Siglo XVII, Sección 4, Escribanías de Cabildo, Tomo 16, No. 73. AMS, Siglo XVI, Sección 3, Escribanías de Cabildo, Tomo 7, No. 17.

7. AMS, Siglo XVI, Sección 3, Escribanías de Cabildo, Tomo 7, No. 17.

8. Ortiz de Zuñiga. 4:709. AMS, Siglo XVI, Sección 3, Escribanías de Cabildo, Tomo 7, Nos. 14, 17. Góngora, folios 57^V, 60, 83, 83^V.

Disposal of the dead posed a serious problem. "The poor people," wrote Diego Ignacio de Góngora in his report of the 1649 epidemic, "lacking money and unable to carry their dead to the sanctity of the doors of the churches, dragged them along by a cord tied to the feet, and left them in the middle of the streets and plazas."[9] Wealthier citizens hired cart drivers to haul bodies away for burial, but the city lacked space to bury all of them. A sixteenth-century complaint that cemeteries were too full and bodies too easily dug up by scavenging dogs was echoed in epidemics of the seventeenth century. Six new cemeteries were established in the epidemic of 1649.

Despite the emergency efforts, Seville suffered serious dislocations. A basic problem was lack of manpower. Few healthy people were willing to work with the ill. In the epidemic of 1649 city council members, including the most illustrious veinticuatros, had to stand guard at city gates. Parishes were ordered to appoint deputies to carry sick people on litters to the hospitals, but they were overwhelmed by the numbers of the ill, and carts had to be called into service.[10]

The shortage of people to care for the ill in the 1649 epidemic was so acute that the city government had to turn to its prisoners. Life sentences to the galleys or a presidio were commuted if prisoners would agree to work in the hospitals during the epidemic. Nearly all of the commuted prisoners became sick and died, but some hardy ones survived and were able to escape the city. Those who served in the hospitals characteristically exploited their new-found opportunities, robbing sick people and, in the words of a contemporary report, soliciting "illicit communication" with the women there.[11]

Forced to use less respectable people to care for the sick and the dead, the city oligarchy also depended upon lesser city

9. Quoted in Guichot y Parody, 2:260. AMS, Papeles Importantes, Siglo XVI, Tomo 3, No. 26. Oritz de Zuñiga, 4:707–710.

10. Góngora, folios 56^V-57, 61. Cf. Anne Cornelisen's description of a typhoid epidemic in a twentieth-century Italian village, in *Torregreca*, p. 77.

11. Góngora, folio 86.

officials to supervise them. According to a chronicle of the 1649 epidemic, a minister of justice had to ride in each cart that hauled away bodies and infected clothing, to prevent the cart drivers from stealing the clothing. Unfortunately, supervisory officials became more difficult to find. Many city officials ignored their jobs during an epidemic. They moved their families out of the city if possible, or spent their time caring for their own sick relatives. Others preferred better jobs; one account of a seventeenth-century epidemic says that people would not serve as officials because they could receive higher wages for manual labor during this time of labor scarcity.[12]

Many city functions ceased because there was no one to perform them. The militia dissolved. Sheriffs no longer made their rounds of the city to enforce laws. Justices did not prosecute thieves and murderers, nor were they able to prevent the theft and sale of contaminated bedding and clothing. Streets were not cleaned. The poor picked up the clothing of diseased people left in the streets and took it home "with pitiful security," as a contemporary warned. Trades continued only spasmodically, their guilds lacking masters or officials.[13]

The most serious dislocation, however, was in the marketing of food. Fewer people were available to harvest crops, bring food to market, or bake the bread. The hardy who ventured into the streets to sell food demanded the highest prices possible. People were so fearful of food shortage that they paid the high prices.[14]

City residents held their government responsible for their welfare during an epidemic, but they realized that the task required broader regulatory power. Public health measures became one of the strongest pillars of political power in Seville. In 1645 the city council directed each parish to elect two deputies to be in charge of street cleaning, who were empowered to compel householders to assist. A resident who refused would be fined

---

12. Ibid., folio 69; Guichot y Parody, 2:259–261. A sixteenth-century account of the paralysis of city functions during an epidemic is in AMS, Siglo XVI, Sección 3, Escribanías de Cabildo, Tomo 7, No. 10.

13. AMS, Siglo XVI, Sección 3, Escribanías de Cabildo, Tomo 7, No. 10.

14. Góngora, folio 63^{v}. Ortiz de Zuñiga, 4:707–710.

500 maravedís and imprisoned for ten days.[15] The power was extended in 1667 when the council complained to the Crown that nobles and clergy were refusing to help pay the costs of street cleaning. In response the Crown ordered everyone, without exception, to pay—a clear victory for secular government.[16]

By 1676 the issue of public health had so increased the powers of the city government that its health commission was able to assert control over many city activities, even in periods free of epidemics. A health ordinance of that year called for the Church to continue its "pious zeal," and for citizens to clean the streets and remove dead animals. It demanded the inspection of all corrales to ensure their cleanliness, and it decreed an absolute prohibition on throwing sewage water into streets. Residents were ordered to burn thyme and rosemary. The sale of spoiled fruit, fish, and meat was prohibited, and bakers were directed to put salt in their bread. The health commission prohibited the sale of old clothing during outbreaks of disease. It directed charitable groups to find shelter for the poor, and ordered postmen to refuse letters from areas known to be diseased. Public prisons were to be cleaned every Saturday, with special care given to the cleaning and sustenance of poor prisoners. Deputies were appointed to guard the city gates and to allow traffic through only seven of them.[17]

Residents looked to their government for emergency regulations also, for they really had no alternative. The community catastrophe of an epidemic required collective action, and Seville had few institutions capable of taking collective city-wide action. Epidemics transcended neighborhoods and parishes. Cofradías and guilds provided some care for victims, but they had no organization to coordinate their work throughout the city, nor did they have authority to order the city gates closed. The Church was better equipped, from the council of the Cathedral to the parish system, but it relied on leading processions and prayers, ministering to the sick, and burying the dead. An epi-

15. AMS, Papeles Importantes, Siglo XVII, Tomo 4, No. 58.
16. Reported in Guichot y Parody, 2:276-277.
17. AMS, Siglo XVII, Sección 4, Escribanías de Cabildo, Tomo 16, No. 59.

demic required citywide action, and by tradition people of the city looked to the city council to exercise that authority. In their concern for defensive health measures, residents did not complain about growing governmental power. Even when officials stopped functioning during an epidemic, citizens directed their complaints against the irresponsible individuals, not against the institutions of city government.[18]

Although epidemics increased the regulatory powers of city government, it is likely that they also strengthened the resolve of underworld people. Those who were not victims of disease refused to be victims of the city oligarchy. They agreed to be used by the city government in caring for the sick or dead, but only if they could also use the situation to their own benefit. The specter of death from disease was not enough to soften the outlook of underworld people who saw death as a constant companion, sardonically grinning, certain to take them in the end. The underworld and city oligarchy continued to use one another, but the issue of survival pushed them into more rigid lines of opposition.

RESPONSES TO EPIDEMICS AND FAMINES

The residents of Seville who responded to epidemics with fear most often responded to famine with anger. Citizens unable to protect themselves from an epidemic willingly accepted more regulations from the city government, hoping to find in it an adequate defense from disaster, but the anger of rebels in a seventeenth-century bread riot rang out clearly when they shouted, "Long live the King of Spain and death to bad government!"[19]

One reason that people of the city responded differently was that famines were more socially selective. True, wealthy people had some advantages in an epidemic. They were better nourished and could leave the city more easily until the epidemic had gone, and many lived farther from the port and extramural

18. AMS, Siglo XVI, Sección 3, Escribanías de Cabildo, Tomo 7, No. 10.

19. Joseph Maldonado Danila y Saavedra, "Tratado verdadero del motin que hubo en esta ciudad este año de 1652," 1663, Sevilla, BC, 84-7-21, folios 115^v-116.

parishes where epidemics were likely to appear first. Neverthe-less, disease also struck the rich and well-fed. Moreover, no one seemed to profit from an epidemic except ex-prisoners, who stole from the sick and dying. In contrast, dearth was more obviously selective of its victims. The poorest people of the city were the first to feel hunger and to hear the wails of the children they could not feed. A wealthy merchant might complain of ris-ing food prices, but he rarely went hungry. Worse, some people seemed to prosper when poorer people were dying from starva-tion. Where epidemics could level differences between the rich and poor, famine brought them into bold relief.

A second reason for the differing responses is that people identified the causes for these disasters differently. They usually blamed epidemics on germ-laden vagabonds, wandering used-clothing merchants, sailors from foreign ships, and prostitutes, or on divine punishment, or such "natural causes" as refuse or unburied corpses. Measures taken against them strengthened a sense of solidarity among city residents. Enforcing public health standards provoked a few squabbles, but these regulations also promoted a collective view of how the people of the community should live together. Even divine punishment promoted a collec-tive response. God punished all His children with the epidemic, and together they made penance, whipping themselves, chanting, marching, and praying together.

Famine, too, could be blamed on a punishing God, but it could also be blamed on visible human targets. Bakers were charged with selling short loaves or holding back their bread in order to get higher prices.[20] Millers were accused of overcharging bakers or cheating on the flour they milled. Large agricultural producers could afford to keep their grain off the market until prices rose. Wealthy families bought up large quantities of grain and stored it until prices increased enough to return a handsome profit. Street vendors raised the prices of food as it became scarce, and officials enforced neither price controls nor other

20. An example is in AMS, Archivo General, Sección 1, Carpeta 27, No. 364.

retail regulations. The presence of so many who seemed to profit
while others starved split the community into angry groups.

Government was blamed for famine because it had traditionally assumed responsibility for providing food. The basic assump-
tion of the long and detailed city ordinances regulating the
transportation and sale of food was that the city government
would be discredited if it did not feed the people, a misfortune
that would also reflect on the Crown. City ordinances blamed
rising food prices and scarcity on "bad government" in the public
granary and the slaughterhouse. They specifically warned against
allowing "ruffians" to steal or buy up quantities of food for
resale.[21] One reason for these warnings was that many underworld people made a part-time living as slaughterhouse workers
and street hawkers, and Seville's slaughterhouse became notorious as a gathering place for them. The description by one of the
dogs in Cervantes' story "The Dogs' Colloquy" undoubtedly
reflects a popular conception of Seville's slaughterhouse:

> The things I could tell you, brother Scipio, about what I
> saw in that slaughter-house, and about the extraordinary
> things which go on there! First of all, you must bear in
> mind that all those who work there, from the youngest to
> the oldest, are people with easy consciences, without mercy
> or fear for the king or his law. Most of them are living with
> concubines, and they're like birds of prey, maintaining
> themselves, along with their mistresses, on what they steal.
> Every meat day there are vast numbers of girls and youths
> in the slaughterhouse before daybreak, all with bags which
> are empty when they start, but which are full of pieces of
> meat when they go home. . . . But nothing shocked me
> more than to see that these slaughterers will kill a man as
> easily as they kill a cow. For a trifle, and without a thought,
> they put a knife in a man's stomach as readily as if they
> were killing a bull. It's a rare thing for a day to pass without

21. AMS, Ordenanzas, "Ordenanzas primeras del Alhóndiga del pan de
Sevilla," See also Morgado, p. 154. AMS, Siglo XVII, Sección 4, Escribanías
de Cabildo,, Tomo 22, No. 22.

quarrels and wounds, and sometimes deaths; they all take pride in being tough, and even boast of being ruffians.[22]

Warnings against ruffians in the markets suggest a pervasive suspicion of all retailers. In times of food scarcity they were in direct contact with consumers, who quickly blamed them for raising prices. A sixteenth-century economist expressed a common attitude when he wrote that the interests of the community and retailers conflicted because the retailer wanted to buy cheaply and sell dear, while the people of the community wanted to buy as cheaply as possible. To settle this conflict, he argued, the government should expel offensive retailers, especially foreigners, and impose a fair price.[23]

Responsible for providing adequate food at a fair price, the city government must have found the presence of "suspicious people" useful in deflecting popular anger. Officials could say that ruffians who filched in the slaughterhouse were responsible for the lack of meat and the increase in prices. They could represent themselves as the legitimate leaders of a community united in angry indignation against retail bandits who resold bread at a higher price in the back streets of the city. People might forget official inadequacy in enforcing retail regulations if they could focus on a few visible violators.

City records suggest, however, that retail violators were not limited to people of the underworld. Ordinances for the city granary complained that rich people were buying up the bread that was to be sold from the granary to poor people for ten maravedís less than the usual price. These ordinances also complained of the numbers of people who were profiting from selling contraband bread. Bakers refused to bring their bread to the granary and sold it secretly in the city above the set price. Later in the sixteenth century the Crown complained that city officials had distributed bread from the public granary to their friends and vassals and had resold it at higher prices.[24] Despite more

22. Cervantes, "The Dogs' Colloquy," pp. 197–198.
23. Thomás de Mercado, pp. 33–36.
24. AMS, Ordenanzas, "Ordenanzas segundas del Alhóndiga." AMS, Siglo XVI, Sección 3, Escribanías de Cabildo, Tomo 13, No. 13.

stringent royal controls, contraband bread remained a problem in Seville, and anger continued to be the principal response to famine.

MORAL ECONOMY AND POLITICAL REBELLION

City chronicles contain detailed reports of uprisings in Seville in 1521 and 1652. The dissimilarities between the two revolts are striking and cannot be explained simply as the result of accounts written by different people from varying points of view. These differences suggest significant changes that occurred in Seville in the early modern period. They also challenge some recent theories of pre-industrial urban unrest.

In his analysis of the English crowd in the eighteenth century, E. P. Thompson described a "paternalist model" of a moral economy in which local leaders were expected to enforce fair prices on food and to protect the people from profiteering retailers.[25] When local officials failed to regulate the market, the people rose up and took direct action themselves. Unlike the "spasmodic" version of bread riots, however, Thompson emphasized the restraint of these uprisings. His rioters were not men crazed by hunger, blindly striking out at anything; they were reasonable, disciplined men and women, who restricted their demands to immediate economic objectives.

This model is of limited usefulness in studying the two riots of early modern Seville. It is true that Seville exhibited many of the characteristics that Thompson described for the moral economy: fair price, regulated marketing, general suspicion of retailers or middlemen, direct popular action when local officials failed to provide food at a fair price. In 1521 and 1652, however, the people rose up in bread riots that exploded into political rebellions. Direct action by the rebels was not limited to immediate economic demands, nor were their targets limited to profiteering middlemen.

Thompson's model does not apply to Seville because his analysis assumes that bread riots in pre-industrial societies

25. Thompson, pp. 83–84.

occurred in small, closed economies where the problem of hunger was simply a matter of sufficient local harvests and reasonable food prices. Although the people of Seville did depend upon food production in the surrounding countryside, they realized even in 1521 the larger economic and political ramifications of food supply. Seville had long since left the phase of the small, local economy which still prevailed in parts of northern Europe in the early modern period. For centuries Seville had participated in the larger Mediterranean economy, exporting wheat, wine, olives and many manufactured goods. A comparison of the 1521 and 1652 rebellions argues persuasively that rebels demanded more than bread, because during this period Seville became even more involved in world commerce and royal monetary policies. People of this city suspected in 1521 that their hunger was the result of more than bad harvests and profiteering hoarders. By 1652 they knew that food supply was intimately related to wages, monetary valuation, and taxes; they angrily demanded not bread alone, but also an end to devaluation and a prohibition of the *millones*, a royal sales tax first imposed in the sixteenth century.

Accounts of Seville's two uprisings also challenge the theories of pre-industrial urban unrest presented by E. J. Hobsbawm. Describing urban riots as direct action by the urban poor to bring about economic or political changes, he calls these people "the mob," and he classifies them as "pre-political," because they lacked an ideology, "a specific language in which to express their aspirations about the world."[26] It is true that in neither 1521 nor 1652 did rebels nail on the Cathedral door a written program for a better Seville. However, rebels in both uprisings recognized that their economic demands required not only their direct action, but also action by people in power. In 1652 the rebels even placed their own nominees in these positions of power. Although they were not revolutionaries, they were nonetheless more sophisticated politically than the naive and inarticulate mob described by Hobsbawm. What is more, they were not a homogeneous group of urban poor who wanted only

26. Hobsbawm, pp. 2, 110.

to attack the rich and the powerful. Internal differences, rather than political naiveté, may account for their failure to bring about lasting changes. Evidence suggests that the presence of underworld people among the rebels helped to preserve the local government when it was threatened by popular rebellion.

City chronicles refer to these rebellions as the revolts of the *Pendon Verde*, a green banner carried by the rebels, and of the *Feria*, the section of the city in which the rebellions began. Both names have symbolic significance. The Pendon Verde had been captured from the Moors during the Reconquest and was preserved in a chapel in Omnium Sanctorum, the parish church for most of the Feria neighborhood. This traditional trophy was well known to the people of the city, and it was taken in both revolts without authorization of priests or officials by a group of rebels who carried it as they marched through the streets rallying supporters. When city officials approached the rebels in the revolt of 1521, they marched with the *Pendon Real*, the royal banner. The Pendon Verde thus seemed to symbolize local pride and popular direct action, as opposed to governmental authority allied to a central Crown.

The Feria is the name of a long, narrow winding street some distance from the center of Seville. Significantly, one of the accounts of the 1652 uprising described the Feria as separate from the main commerce of the city, almost "remote."[27] In many respects, the Feria was a separate community. In its main square stood the parish church, and small shops lined the streets. Every Thursday morning hundreds of small merchants came to sell their wares on the street, and on Tuesdays and Saturdays there were other fairs to sell horses and mules. The Feria was a gathering place for residents who felt themselves a small community separate from the city council, the substantial merchants of the Contratación, royal officials, and the hierarchy of the Cathedral. It symbolized separatism.

Both the 1521 and the 1652 riots began in times of food scarcity and sharply increased prices, but their immediate targets differed. In 1521 the rebels agreed to go together to sack houses

27. Maldonado, folios 114–114^v.

where they believed wheat was stored in the city. In 1652, however, the anger of the rebels focused on the bakers. For weeks bakers from outlying villages had been reluctant to bring their bread to sell in the city. One reason was that money had just been devalued by the Crown, and bakers demanded silver rather than devalued money.[28] As they raised their prices and brought less bread, people began to rush them, taking their bread without paying. City officials sent troops to guard the bakers and force them to bring their bread to sell, but the soldiers blamed the officials for the bakers' lack of cooperation. People of the city suspected that the bakers were deliberately holding back bread in order to get higher prices. When only a few bakers appeared in the main square of the Feria early on May 22, 1652, and told the people that the price of bread had again risen, they were attacked by three armed men who dashed their bread to the ground with their swords.

Rebels in both uprisings were acting in the place of magistrates who, they believed, had failed to provide bread at a just price. Accounts of the 1521 rebellion describe the rebellious people as running through the streets searching houses for wheat and then converging on the chambers of the city council. There they noisily demanded bread, but they were soon placated by the asistente and a leading noble, Fernando Henriquez de Ribera. Many believed that the authorities' assurances of bread had quelled the uprising by the end of the first day.[29]

By 1652 Seville's was a capitalist, commercial, Atlantic-wide economy regulated by a government that could remain legitimate only if it provided food for its people. The 1652 rebels demanded the lifting of the millones tax, a royal sales tax imposed in the late sixteenth century from which neither nobles nor churchmen were exempt. They also demanded a return to the

28. Letter from the city of Seville to Philip IV, June 1652, quoted in Domínguez Ortiz, *Alteraciones*, p. 217. This study is based on a wealth of archival evidence from Granada, Cordoba, and Seville. It discusses the 1652 revolt in Seville as part of a larger picture of social unrest in Andalucia.

29. Ortiz de Zuñiga, 3:325–326. Maldonado, folio 114[v].

previous value of vellon money, coins made from a mixture of silver and copper that progressively lost their silver content to the royal treasury as they were periodically reissued. Rebels demanded the release of people imprisoned for violating regulations on restamping money and stamped paper. These rebels had recognized that the problem of providing food was directly tied to taxation and monetary policies. They had no illusions of living in a local, closed economy dependent for food on the harvests of its own region. Wheat had been imported since the last quarter of the sixteenth century, and bread was bought by people who earned a living in the wine, oil, and shipping industries—all closely tied to an Atlantic-wide commerce.[30]

In 1652 rebels demanded not only food but a check on the developing capitalist system. They believed that merchants and large landholders had accumulated capital at their expense by squeezing higher food prices out of them and diverting local agricultural production into crops for more profitable foreign markets. Furthermore, they argued that the Crown's economic policies had promoted the drain of capital away from them by absorbing their small monetary holdings in taxes and monetary devaluation.

Rebels in 1652 did not bother to march to the city council to voice their demands. Instead, they waited until the second day of the rebellion and then went to the *regente*, the king's first minister in Seville. The implication is that people of the city recognized the impotence of the local city council. If they were to have bread, they would have to go to royal authorities, who were the only ones who could make the necessary changes in taxes, monetary policy, and commerce. This change is a key to understanding the growth of central political power in the development of modern states. Local governments like the city council of Seville lost authority and credibility when they could not feed their people.

30. Ortiz de Zuñiga, 4:743. Maldonado, folio 122. Elizabeth Fox Genoese, "The Many Faces of Moral Economy: A Contribution to a Debate," *Past and Present*, No. 58 (1973), discusses the flaws in Thompson's model of a moral economy; see esp. pp. 163–167.

Officials listened to the rebels' demands in both uprisings because the rebels were armed and violent. The rebels of 1521 limited their violence on the first day of rebellion to breaking into houses where they suspected wheat was stored. On the second day, however, they broke into the house of the Duke of Medina Sidonia and seized four pieces of artillery, which they placed in the streets to fortify their stronghold in the Feria. Evidently they had lost faith in the calm assurances that local authorities had given on the previous day. Their resistance, however, was not reported as an aggressive, mindless violence; Ortiz de Zuñiga, a seventeenth-century noble, described "the common people taking up positions of defense in their parish and its plaza with four pieces of artillery that they had taken from the house of the Duke of Medina Sidonia."[31]

Violence in the 1652 rebellion was much more immediate, wide-spread, and uncontrolled. One official estimated that 10,000 men poured through the city streets, sweeping along city officials in their rush. Officials who could make themselves heard urged the rebels to take all the wheat they found to the Alhóndiga, the public granary, where it could be better distributed. Ironically, the Alhóndiga also served as the city's armory and was a perfect target for hungry, angry rebels. A contemporary described the surge into the armory of "a great crowd and mob of roguish and base people who, in a very brief time, left not a single arm remaining."[32] Some took guns with no powder or ammunition, and teen-aged boys happily ran off with antiquated armor and broadswords far too large for them.

After arming themselves at the Alhóndiga, the 1652 rebels went about the city in groups of twelve to twenty men. These *quadrillas* broke into houses demanding bread, wheat, bacon, ham, and cheese. They also took clothing, silver, and money.

31. Ortiz de Zuñiga, 3:325.

32. Domínguez Ortiz, *Alteraciones*, letter from Seville to the royal government, May 22, 1652, quoted in the appendix, pp. 208–209. Maldonado, folio 116^V. Davis, Chapter 6, also printed as "Religious Riot in Sixteenth-Century France," *Past and Present*, No. 59 (1973), 87–88, suggests a parallel between the youths who participated in religious riots and the youth festivals of misrule that she discussed in "Misrule."

The account by one eye-witness described the quadrilla that came to his house. A barefoot mulatto dressed in rags and armed with a helmet and breastplate led the noisy group. The captain and a few he chose came into the house to demand wheat while the others waited at the door and made "shameless comments." When the householder could find no wheat to give them, he gave some wine and money to the captain. The other members of the quadrilla complained loudly and said it was a shame that white men were subjected to a "dog mulatto." They killed the mulatto captain and left his body in a little plaza.[33]

Although the violence of the quadrillas threatened the entire city, it focused on bakers, law officers, and a royal prosecutor. Rebels chased bakers and sheriffs, wounding some, killing others, and even killing their horses. They sacked the homes of two criminal law clerks and then broke into their offices with hatchets. They destroyed their papers in a huge bonfire in the Plaza de San Francisco, adding papers to it from other lawyers' offices. A member of the king's Supreme Council who had come to Seville with the special commission of prosecuting violators of the new monetary laws left town just ahead of an angry band. Many city residents hated him for his vigorous punishment of small debtors.[34]

Rebels in both uprisings stormed city prisons and released prisoners. They did not limit their action to people imprisoned for debts or counterfeiting money or stamped paper; they freed all prisoners in the Royal Prison, prison of the Hermandad, prison of the Contratación, prison of the archbishop, and prison for prostitutes. After breaking down prison doors with hatchets and maces in 1652, they left imprisoned only one man, a Portuguese who had been accused of crimes against the king.[35] The injustices protested by rebels in both of these uprisings included much more than the scarcity of bread at a "just price."

33. Maldonado, folios 153ᵛ–154.

34. Ibid., folios 117ᵛ–118, 123–123ᵛ. Ortiz de Zuñiga, 4:741. For the city's hatred of the royal prosecutor, see the letter of Fray Juan de los Santos, April 23, 1652, quoted in the appendix of Domínguez Ortiz, *Alteraciones*, pp. 205–207.

35. Ortiz de Zuñiga, 4:743. Maldonado, folio 122ᵛ.

Underworld people who were released from prison undoubtedly joined the rebels, exulting in the uprisings as fine opportunities for arming themselves, looting, and attacking hated figures of authority. There is no evidence that either the rebels or the prisoners greeted one another as brothers, however, nor that the underworld people took leading roles in the uprisings. Accounts of the 1521 rebellion described it as an uprising of "starving and needy common people" (*plebe*), and "very humble subjects" led by residents of the Feria.[36] The more detailed accounts of the 1652 uprising indicate that it began with two silk weavers attacking the bakers in the plaza of the Feria. Leaders punished for the 1652 riot included workers of gold thread, barbers, masons, fishermen, shoemakers, and hat makers. All of these men were artisans and relatively prosperous, whose economic fortunes had declined by the middle of the seventeenth century. One man punished for his role in the rebellion was a sheriff of the Santa Hermandad who had complained too loudly about "evil government."[37] Others punished included a Portuguese cleric and many people who had recently arrived in Seville.

The significance of the underworld in these events was more symbolic than real. Many participated, and they must have added a frightening and ridiculous aspect to the rebellion. One eyewitness who described the ragtag gangs that went about the city said that they were composed of "picaros, many of them barefoot, some with helmets, others with breastplates and swords, the bodyguards in armor, some with only gauntlets, others with pikes and arquebuses, according to what they had taken from the armory in the Alhóndiga."[38] According to Ortiz de Zuñiga, the crowd that rushed to the initial attack on the bakers in the plaza of the Feria in 1652 included "vile subjects." Later in his account he referred to the rebels as "that infamous rabble."[39] Although his own attitude toward rebellion colored

36. Ortiz de Zuñiga, 3:325. Maldonado, folio 114[v].
37. Maldonado, folios 141, 145. AMS, Siglo XVII, Sección 4, Escribanías de Cabildo, Tomo 28, No. 19.
38. Maldonado, folio 153[v].
39. Ortiz de Zuñiga, 4:739–740, 743.

his account, they undoubtedly appeared to be the lowest, dirtiest, hungriest, and most frightening people of the city. The presence of underworld people among them confirmed a general contemporary attitude that crowd violence was chaotic, horrible, and carried out by the dregs of society.[40]

People of Triana, the suburb across the river, also joined the 1652 uprising. According to Maldonado, another chronicler, more than 600 rebels armed themselves in Triana and marched to a bugle across the bridge to the city. Rather than other armed rebels ready to join them there, however, they found some Franciscans, who assured them that the rebels of the Feria had disarmed because bread was now being distributed from the Convent of Santa Paula. Maldonado wrote that the Triana rebels received this news "gladly" and returned to Triana.[41] Ortiz de Zuñiga believed that local nobles defeated the rebels because they prevented the rebels of Triana from communicating with those of the Feria; they soon closed the city gates to prevent outsiders from joining the rebels inside.[42]

Clergymen played different roles in the two rebellions. Reports of the 1521 riot do not mention participation by clergy until the rebels had been routed by the nobles in street battles. The rebellion then died, closed by a romería, a traditional religious procession making a pilgrimage to a rural shrine. More than 1500 people from nearby Carmona entered the city on their way to pray for relief from famine at the shrine of Our Lady of Antiquity. Accompanied by their clergy and dressed as penitents with ropes around their necks, they intoned prayers and supplications to the Cathedral. From the Cathedral they received a Mass and sermon, food, and alms. People in the surrounding area who made similar romerías also received wheat that Seville bought at public expense from Africa, a demonstration that people who expressed their needs in traditional religious ways would receive help.[43] The contrast between the pilgrims and the wounded,

40. Davis, "Religious Riots," p. 52, discusses sixteenth-century attitudes about crowd violence.
41. Maldonado, folios 119ᵛ–120.
42. Ortiz de Zuñiga, 4:747.
43. Ibid., 3:325–327.

slain, and discredited rebels could not have been greater. Probably the clergy responded more quickly than usual to the pilgrims in 1521 because the rebellion had jolted them from paralysis to action. Traditionally, the people looked to the Church to sustain them in times of calamity, and in 1521 the clergy was able to insist that their traditional support would come only in traditional forms.

During the rebellion of 1652, however, the clergy added some innovations to these traditional forms and played a much more active role in the rebellion. In order to stop the marauding violence of armed quadrillas, monks offered food and drink to them and persuaded them to put down their arms while they ate. In this way, Maldonado wrote, they were able to disarm entire quadrillas. Franciscans distributed themselves among the rebels to enforce peace after the rebel-approved governor tried to restore order to the rebellious city. The religious of the Convent of Santa Paula gave city authorities permission to station an armed guard there.[44]

On the fourth day of the rebellion, twenty-five monks entered the Feria and persuaded the rebels to go to the archbishop, ask pardon, and make peace. As the archbishop pardoned them in the name of the king, church bells and the Cathedral bells rang out the news, and some rebels laid down their arms. Others insisted that they should keep their weapons until they knew for certain that the king's pardon was genuine, the value of vellon money had been restored, and the hated taxes removed. The archbishop, regente, and asistente later went to the Feria to convince the people that the pardon was genuine and they could put down their arms. Many rebels refused, however, replying that they would not disarm until they received assurances from the king, "written in letters fat with gold," that they had won their demands and had been pardoned for their rebellion.[45]

Some clerics disagreed with the peace-making attempts of monks and the archbishop that seemed to align them with local authorities against the rebels. When Maldonado discussed the

44. Maldonado, folios 118[V]–119[V]. Ortiz de Zuñiga, 4:744.
45. Maldonado, folio 133[V].

causes of the 1652 rebellion, he described an incident in which secular officers of justice had "violated" and "profaned" a monastery when they broke into it to search for counterfeiters. They had been told that some men in the monastery had received the abbot's permission to restamp money there.[46] This incident sparked a long-smoldering resentment that involved disputes over legal jurisdiction, abuses of religious asylum, the imposition of the millones tax on a clergy that believed it should be exempt, a royal requirement for using stamped paper (another illegal tax, according to some clergy), and the recent devaluation of vellon money. Required to pay its "donations" to the Crown in silver, the Church was pinched by the devaluation of vellon money. In addition, the lower secular clergy in Seville had to live on fees paid in vellon for Masses, burials, and baptisms.[47]

It is no accident that one of the leaders of the rebellion was a priest, undoubtedly a member of the lower clergy. Bernabe Lopez Filgueras, whom Ortiz de Zuñiga called "the seditious cleric,"[48] was also Portuguese, born in the country that had just risen once more against its Spanish rulers. Maldonado described him as the "grand mutineer [grandíssimo amotinado], and the main leader of [the rebels], who as a priest and ecclesiastic had much hand and authority with them."[49] According to witnesses, he urged the rebels to break down the doors of the Alcázar, a traditional symbol of authority. He demanded that a city official not only agree to the rebels' demands, but swear on a missal to uphold and support the ends of the people. When the archbishop pronounced pardon in the king's name, Lopez Filgueras scoffed that only the king could grant the pardon. He urged the rebels to keep their arms until they had heard from the king, himself, and he ridiculed those who believed the king would pardon them after they had committed such crimes.[50] This priest was offering

46. Ibid.
47. Domínguez Ortiz, *Estamento*, discusses taxes on the Church, pp. 153, 155; see pp. 71-73 for concerns about economic support of the clergy, and pp. 62-63 for a discussion of the poverty of the lower clergy.
48. Ortiz de Zuñiga, 4:744.
49. Maldonado, folio 141.
50. Ortiz de Zuñiga, 4:741, 747-748. Maldonado, folios 125^V, 133^V.

support to a needy people, but hardly in the traditional manner. In 1521 no priest had appeared as a rebel leader, but by 1652 the economic and political development of Spain had produced a group of clergy who felt the injustices of the existing system as keenly as the rebellious artisans and unskilled workers.

There were no pilgrimages to close the rebellion of 1652, as in 1521. On the contrary, Church leaders and city officials sensed the danger of permitting religious festivals to take place soon after the rebellion had been put down. They decided to postpone the festival of Corpus Christi for one month because "it is very evident that the rebels intend to use this day to make a great havoc and slaughter in the justice and nobility of this city."[51] In the sixteenth-century rebellion a religious procession had been used to reinforce traditional values and responses; in 1652 city fathers feared that the group identity, collective action, and legitimation arising from a religious procession would be used against them. And though the institutional Church was still allied with the ruling class, some of the disaffected clergy were not. Also, the religious wars that had devastated Europe in the early modern period had demonstrated that religion, uncontrolled by a Church firmly allied with the government, could be a potent agency for popular protest, legitimizing political challenges and even sanctifying revolution.

Rebels in 1652 demonstrated more organizational skill than in 1521. Accounts of the sixteenth-century uprising have little evidence of rebel organization. The rebels appeared to agree on the targets for their direct action, and they went together to the city council, but they had no spokesmen, nor do accounts accuse any individuals of being leaders of the rebellion. Rebels cooperated in placing artillery pieces in the streets, but they had no plan or leaders to turn to when the nobles of the city routed them.

In contrast, accounts of the 1652 uprising suggest that it had been planned. In ordinary circumstances, for example, two silk weavers would not go to the plaza armed and on horseback to buy bread. In addition, the bakers' high price didn't provoke a

51. Maldonado, folio 144.

loud outburst of profanity, as might be expected, but a cry,
"Long live the King of Spain, and death to bad government!"
This was clearly a rallying cry, undoubtedly agreed upon by
residents of the Feria as a signal. One historian has found
evidence that it was also a rallying cry in several other uprisings
in Andalucia during this year.[52]

Although the quadrillas probably arose spontaneously in the
1652 rebellion, these rebel gangs do show evidence of organization. Maldonado's eye witnesses said the gangs had leaders.
Moreover, the gangs imposed their own kind of justice on their
members. They imprisoned one gang member who had violated
their code, and when a bystander inquired what the arrested
man had done, members of the gang replied, "He has been imprisoned by order of the crowd . . . because he stole a silver vase
from a house."[53] Perhaps the victim was an underworld character
who had violated the rebels' code, demonstrating less interest in
justice than in loot.

One account of the 1652 rebellion listed the "impudences"
committed by the rebels, and among "other infinitely evil
things" declared that the rebels had established price controls.[54]
Maldonado asserted that the rebels had agreed on whom they
would appoint regente and asistente, although he gave no names.
The rebels made Juan de Villasis the head of their army, and
they accepted the aide of the asistente as governor of the city
after he had bowed to their demands and had sworn on a missal
to uphold their interests. They directed him to name chiefs of
the quadrillas and body guards and place them in charge of the
parishes, evidently realizing that organization was crucial to
consolidating their position.[55]

Despite the superior organization of rebels in 1652, this
uprising failed in an armed rout similar to that of 1521. Ortiz
de Zuñiga, who had belonged to one of the noble groups that

52. Domínguez Ortiz, *Alteraciones*, pp. 53, 220.

53. Maldonado, folio 154.

54. Andrés de Vega, in AMS, *Papeles del Conde de Aguila*, Sección
especial, Tomo 10 en folio, No. 30.

55. Ibid. Ortiz de Zuñiga, 4:744.

restored order in 1652, gave credit to the nobility for putting down both rebellions. Not only were the nobles superior militarily to the rebels, he wrote; they were also true paternalists, demonstrating their care and regard for the common people.[56] Ortiz de Zuñiga failed to recognize the differences between the nobles in the 1521 revolt and those putting down the 1652 rebellion. He happily noted that one result of the 1521 revolt was to bring the dukes of Medina Sidonia and Arcos back to Seville, strong and willing to accept their paternalist obligations to the city.[57] But he did not see the connection with the Comunero Revolt, a series of local uprisings which broke out all over Spain against Charles I in 1520-21. In this period the Crown was vulnerable and had to depend on the local authority of nobles, such as the Duke of Medina Sidonia, who could restore order. People of the city accepted their nobles as responsible patrons, and the nobles demonstrated their generosity and understanding by pardoning the rebels. Although the famine of Seville continued for at least another year, leaving the streets full of corpses and starving beggars, the people revolted no more. Their anger seemed to disappear with the gunsmoke in the streets, and they willingly returned to the traditional responses to hunger: religious processions, begging, seeking bread from the city council and archbishopric. As long as their patrons provided some food, they held their peace.

By 1652, however, the paternalism of the local nobles was more form than substance. In a very literal sense nobles no longer provided wheat for the people. Much of the land belonging to nobles had been converted to the more profitable wine and olive cultivation. Wheat, now imported from other countries, was carried to the city by merchants and other commercial officials. In addition, nobles were increasingly absent from the city and their land. They leased their holdings to other cultivators and delegated their responsibilities in city government to lesser officials so that they could spend increasing time at the royal court. The preeminence of the Crown over local nobles

56. Ortiz de Zuñiga, 4:741–742, 746.
57. Ibid., 3:326–327.

was clearly recognized by the rebels, who refused to disarm until they heard from the king himself that he had granted their demands and had pardoned them.

The rebels of 1652 were defeated in an engagement on Saturday, May 26, 1652, when a combined city force captured their artillery and routed their defenses. They were defeated a second time two days later when the ruling junta rescinded all concessions made to the rebels. Vellon money would return to its previous level, and all royal taxes would be reimposed. Concessions had been promised, the announcement declared, only to quiet the rebels. They were now rescinded because they were "against the service of his majesty."[58] A royal directive sent by special mail soon arrived in Seville to confirm this action. The king also exempted 56 rebel leaders from his pardon, 38 from the Feria and 18 from Triana. Five of these rebels had already been shot, their bodies hanged from windows on the Plaza de San Francisco. Two brothers were hanged in the Plaza and their heads displayed in the square of the Feria. Authorities delayed the execution of one leader in an unsuccessful attempt to force him, under torture, to name other rebel leaders.[59]

While none of the rebels executed was described as a ruffian or member of the underworld, the role of the underworld in the rebellion should not be discounted. In the first place, the presence of underworld people among the rebels discredited the uprising and helped city officials justify their actions in putting it down. They could make insincere promises to people as low and dishonest as those ruffians. They could insist that all arms be kept in the Tower of Gold by city-paid guards, for no reasonable resident wanted to permit armed thugs and murderers in the city. Finally, they could punish the Feria under the guise of clearing out a nest of criminals. As Maldonado wrote: "because the site of the Feria has always been a refuge of the delinquents in this city, both natives and those from afar, the council and government agreed to close all the taverns and bars there."[60]

58. Maldonado, folios 143ᵛ–144.
59. Ibid., folios 141, 144ᵛ, 147–147ᵛ.
60. Ibid., folio 150.

Opposition between underworld and city government became more rigid during such crises as bread riots and political rebellions.

City officials opposed the underworld during crises, but they usually opposed them from a weaker position. One account of the 1652 rebellion used the following often contradictory metaphors to describe the weakness of the city:

The *veinticuatro* not worth one
The ministers servants, and the servants ministers
The staffs of office (*varas*) at a standstill (*varadas*)
Sheriffs invisible
The city alone, the city full
Judges without a court; the court for horses
Broken soldiers
Money with no value
The *Lonja* a skeleton
The *Alcázar* in forgetfulness.[61]

This purposeful combination of contradictions emphasizes the confusion and impotence of the city government.

The underworld exploited the lack of law and order, but it could not survive as a parasite on a host reduced to bones. Survival for the underworld depended upon the city overcoming its crises. Underworld people nipped at the heels of the city oligarchy, but they refused to sink tooth or claw into it. They diverted potentially revolutionary fervor into a toothless, clawless pose, threatening and fearsome but ultimately supportive of the existing social order.

Crises in early modern Seville demonstrate that governments gather political power from sources as mundane as public health and bread. The city government in Seville survived the painful dislocations of famine and epidemic and even wrested from these traumas an extension of power. One reason is that the parasitical underworld realized that its own survival depended upon preserving the existing order. A second reason is that the underworld

61. "Casos del tumulto de Sevilla de 22 de mayo del año de 1652," Papeles varios, BC, 83-7-14, folios 181-182.

provided city fathers with a justification for enforcing more regulations and monopolizing violence. As a symbol of evil, the underworld enabled the dominant culture to define itself as just and moral, author of a legitimate social order.

Conclusion

B
Y the end of the seventeenth century Seville had faded. Once thronged with jostling crowds, the city streets now wound mutely past deserted buildings. The clamor of bankers and merchants on the Cathedral steps had died away as fewer ships sailed into port. The famous Casa de Contratación no longer throbbed with commercial enterprise at the heart of the city. Now it functioned far away in Cadiz.

The city government had survived, however, even though it had become more closely tied to a faltering monarchy. Local authorities had even extended their regulatory powers. One reason for the persistence and development of this political power was the presence in the city of underworld people. Far more than a curious fringe group, they complemented the city's inadequate systems of commerce, justice, and charity. They diverted potentially revolutionary fervor into antisocial sniping, and by their participation discredited some popular outbursts against political authorities.

The partnership of crime and political authority goes far beyond early modern Seville. Police have long depended on underworld informers, and many governments have hired thugs to reinforce their own power with terrorism and strategic assassinations. There is even some indication that agencies of the United States government have collaborated with the Mafia and utilized underworld connections in the conduct of foreign policy.

The underworld of early modern Seville helps to explain this partnership. Ostensibly enemies of the city oligarchy, underworld people actually supported it. They were conservatives, as determined to preserve the social order as they were to exploit it. For its part, the city oligarchy used the underworld as a symbol of a common enemy, an embodiment of evil that all city residents could recognize and oppose. The presence of underworld people justified the extension of political power and more vigorous governmental action to control the use of violence.

The peculiar partnership between political authority and the underworld in Seville demonstrates that criminality is much more than deviant behavior. Crime in this city was associated with a distinct subculture, but it was also well integrated with other social, economic, and political activities of the city. While criminals were punished as individuals, their offenses were not simply isolated incidents of deviance. Sometimes crime was social protest, and sometimes it was anti-social villainy. In every case, it was the deviance that political authority defined as crime. Seville shows that the right to define and prosecute crime is so crucial in the consolidation of power that crime persists not merely as a symptom of social illness, but also because it is indispensable to political power.

Appendixes

I. *Coins Used in Early Modern Seville*

Coins were minted in sixteenth and seventeenth-century Spain from gold, silver, and vellon. Vellon coins, which were a mixture of silver and copper, were first issued in 1556 under Philip II. After 1602 all silver was removed from the vellon coins so that the silver could be added to the royal treasury. The maravedí was a gold coin in ancient times, but by the fifteenth century it had very little value.

In order of value, the coins were:

Doblon de a ocho	gold coin worth 8 escudos
Doblon	gold coin worth 2 escudos
Escudo, or ducat	gold coin worth 440 maravedís in 1609
Real	silver coin usually worth 34 maravedís
Quartillo	vellon coin worth 8 1/2 maravedís
Quarto	vellon coin worth 4 maravedís
Medio quarto	vellon coin wirth 2 maravedís
Maravedí	vellon coin worth 2 blancas
Blanca	vellon coin worth 1/2 maravedí

Monetary value fluctuated widely. For example, the escudo, worth 374 maravedís in 1497, underwent the following changes:

1566	400 maravedís
1609	440 maravedís
1642	550 maravedís
1643	612 and then 510 maravedís
1651	about 544 maravedís
1652	about 476 maravedís

The purchasing power of these coins also fluctuated widely. In 1650 a kilo of bread cost four quartos, a liter of wine cost one real, and a liter of oil cost two reales. An unskilled worker could earn four reales a day. An artisan earned about six reales a day, and a doctor earned twenty-five ducats a month. A priest usually received two or three reales for saying a Mass. A lieutenant in the artillery earned forty ducats a month.

Based on Antonio Dominguez Ortiz, *Alteraciones andaluzas*, p. 14; Henry C. Lea, *A History of the Inquisition of Spain*, I, Appendix III, pp. 560–565.

II. *Population of Seville by Parish, 1588*

Parish	Houses	Household Heads	People	People per House
Santa María	2292	3183	16776	7.3
Salvador	1085	1866	8450	7.8
Santa Cruz	215	378	2806	13.0
Santa Maria la Blanca	86	137	869	10.1
San Isidro	268	468	1974	7.4
San Nicolás	106	280	1249	11.8
San Ildefonso	209	251	2256	10.8
San Bartolomé	218	408	2424	11.1
Santa María Magdalena	1000	1360	8484	8.5
San Esteban	168	282	1356	8.1
Santiago	130	315	1353	10.4
San Miguel	208	278	2043	9.8
San Pedro	200	243	2032	10.1
San Martín	372	746	3214	8.6
San Andrés	222	366	1110	5.0
San Juan	326	633	3424	10.5
Santa Catalina	349	843	3514	10.0
San Román	292	502	1917	6.6
Omnium Sanctorum	854	1771	6416	7.5
San Vicente	1535	2770	12414	8.1
San Lorenzo	746	1215	2270	3.0
San Marcos	250	497	3085	12.3
Santa Marina	250	599	4716	18.9
San Julián	179	471	1481	8.3
Santa Lucia	124	657	1636	13.2
San Gil	445	1030	3342	7.5
San Roque	246	922	3096	12.6
San Bernardo	158	400	1323	8.4
Santa Ana	1848	3115	15520	8.4
Totals	14,381	25,986	120,559	
Average				9.5

Based on documents in Archivo de Simancas, presented by Tomás González in *Censo de población de España en el Siglo XVI* (Madrid 1829). According to Domínguez Ortiz, in *Orto y Ocaso de Sevilla,* p. 42, these figures do not include transients or some 4000 Moriscos. See his Appendix, pp. 110–111.

Bibliography

The archives of Seville offer a wide variety of information about underworld people and their interaction with other city residents. The municipal
archive, which is in the city hall, contains official documents of the city
government which are organized by century and by topic within each
century. Of special interest to social historians is the collection of papers
of the Count of Aguila. The "Relacion de las cosas de la cárcel de Sevilla
y su trato," by Cristóbal de Chaves, is in this collection, as well as the
Efemérides, a record of many notable events in Seville in the early modern
period.

The Cathedral of Seville maintains the Biblioteca Colombina and the
Biblioteca Capitular, which include both secular and ecclesiastical records.
Documents most helpful to this study describe charity, public executions,
autos de fé, religious festivals, and disciplinary problems in religious houses.
The best accounts of the rebellions of 1521 and 1652 are in the Biblioteca
Capitular.

An upstairs room in the Hospital de la Santa Caridad contains stacks of
documents about the Brotherhood of Holy Charity and the founder of the
Hospital, Miguel de Mañara. This archive is uncatalogued, and researchers
must ask the Hermano Mayor of the Brotherhood for special permission
to use it. Particularly valuable to a study of the underworld are the records
of charitable dowries granted by Manara from 1666 to 1670, and a survey
of poor people in the city which he directed in 1667. Antonio Domínguez
Ortiz referred to the survey in his work, but the present study is believed
to be the first published discussion of the documents.

Padre Pedro de León was ordered by a superior in the Society of Jesus
to write a report of his work in Andalucia between 1578 and 1616. His
Compendio is available in two hand-written copies. One is in the university
library of Salamanca, and the other is in the library of the University of
Granada. This book uses the latter copy. Pedro de León listed in an appendix to Part II the people whom he assisted in the Royal Prison before
they were executed. On both copies these names have been crossed out
with ink. His report covers his work inside the Royal Prison and also in the
brothels and on the streets of Seville.

Several people in the early modern period wrote and published histories of Seville. Luis Peraza concentrated on the government and judicial system of the city when he wrote in the midsixteenth century. Francisco de Ariño wrote a chronicle of the years from 1592 until 1604 which is the best account of the tensions within Seville when the Count of Puñoenrostro was sent by the Crown to head the city government. Alonso Morgado published a very laudatory history of Seville in 1587. The most extensive history written in the seventeenth century is by Diego Ortiz de Zuñiga. This five-volume work presents documentary evidence and an interpretation that is favorable to local nobles.

The primary evidence that is available tends to be anecdotal. It rarely lends itself to quantitative analyses. Police records do not exist for this period for Seville. Surveys of the poor and lists of licensed beggars were made at different times and by different methods, so that comparisons between them are of questionable value. The national archives of Spain are rich sources for military and Inquisitional histories of Seville, but they are of limited value in describing crime in the city.

Several secondary works have been very helpful in analyzing the primary evidence that is available. The histories of John Elliott and John Lynch are invaluable as overviews of Spain in the early modern period. Ruth Pike and Antonio Domínguez Ortiz have both contributed more specialized histories of Seville. Outside the field of history, this study has depended very heavily on the political ideas of Antonio Gramsci, the anthropological concepts of William Christian and Victor Turner, and the child-development theories of Erik Erikson and Jean Piaget.

I. ARCHIVAL MANUSCRIPTS

Archivo General de Indias, Sevilla

Sección 2, Casa de Contratación
Sección 5, Indiferente General

Archivo del Hospital de la Santa Caridad, Sevilla

Dottes que pago N^{ro} Venerable herm^o May^{or}, el Sr. D. Miguel Mañara en los años desde el de 1666 Hasta el de 1670 a Diferentes Pobres para que se casasen, Estante 4, Legajo 18.
Memoria de todas las parroquias de Sevilla y de las necesidades y pobres que había en ellas; que pedía, el V^{er} Sr. D. Miguel Mañara para tener cuidado de socorrer las como lo hijo, y mientras ricibio los remedios como por estas memorias parece, Estante 4, Legajo 18.

Archivo Municipal de Sevilla

Archivo General
Archivo de Privilegios
   No. 127, Ordenanzas de Sevilla, recopiladas, Andres Grande, Sevilla, 1632.

Escribanías de Cabildo
  Siglo XVI, Sección 3
  Siglo XVII, Sección 4
Papeles del Conde de Aguila, Sección Especial
  Chaves, Cristóbal de, "Relación de las cosas de la cárcel de Sevilla y su trato," Tomo B-C.
  Efemérides de Sevilla, Tomo 20, folio 33.
Papeles Importantes

Biblioteca Capitular, Sevilla

Castro Palacios, Bernardo Luís de, "Tratado de algunas ceremonias y cosas antiguas que se observasen en la Sta Iglesia Patriarcal, y Metropolitoria desta Ciudad de Sevilla," 1712, 83-4-9.
Cuesta y Saavedra, Ambrosias de la, Memorias históricas sevillanas, 82-5-21.
"En Auto público de fée en la Plaza de S. Fran^{co} de Sevilla á 2d de Sept^{re} de 1559," 64-7-118.
Fernandez Melgarejo, Luís, Discurso genealógico de la nobilissima y antigua casa de los Tellos de Sevilla, 1660, 84-3-42.
Maldonado de Saabedra, Joseph, Obras y apuntamientos, Sevilla, 1596, 82-4-23.
Mañara, Miguel de, "Motibo principal por que zesaron las comedias en Sevilla año de 1679," 80-1-92.
Memorias de diferentes cosas sucedidas en esta muy noble y mui leal ciudad de Sevilla copiaronse en Sevilla año de 1696, 84-7-21.
  Góngora, Diego Ignacio de, "Relacion del contagio que padeció esta ciudad de Sevilla el año de 1649."
  Maldonado Danila y Saavedra, Joseph, "Tratado verdadero del motin que hubo en esta ciudad este año de 1652," 1663, orig. 1652.
  "Suceso notable en esta Ciudad de Sevilla y por que se dixo Feria y Pendon Verde."
Memorias eclesiásticas y seculares de la muy noble y muy leal ciudad de Sevilla, Sevilla, 1698, 84-7-19.
  "Serie historial, desde el año de 1531 que contiene varios casos sucedidos por diversos tiempos en la Ciudad de Sevilla."
Memorias que tocan a la Sta Iglesia Metropolitana, y Patriarchal de Sevilla y Fundaciones de algunos monesterios de dicha ciudad, 84-7-20.
Papeles varios, 85-4-11.
  "Casos raros y particulares, sucedidos en Sevilla, en diferentes tiempos recogidos de los manuscritos que dejaron el coronista Pedro Mexia, Don Josef Maldonado de Avila y Saavedra, y Don Diego de Gongora, y otros sucedidos en estos tiempos."
  "Desde el año de 1616 asta el de 1634."
Papeles varios, 85-4-13.
  Alcocer, Pedro de, "Relación de las comunidades de España el año de

mill y quinientos y veinte y uno por el licenciado Pedro de Alcocer vezino de la ciudad de Toledo."

"Feria y Pendon Verde de Sevilla año MDXXI."

Santa Cruz, Alonso de, "Lo que paso en Sevilla en tiempo de las comunidades, escrito por Alonso de Santa Cruz."

Siguenza, Francisco de, "Relación de la translacion de la imagen de N^{tra} S^{ra} de los Reyes i cuerpo de S. Leandro i de los cuerpos reales a la Real Capilla en la Sta Iglesia de Sevilla año de 1579, escrito en dialogo por Francisco de Siguenza."

Papeles varios pertenecientes a la historia de Sevilla, 83-7-14.

"Caos del Tumulto de Sevilla de 22 de mayo del año de 1652."

"Consulta theologia, en que se pregunta si será justo y conveniente que se apliquen las obras pias de esta ciudad al remedio de la necesidad publica que al presente ay en esta ciudad de Sevilla."

"La Forma que se tubo en levantar el Estandarte Real en la Ciudad de Sevilla por la Mg^d del Rey d. Phelipe III."

"Relación de las fiestas reales de toros y cañas que se hizieron en Sevilla a 2 de octubre del 1620 años hecha por don Francisco Morbeli y Puebla, cavallero de ella."

"Segunda relación de las cañas y toros que los cavalleros de Sevilla hizieron en 2 de octubre de 1620, por la Junta de sus altezas los principes herederos de España."

Poesias y relaciones varias, 82-3-26.

"La Forma que se tuvo en levantar el estandarte Real en la ciudad de Sevilla por la Mag. del Rey don Phelipe Tercero."

"Relación de un auto de fee que se celebro en el Sta Oficio de la Inquisicion de la Ciudad de Sevilla en el $Conv^{to}$ de S^n Pablo . . . el ultimo dia del mes de Febreo del año de 1627," 64-7-118.

Sanchez Gordillo, Alonso, Memorial de historia eclesiastica de la ciudad de Sevilla, 1612, 82-6-19.

"Recopilacion de las cosas seculares de Sevilla."

"Religiosas estaciones que frecuenta la devocion sevillana."

Biblioteca Universitaria de Granada

Pedro de León, Compendio de algunas experiencias en los ministerios de que vsa la $Comp^a$ de IESVS con q practicamente se muestra con algunos acaecimientos y documentos el buen acierto en ellos, Granada, 1619.

British Museum, London

"Los Cargos que resultan de la residencia que se tomó por mando del R^{rmo} señor don Rodrigo de Castro Arçobispo de Sevilla contra don Alonso Faxardo de Villalobos Obispo de Esquilache Arcediano y Canonigo de Sevilla," Additional 28358.

"Papeles varios," Additional 14015.

Texera, Pedro, "Discripcion de las costas y puertas de España," Additional 28497.

"Tractatus varii, et collectanea," Egerton 1873.

II. ARCHIVAL CATALOGUES AND COLLECTIONS

Aguilar Piñal, *Catálogo de documentos sevillanos que se conservan en el Museo Britanico,* n.p., n.d.

Archivo Documental Español, Madrid, Real Academia de la Historia, 1968.

Archivo Hispalense, Revista Historica, Literaria y Artistica, Sevilla, E. Rasco, 1886–1888, 4 vols.

Colección de documentos inéditos relativos al descubrimiento, conquista y colonizacion de las posesiones españolas en América y occeanía, sacado en su mayor parte, del Real Archivo de Indias, Madrid, Manuel B. Quirós, 1865.

Gayangos, Pascual, *Catalogue of the Manuscripts in the Spanish Language in the British Museum,* London, William Clowes and Sons, 1875.

III. CHRONICLES, MEMOIRS, AND TREATISES

Ánes Álvarez, Gonzalo, ed., *Memoriales y discursos de Francisco Martínez de Mata,* Madrid, Moneda y Crédito, 1971.

Anonymous, introd. by Benitez de Lugo, Antonio, *Discurso de las Comunidad de Sevilla año 1520, Q escrivió un clérigo apasionado de la casa de Niebla,* Sevilla, Rafael Tarascó y Lassa, 1881.

Ariño, Francisco de, *Sucesos de Sevilla de 1592 á 1604 recojidos de Francisco de Ariño, vecino de la ciudad en el barrio de Triana,* Sevilla, Rafael Tarascó y Lassa, 1873.

Benzoni, Girolamo, *History of the New World,* trans. W. H. Smyth, New York, Burt Franklin, 1857, orig. 1565.

Braun, Georgius, *Givitates Orbis Terrarum,* Cologne, 1574.

Cárdenas, Juan de, *Breve relación de la muerte, vida, y virtudes del venerable caballero Don Miguel Mañara Vicentelo de Leca, Caballero del Orden de Calatrava, Hermano Mayor de la Santa Caridad,* Sevilla, E. Rasco, 1903, orig. 1679.

Caro, Rodrigo, *Adiciones al principado y Antiguedades de la Ciudad de Sevilla y su convento jurídico,* Sevilla, Imprenta Alemaña, 1932.

Ciruelo, Pedro, *Reprobación de las supersticiones y hechicerías,* Madrid, Colección Joyas Bibliográficas, 1952, orig. ca. 1530.

del Rio, Martín, *Disqvisitionvm magicarvm libri sex quibvs continetur accvrata cviosarvm artivm, et vanorum superstitionum confutatio, vtilis Theologis, Jurisconsultis, Medicis, Philologis,* n.p., 1633.

Enriquez de Guzmán, Don Alonzo, *The Life and Acts of Don Alonzo Enriquez de Guzmán, a Knight of Seville, of the Order of Santiago,*

A.D. 1518 to 1543, trans. Clements R. Markham, London, Hakluyt Society, 1862.

Espinosa de los Monteros, Pablo, *Historia, Antiguedades y grandezas de la muy noble y muy leal ciudad de Sevilla,* Sevilla, Oficina de Matias Clavijo, 1627.

Farfan, Francisco, *Tres libros contra el peccado de la simple fornicacion: donde se averigua, que la torpeza entre solteros es peccado mortal, segun ley divina, natural, y humana: y se responde a los engaños de los que dizen que no es peccado,* Salamanca, Herederos de Mathies Gast, 1585.

Grijalva, Juan de, *The Discovery of New Spain in 1518,* trans. Henry R. Wagner, Pasadena, Cortes Society, 1942.

Luque, Faxardo, Francisco de, *Fiel desengaño; Contra la ociosidad y los juegos,* Fundación Conde de Cartegena, Madrid, 1955, orig. 1603.

Mal lara, Juan de, *Filosofia vulgar,* Selecciones Bibliófilas, Barcelona, 1958, orig. 1567.

Monardes, Nicolás, *Sevillana medicina, que trata el modo conservativo y curativo de los que habitan en la muy insigne ciudad de Sevilla, la cual sirve y aprovecha para cual quier otro lugar de estos reinos,* Sevilla, E. Rasco, 1885, orig. 1545.

Morgado, Alonso, *Historia de Sevilla,* Sevilla, Andrea Pescioni y Juan de Leon, 1587.

Navagero, Andres, *Viaje a España,* trans. José María Alonso Gamo, Valencia, Editorial Castalia, 1951.

Ortiz de Zuñiga, Diego, *Anales eclesiasticos y seculares de la muy noble y muy leal ciudad de Sevilla,* Madrid, Imprenta Real, 1795, orig. 1677, 5 vols.

Pacheco, Francisco, *Libro de descripcion de verdaderos retratos, de illustres y memorables varones,* Sevilla, 1599.

Peraza, Luís, *Justicia de Sevilla; Historia de esta ciudad,* n.p., n.d., ca. 1560.

Sigüenza, José de, *Historia de la orden de San Jerónimo,* Madrid, Bailly, Bailliere é Hijos, 1907, orig. 1464.

Suarez de Figueroa, *El pasagero,* Sociedad de Bibliófilos Españoles, Madrid, 1914, orig. 1617.

Thomás de Mercado, *Summa de Tratos y contratos,* Sevilla, Hernando Diaz, 1571.

Vives, Juan Luís, *Del socorro de los pobres, ó de las necesidades humanes,* Madrid, Libería de los Sucesores de Hernando, 1922, orig. 1526.

IV. SIXTEENTH AND SEVENTEENTH CENTURY LITERATURE

Alemán, Mateo, *Guzmán de Alfarache,* Heitz, Strasburgo, 1699.

Castillo Solórzano, Alonso de, *La garduña de Sevilla y anzvelo de las bolsas,* Madrid, Lectura, 1922, orig. 1642.

Cervantes Saavedra, Miguel de, *The Adventures of Don Quixote,* trans. J. M. Cohen, Middlesex, England, Penguin, 1970.

Cervantes Saavedra, Miguel de, *Exemplary Stories,* trans. C. A. Jones, Middlesex, England, Penguin, 1972.

Hidalgo, Juan, *Romances de Germanía de varios autores con el vocabulario por la orden del a.b.c. para declaracion de sus términos y lengua,* Madrid, Antonio de Sancha, 1779, orig. 1609.

Hill, John M., ed., *Poesías Germanescas,* Indiana University Press, Humanities Series No. 15, Bloomington, 1945.

Quevedo Villegas, Francisco de, *Quevedo: The Choice Humorous and Satirical Works,* trans. Sir Roger L'Estrange, et al., London, George Routledge and Sons, n.d.

Tiros de Molina, et al., *Don Juan en el Drama,* Buenos Aires, Editorial Futuro, 1944.

Two Spanish Picaresque Novels; Lazarillo de Tormes (Anonymous), and *The Swindler,* by Francisco de Quevedo, trans. Michael Alpert, Middlesex, England, Penguin, 1971.

V. LITERARY CRITICISM

Arco, Ricardo del, "La Critica Social en Cervantes," *Estudios de historia social de España,* Tomo II, Madrid, 1952.

Arco y Garay, Ricardo del, *La Sociedad Española en los obras de Cervantes,* Madrid, 1951.

Bataillon, Marcel, *El Sentido del Lazarillo de Tormes,* Librairie des Editions Espangoles, Paris-Toulouse, 1954.

Darnton, Robert, "Reading, Writing, and Publishing in Eighteenth-Century France: A Case Study in the Sociology of Literature," *Daedalus,* 100 (1971), 214–256.

Diaz Plaja, Guillermo, *España en su literatura,* Navarre, Gráficas Estella, 1969.

Hazañas y la Rua, Joaquin, *Los Rufianes de Cervantes: "El Rufian Dichoso" y "El Rufian Viudo" con un estudio preliminar y notas,* Sevilla, Isquierdo, 1906.

Lázaro Carreter, Fernando, "Glosas Críticas a *Los Pícaros en la literatura* de Alexander A. Parker," *Hispanic Review,* 41 (1973), 469–497.

McKendrick, Melveena, "The 'Mujer Esquiva—a Measure of the Feminist Sympathies of Seventeenth-Century Spanish Dramatists," *Hispanic Review,* 40 (1972), 162–197.

Riffaterre, Michael, "Criteria for Style Analysis," *Style and Stylistics,* reprinted from *Word,* 15, No. 1, April 1959.

Rodríguez Marín, Francisco, *Cervantes estudió en Sevilla,* Sevilla, Imprenta de F. de P. Dias, 1905.

Rodríguez Marín, Francisco, *La Cárcel en que se engendró el "Quijote" por Francisco Rodríquez Marín,* Revista de Archivos, Bibliotecas y Museos, Madrid, 1916.

Rodríguez Marín, Francisco, *Edicion crítica de Rinconete y Cortadillo por Miguel de Cervantes Saavedra,* Revista de Archivos, Bibliotecas, y Museos, Madrid, 1920.

Rójas, Fernando de, *La Celestina; Tragicomedia de Calisto y Melibea,* Vigo, Eugenio Krapf, 1899.

VI. SECONDARY HISTORICAL WORKS

Abbiateci, A., F. Billacois, Y. Bongert, N. Castan, Y. Castan, P. Petrovitch, *Crimes et criminalité en France sous l'Ancien Régime 17ᵉ-18ᵉ siécles,* Paris, Librairie Armand Colin, 1971.

Alonso Baquer, Miguel, *El ejército en la sociedad española,* Madrid, Ediciones de Movimiento, 1971.

Ánes Álvarez, Gonzalo, *Las crisis agrarias en la España moderna,* Madrid, Taurus Ediciones, 1970.

Asher, Eugene L., *The Resistance to the Maritime Classes: The Survival of Feudalism in the France of Colbert,* Berkeley and Los Angeles, University of California Press, 1960.

Astrain, Antonio. *Historia de la Compañía de Jesús en la asistencia de España,* Madrid, Administracion de Razon y Fe, 1912, 7 vols.

Ballesteros, Antonio, *Sevilla en el siglo XIII,* Madrid, Juan Pérez Torres, 1913.

Bloch, Marc, *Feudal Society,* trans. L. A. Manyon, London, Routledge and Kegan Paul, 1962.

Braudel, Fernand, *The Mediterranean and the Mediterranean World in the Age of Philip II,* trans. Sian Reynolds, New York, Harper and Row, 2 vols. 1972.

Calvert, Albert F., *Seville: An Historical and Descriptive Account of 'The Pearl of Andalusia,'* New York, John Lawe, 1913.

Cambridge Economic History of Europe, Vol. 4, *The Economy of Expanding Europe in the Sixteenth and Seventeenth Centuries,* Cambridge, Cambridge University Press, 1967.

Carande Thobar, Ramón, *Carlos V y sus banqueros; La vida económica en Castilla 1516-1556,* Madrid, Revista de Occidente, 1943.

Castro, Américo, *The Spaniards; An Introduction to their History,* trans. Willard F. King and Selma Margaretten, Berkeley, Los Angeles, and London, University of California Press, 1971.

Chaunu, Huguette and Pierre Chaunu, *Seville et l'Atlantique 1504-1650,* Paris, S.E.V.P.E.N., 1955-59, 8 vols.

Chaves, Manuel, *Cosas nuevas y viejas (Apuntes sevillanos),* Sevilla, Tipografía, 1904.

Chevalier, Louis, *Laboring Classes and Dangerous Classes in Paris during the First Half of the Nineteenth Century*, trans. Frank Jellinek, New York, Howard Fertig, 1973.

Collantes de Teran, Francisco, *Los establecimientos de caridad de Sevilla, que se consideran como particulares; Apuntes y memorias para su historia*, Sevilla, El Orden, 1886.

Collantes de Teran, Francisco, *Memorias históricas de los establecimientos de caridad de Sevilla y descripcion artistica de los mismos*, Sevilla, José M. Ariza, 1884.

Davis, Natalie Zemon, *Society and Culture in Early Modern France: Eight Essays*, Stanford, Stanford University Press, 1975.

Deleito y Piñuela, José, *La mala vida en la España de Felipe IV*, Madrid, Espasa-Calpe, 1959.

Deleito y Piñuela, José, *La vida religiosa española bajo el quarto Felipe; Santos y pecadores*, Madrid, Espasa-Calpe, 1952.

Diaz Plaja, Fernando, ed., *La historia de España en sus documentos*, Madrid, Instituto de Estudio Politicos, 1954–58, 4 vols.

Diaz Plaja, Fernando, *La sociedad española (desde 1500 hasta nuestros días)*, Barcelona, Ediciones G.P., 1970.

Domínguez Ortiz, Antonio, *Alteraciones andaluzas*, Madrid, Narcea, 1973.

Domínguez Ortiz, Antonio, *The Golden Age of Spain 1516–1659*, London, Weidenfeld and Nicolson, 1971.

Domínguez Ortiz, Antonio, *Orto y ocaso de Sevilla; Estudio sobre la prosperidad y decadencia de la ciudad durante los siglos XVI y XVII*, Sevilla, Diputacion Provincial, 1946.

Domínguez Ortiz, Antonio, *La sociedad española en el siglo XVII*, Vol. 2, *El estamento eclesiastico*, Madrid, Consejo Superior de Investigaciones Cientificas, 1970.

Domínguez Ortiz, Antonio, and Francisco Aguilar Piñal, *El barroco y la Ilustracion: Historia de Sevilla IV*, Sevilla, Universidad de Sevilla, 1976.

Elliott, John Huxtable, *Imperial Spain, 1469–1716*, New York, St. Martin's Press, 1964.

Elliott, John Huxtable, *The Old World and the New, 1492–1650*, Cambridge, Cambridge University Press, 1970.

Elliott, John Huxtable, *The Revolt of the Catalans: A Study in the Decline of Spain, 1598–1640*, Cambridge, Cambridge University Press, 1963.

Emmison, F. G., *Elizabethan Life: Disorder*, Essex, Collingford and Co., 1970.

Emmison, F. G., *Elizabethan Life: Morals and the Church Courts*, Essex, Benham and Co., 1973.

Foucault, Michel, *Discipline and Punishment: The Birth of the Prison*, New York, Pantheon, 1977.

Foucault, Michel, *Madness and Civilization: A History of Insanity in the Age of Reason*, New York, Pantheon, 1965.

Gallichan, Walter M., *The Story of Seville*, London, J. M. Dent, 1903.

García y Bellido, A., L. Torres Balbás, L. Cevera, F. Chueca, P. Bigador, *Resumen histórico del urbanismo en España,* Madrid, Graficas Uguina, 1968.

Gestoso y Perez, José, *Curiosidades antiguas sevillanas; Estudios arqueológicos,* Sevilla, El Universal, 1885.

Gestoso y Perez, José, *Sevilla monumental y artística: Historia y descripción de todos los edificios notables, religiosos y civiles,, que existen actualmente en esta ciudad y noticia de las preciosidades artísticas y arqueológicas que en ella se conservan,* Sevilla, La Andalucía Moderna, 1889, 3 vols.

Gomez Marín, José Antonio, *Bandolerísimo, santidad y otras temas españolas,* Madrid, M. Castellate, 1972.

Gonzalez, Tomás, ed., *Censo de población de las provincias y partidos de la corona de Castilla en el siglo XVI, con varios apéndices para completar la del resto de la peninsula en el mismo siglo, y formar juicio comparativo con la del anterior y siguiente, segun resulta de los libros y registros que se custodian en el Real Archivo de Simancas,* Madrid, Imprenta Real, 1829.

Graham, Thomas F., *Medieval Minds: Mental Health in the Middle Ages,* London, George Allen and Unwin, 1967.

Guichot y Parody, Joaquin, *Historia del Exmo. Ayuntamiento de la muy noble, muy leal, muy heróica é invicta ciudad de Sevilla,* Vols. 1 and 2, Sevilla, Tipografía de la Región, 1896.

Gutkind, E. A., *Urban development in Southern Europe: Spain and Portugal,* New York, Free Press, 1967.

Haebler, Konrad, *Prosperidad y decadencia económica de España durante el siglo XVI,* Madrid, Tello, 1899.

Hamilton, Earl J., *American Treasure and the Price Revolution in Spain,* Cambridge, Massachusetts, Harvard University Press, 1934.

Hay, Douglas, P. Linebaugh, J. G. Rule, E. P. Thompson, C. Winslow, *Albion's Fatal Tree: Crime and Society in Eighteenth-Century England,* New York, Pantheon, 1975.

Herrera Puga, Pedro, *Sociedad y delincuencia en el siglo de oro,* Madrid, Biblioteca de Autores Cristianos, 1974.

Himes, Norman E., *Medical History of Contraception,* New York, Schocken Books, 1970, orig. 1936.

Hobsbawm, E. J., *Social Bandits and Primitive Rebels: Studies in Archaic Forms of Social Movement in the Nineteenth and Twentieth Centuries,* Glencoe, Illinois, Free Press, 1959.

Hufton, Olwen H., *Bayeux in the Late Eighteenth Century: A Social Study,* Oxford, Clarendon Press, 1967.

Huizinga, Johann, *The Waning of the Middle Ages,* New York, Doubleday, 1954.

Hunter, Richard, and Ida Macalpine, *Three-Hundred Years of Psychiatry, 1535–1860,* London, Oxford University Press, 1964.

Kagan, Richard L., *Students and Society in Early Modern Spain*, Baltimore, Johns Hopkins University Press, 1974.

Kamen, Henry, *The Spanish Inquisition*, New York, London, and Scarborough, Ontario, Times Mirror, 1965.

Koenigsberger, Helmut George, *Europe in the Sixteenth Century*, New York, Holt Rinehart, and Winston, 1968.

Koenigsberger, Helmut George, *The Hapsburgs and Europe, 1516-1680*, Ithaca, Cornell University Press, 1971.

Laiglesia, F. de, *Estudios historicos (1515-1555)*, Vol 1, Madrid, Imprenta Clásica Española, 1918.

Lazo Diaz, Alfonso, *La Desamortización eclesiástica en la provincia de Sevilla (1835-1845)*, Sevilla, Excma. Diputacion Provincial de Sevilla y del Instituto de Estudios Sevillanos con la colaboracion de la Facultad de Filosofia y Letras, 1970.

Lea, Henry Charles, *A History of the Inquisition of Spain*, New York, MacMillan, 1922, 4 vols.

Levi-Provencal y Emilio García Gomez, *Sevilla a comienzos del siglo XII; El tratado de Ibn 'Abdun*, Madrid, Moneda y Crédito, 1948.

Lockhart, James, *The Men of Cajamarca: A Social and Biographical Study of the First Conquerors of Peru*, Austin and London, Univeristy of Texas Press, 1972.

Lopez Martínez, Celestino, *Mudejares y moriscos sevillanos*, Sevilla, Tipografía Rodriguez, Gimenez y Compañia, 1935.

Lynch, John, *Spain under the Hapsburgs*, New York, Oxford University Press, 1964, 2 vols.

Martínez de Campos y Serrano, Carlos, *España bélica; El siglo XVII*, Madrid, Aguilar, 1967, 2 vols.

Menéndez y Pelayo, Marcelino, *Historia de los heterodoxos españoles*, Madrid, Libería General de Victoriano Suarez, 1928.

Merriman, Roger Bigelow, *The Rise of the Spanish Empire in the Old World and the New*, New York, Cooper Square Publishers, 1962.

Montoto, Santiago, *Sevilla en el Imperio (siglo XVI)*, Sevilla, Nueva Libería, 1937.

Moore, Barrington, Jr., *Social Origins of Dicatorship and Democracy: Lord and Peasant in the Making of the Modern World*, Boston, Beacon Press, 1966.

Moret, Michele, *Aspects de la société marchande de Séville au début du XVIIe siécle*, Paris, Editions Marcel Riviére, 1967.

Nadal, Jorge, *La poblacion española (siglos XVI a XX)*, Barcelona, Ediciones Ariel, 1966.

Noonan, John T., *Contraception: A History of its Treatment by the Catholic Theologians and Canonists*, Cambridge, Massachusetts, Harvard University Press, 1966.

Ortega Rubio, Juan, ed., *Relaciones tipográficas de los pueblos de España*, Madrid, Sociedad Español de Artes Graficas, 1918.

Parker, Geoffrey, *The Army of Flanders and the Spanish Road 1567–1659: The Logistics of Spanish Victory and Defeat in the Low Countries' War,* Cambridge, Cambridge University Press, 1972.

Pfandl, Ludwig, *Cultura y costumbres del pueblo español de los siglos XVI y XVII; Introducción al estudio del siglo de oro,* Barcelona, Editorial Araluce, 1929.

Pike, Ruth, *Aristocrats and Traders: Sevillian Society in the Sixteenth Century,* Ithaca and London, Cornell University Press, 1972.

Pike, Ruth, *Enterprise and Adventure: The Genoese in Seville and the Opening of the New World,* Ithaca, Cornell University Press, 1966.

Pinchbeck, Ivy, and Margaret Hewitt, *Children in English Society,* Vol. 1, *From Tudor Times to the Eighteenth Century,* London, Routledge and Kegan Paul, 1969.

Pullan, Brian, *Rich and Poor in Renaissance Venice: The Social Institutions of a Catholic State, to 1620,* Cambridge, Massachusetts, Harvard University Press, 1971.

Rennert, Hugo Albert, *The Spanish Stage in the Time of Lope de Vega,* New York, Dover, 1963.

Rodríguez Marín, Francisco, *Miscelánea de Andalucía,* Madrid, Paéz, 1927.

Rosen, George, *Madness in Society: Chapters in the Historical Sociology of Mental Illness,* London, Routledge and Kegan Paul, 1968.

Rudé, George, *Paris and London in the Eighteenth Century: Studies in Popular Protest,* New York, Viking, 1970.

Sánchez Arjona, José, *Noticias referentes á los anales del teatro en Sevilla desde Lope de Rueda hasta fines del siglo XVII,* Sevilla, E. Rasco, 1898.

Scholberg, Kenneth R., *Sátira e invectiva en la España medieval,* Madrid, Gredos, 1971.

Smith, Robert Sidney, *The Spanish Guild Merchant: A History of the Consulado 1250–1700,* Durham, N.C., Duke University Press, 1940.

Stein, Stanley J., and Barbara H. Stein, *The Colonial Heritage of Latin America; Essays on Economic Dependence in Perspective,* New York, Oxford University Press, 1970.

Stone, Lawrence, *The Crisis of the Aristocracy 1558–1641,* Oxford, Clarendon Press, 1965.

Thomas, Keith, *Religion and the Decline of Magic,* New York, Charles Scribner's Sons, 1971.

Tilly, Charles, ed., *The Formation of National States in Western Europe,* Princeton, Princeton University Press, 1975.

Tobias, J. J., *Urban Crime in Victorian England,* New York, Schocken Books, 1972.

Ullersperger, J. B., *La Historia de la psicologia y de la psiquiatria en España; Desde los más remotos tiempos hasta la actualidad,* Madrid, Editorial Alhambra, 1954.

van Klaveren, Jacob, *Wirtschaftsgeschichte spaniens im 16 und 17 Jahrhundert,* Stuttgart, Gustav Fischer Verlag, 1960.

Velázquez y Sanchez, José, *Anales epidémicos; reseña histórica de las enfermedades contagiosas en Sevilla desde la reconquista cristiana hasta de presente,* Sevilla, José María Geofin, 1866.

Vicens Vives, Jaime, *An Economic History of Spain,* Trans. Frances M. López Morillas, Princeton, Princeton University Press, 1969.

Viñas Mey, Carmelo, *El problema de la tierra en la España de los siglos XVI y XVII,* Madrid, Consejo Superior de Investigaciones Científicas, 1941.

Viñas, Carmelo and Ramón Paz, *Relaciones historico-geográfico-estadisticas de los pueblos de España hechas por iniciativa de Felipe II,* Madrid, Artes Gráficas Clavileno, 1971.

Vovelle, Michel, *Piété baroque et déchristianisation en Provence au XVIIIe siécle; Les attitudes devant la mort d'aprés les clauses des testaments,* Paris, Plon, 1973.

VIII. MONOGRAPHS AND ARTICLES

Antón Solé, Pablo, *El Saqueo de Cádiz por los Ingleses,* Archivo Hispalense, Series 2, Vol. 54, 1971–72.

Banda y Vargas, Antonio de la *El Barrio de la Macarena,* Archivo Hispalense, Series 2, Vol. 44–45, 1966.

Bauman, Richard, "Differential Identity and the Social Base of Folklore," *Journal of American Folklore,* 84 (1971), 31–41.

Bingham, Caroline, "Seventeenth-Century Attitudes toward Deviant Sex," *Journal of Interdisciplinary History,* 1, No. 3, (1971), 447–471.

Boxer, C. R., "A Question of Contraband: The Old Colonial Trade," *History Today,* 22 (1972), 204–213.

Braudel, Fernand, "Personal Testimony," *Journal of Modern History,* 44 (1972), 448–467.

Carande, Ramón, *Sevilla fortaleza y mercado,* Anuario de historia del derecho Español, Vol. II, 1925.

Caro Baroja, Julio, "The City and the Country: Reflexions on Some Ancient Commonplaces," in *An Urban World,* ed. Charles Tilly, Boston and Toronto, Little Brown, 1974.

Caro Petit, Carlos, *La Cárcel Real de Sevilla,* Archivo Hispalense, Series 2, Vol. 11, pp. 317–348; Vol. 12, pp. 39–85.

Carriazo, Juan de M., *Negros, esclavos y extranjeros en el barrio sevillano de San Bernardo (1617–1629),* Archivo Hispalense, Series 2, Vol. 20, 1954.

Christian, William A., "De los Santos a María: Panorama de las devociones á santuarios españoles desde el principio de la Edad Media hasta nuestros días," in *Temas de antropología española,* ed. María Cátedra Tomás, et al., Madrid, Akal Editor, 1976.

Davis, Natalie Zemon, "Missed Connections: Religion and Regime," *Journal of Interdisciplinary History,* 1, No. 3 (1971), 381–387.

Delasselle, Claude, *Les enfants abandonnés a Paris au XVIIIe siécle,* Annales Economies Sociétiés Civilisations, Anée 38, No. 1, Jan.-Feb. 1975.

Documentos relativos á la mancebía, Archivo Hispalense, Series 1, Vol. 3, 1887.

Domínguez Ortiz, Antonio, *La Alcaicería de la Seda, de Sevilla, en 1679,* Archivo Hispalense, Series 2, Vol. 44-45, 1966.

Domínguez Ortiz, Antonio, *Documentos para la historia de Sevilla,* Archivo Hispalense, Series 2, Vol. 32-33, 1960.

Domínguez Ortiz, Antonio, *Documentos para la historia de Sevilla y su Antiguo Reino,* Archivo Hispalense, Series 2, Vol. 44-45, 1966.

Domínguez Ortiz, Antonio, *Dos monasterios sevillanos en difícil situación económica a fines del siglo XVI,* Archivo Hispalense, Series 2, Vol. 54, 1971-72.

Domínguez Ortiz, Antonio, *Una Relación de la pérdida de la Armada de don Juan de Hoyos,* Archivo Hispalense, Series 2, Vol. 46-47, 1967.

Domínguez Ortiz, Antonio, *Vida y obras del Padre Pedro de León,* Archivo Hispalense, Series 2, Vol. 26-27, 1957.

Espejo, Cristóbal, *La Carestía de la vida en el siglo XVI y medios de abaratarla,* Revista de Archivos, Bibliotecas y Museos, Series 3, Vol. 41, 1920.

Evans, Richard J., "Prostitution, State and Society in Imperial Germany," *Past and Present,* 70 (1976), 106-129.

Genoese, Elizabeth Fox, "The Many Faces of Moral Economy: A Contribution to a Debate," *Past and Present,* 58 (1973), 161-168.

Glick, Thomas F., and Oriol Pi-Sunyer, "Acculturation as an Explanatory Concept in Spanish History," *Comparative Studies in Society and History,* 11 (1969), 136-154.

Goulet, Denis, and Marco Walshok, "Values among Under-Developed Marginals: The Case of Spanish Gypsies," *Comparative Studies in Society and History,* 13 (1971), 451-472.

Guichot y Sierra, Alejandro, *Supersticiones populares andaluzas,* Folklore española: Biblioteca de las tradiciones populares españoles, Vol. I, 1844.

Hexter, J. H., "Fernand Braudel and the *Monde Braudellien,*" *Journal of Modern History,* 44 (1972), 480-539.

Jago, Charles, "The Influence of Debt on the Relations between Crown and Aristocracy in Seventeenth-Century Castile," *Economic History Review,* 26 (1973), 218-236.

Kagan, Richard L., "Universities in Castile 1500-1700," *Past and Present,* 49 (1970), 44-71.

Kamen, Henry, "Galley Service and Crime in Sixteenth-Century Spain," *Economic History Review,* 22 (1969), 304-5.

Lopez Martinez, Celestino, "Poblacion, territorio y edificios de la provincia de Sevilla; estudio conmemorativo del primer centenario de la 'estadística' oficial española," *Archivo Hispalense,* Series 2, Vol. 24-25, 1956, pp. 2-29.

Manjarrés, Ramón de, "Sevilla industrial," in *Quien no vió a Sevilla,* Tipografía Girones, Sevilla, ca. 1920.

Marchena Hidalgo, Rosario, "Economía sevillana en la baja edad media," *Archivo Hispalense,* Series 2, Vol. 54, 1971–72.

Monter, E. William, "La Sodomie á l'époque moderne en Suisse romande," *Annales Economies Sociétiés Civilisations,* Année 29, No. 4, July-Aug. 1974.

Montoto, Luís, "La Calle de las Sierpes," in *Quien no vió a Sevilla,* Tipografia Gironés, Sevilla, ca. 1920.

Montoto de Sedas, Santiago, "El Teatro, el baile y la danza en Sevilla," *Archivo Hispalense,* Series 2, Vol. 32–33, 1960.

Montoto y Rautenstrauch, Luís, "Costumbres populares andaluzas," *Folklore español; Biblioteca de las tradiciones populares españoles,* Vol. I and IV, 1844.

Navarro García, Luís, "El Puerto de Sevilla a fines del siglo XVI," *Archivo Hispalense,* Series 2, Vol. 44–45, 1966, pp. 141–177.

Navarro García, Luís, "Pilotos, maestres y señores de naos en la Carrera de las Indias," *Archivo Hispalense,* Series 2, Vol. 46–47, 1967.

Neasham, V. Aubrey, "Spain's Emigrants to the New World 1492–1592," *Hispanic American Historical Review,* Vol. XIX, 1939, pp. 147–160.

Nyder, Fray Juan, "De los Maleficios y los demonios," transl. from the Latin (orig. fifteenth century) with additions by José María Montoto, *Folklore español; Biblioteca de las tradiciones populares españoles,* Vol. II and III, 1844.

"Ordenanzas del Hospital de San Cosme y San Damian (vulgo de las Bubas)," *Archivo Hispalense,* Series 2, Vol. 44–45, 1966.

Pike, Ruth, "The Genoese in Seville and the Opening of the New World," *Journal of Economic History,* Vol. 22, 1962, pp. 348–378.

Pike, Ruth, "Sevillian Society in the Sixteenth Century: Slaves and Freedmen," *Hispanic American Historical Review,* Vol. 47, 1967.

"Relacion de las fiestas reales de toros y cañas en Sevilla, en 2 de octubre de 1620, por Don Francisco Morovelli de Puebla, cavallero sevillano," *Archivo Hispalense,* Series 1, Vol. 3, 1887.

"Relacion segunda de las cañas y toros que los cavalleros de Sevilla, hizieron en 2 octubre de 1620, por la junta de sus altezas los principes herederos de España," *Archivo Hispalense,* Series 1, Vol. 3, 1887.

Rodríguez la Orden, J., "Los Barrios de la ciudad," in *Quien no vió a Sevilla,* Tipografía Gironés, Sevilla, ca. 1920.

Ruiz Almansa, Javier, "La Poblacion de España en el siglo XVI; Estudio sobre los recuentos de vecindario de 1594, llamados comúmente 'Censo de Tomás González'," *Revista Internacional de Sociología,* Vol. I, 1943.

Ruiz Martín, Felipe, "La Poblacion española al comienzo de los tiempos modernos," *Cuadernos de Historia,* Vol. I, 1967.

Scelle, Georges, "The Slave-Trade in the Spanish Colonies of America:

The Asiento," trans. by Edna K. Hoyt, *American Journal of International Law,* Vol. IV, 1910.

Shore, Miles F., "The Child and Historiography," *Journal of Interdisciplinary History,* Vol. VI, No. 3, 1976, pp. 495–505.

Tenorio, Nicolás, "Las Milicias de Sevilla," *Revista de Archivos, Bibliotecas y Museos,* Vol. 17, Series 3, 1907.

Thompson, E. P., "The Moral Economy of the English Crowd in the Eighteenth Century," *Past and Present,* No. 50, Feb. 1971, pp. 76–136.

Thompson, I.A.A., "A Map of Crime in Sixteenth-Century Spain," *Economic History Review,* Series 2, Vol. 21, 1968, pp. 244–267.

Tomás de la Torre, "Traveling in 1544 from Salamanca, Spain, to Ciudad Real Chiapas, Mexico; The Travels and Trials of Bishop Bartolomé de las Casas and his Dominican Fathers," ed. and trans. by Frans Blom, *Sewanee Review,* Vol. 81, 1973, pp. 429–569.

Trevor-Roper, H. R., "Fernand Braudel, The *Annales,* and the Mediterranean," *Journal of Modern History,* Vol. 44, 1972, pp. 468–479.

Vranich, Stanko B., "Escándalo en la catedral," *Archivo Hispalense,* Series 2, Vol. 54, 1971–72.

Wilson, William E., "Some Notes on Slavery During the Golden Age," *Hispanic Review,* Vol. VII, 1939, p. 171.

Zguta, Russell, "Folklore as History: Russian Byliny and Istoricheskie Pesni," *Southern Folklore Quarterly,* Vol. 35, 1971, p. 97.

IX. STUDIES IN RELATED FIELDS

Brown, Jonathan, *Murillo and His Drawings,* Princeton, Princeton University Press, 1976.

Christian, William A., Jr., *Person and God in a Spanish Valley,* New York and London, Seminar Press, 1972.

Cornelisen, Ann, *Torregreca; Life, Death, Miracles,* Boston and Toronto, Little, Brown and Co., 1969.

Douglas, Norman, *London Street Games,* London, St. Catherine Press, 1916.

Gesell, Arnold and Frances L. Ilg, *Infant and Child in the Culture of Today; The Guidance of Development in Home and Nursery School,* New York and Evanston and London, Harper and Row, 1943.

Gomez-Tabanera, José Manuel, ed., *El Folklore Español,* Madrid, Instituto Español de Antropológia Aplicada, 1968.

Goode, William J., *The Family,* Englewood Cliffs, New Jersey, Prentice-Hall, 1964.

Gramsci, Antonio, *Letters from Prison,* Selected, trans., and introd. by Lynne Lawner, New York, Harper and Row, 1973.

Gramsci, Antonio, *Selections from the Prison Notebooks of Antonio Gramsci*, trans. and ed. by Quentin Hoare and Geoffrey Nowell Smith, New York, International Publishers, 1972.

Kenny, Michael, *A Spanish Tapestry; Town and Country in Castile*, London, Cohen and West, 1961.

Lassaigne, Jacques, *Spanish Painting from Velasquez to Picasso*, trans. by Stuart Gilbert, Geneva, 1952.

Lewis, Oscar, *The Children of Sanchez: Autobiography of a Mexican Family*, New York, Random House, 1961.

Marwick, M. G., *Sorcery in its Social Setting; A Study of the Northern Rhodesian Cewa*, Manchester, Manchester University Press, 1965.

Mayer, A. L., *The Work of Murillo*, New York, Brentano, 1913.

Navascués, Joaquin M. de, *El Folklore español; Boceto histórico*, n.p., n.d.

Peristiany, J. G., ed., *Honour and Shame; The Values of Mediterranean Society*, London, Weidenfeld and Nicolson, 1965.

Piaget, Jean, *The Child's Conception of the World*, trans. by Joan and Andrew Tomlinson, Totowa, N. J., Littlefield, Adams and Co., 1969.

Piaget, Jean, *Play, Dreams and Imitation in Childhood*, trans. by C. Gattegno and F. M. Hodgson, New York, W. W. Norton and Co., 1962.

Piers, Maria W., Ed., *Play and Development*, New York, W. W. Norton and Co., 1972.

Pitt-Rivers, Julian A., *The People of the Sierra*, Chicago and London, University of Chicago Press, 1971.

Poulantzas, Nicos, *Political Power and Social Classes*, trans. by Timothy O'Hagen, London, N.L.B., 1975.

Rocha, José Martínho da, *Virgidade, sexo, família*, Rio de Janeiro, Editoria Rio, 1972.

Rodríguez Marín, Francisco, *Pasatiempo folklorico; Varios juegos infantiles del siglo XVI*, Madrid, Tipografía de Archivos, 1932.

Rowbotham, Sheila, *Women, Resistance and Revolution*, London, Penguin, 1972.

Salillas, Rafael, *El delincuente español; El lenguaje (estudio, filológico, psicológico y sociológico) con dos vocabularios jergales*, Madrid, Libreria de Victoriano Suárez, 1896.

Scott, Samuel Parsons, trans. and notes, *Las Siete Partidas*, Chicago, New York, and Washington, Commerce Clearing House, 1931.

Stirling-Maxwell, Sir William, *Annals of the Artists of Spain*, London, John C. Nimmo, 1891, 4 vols.

Swartz, Marc J., Victor W. Turner, and Arthur Tuden, eds., *Political Anthropology*, Chicago, Aldine, 1966.

Turner, Victor W., *Schism and Continuity in an African Society; A Study of Ndembu Village Life*, Manchester, Manchester University Press, 1957.

Vilá Valentí, Juan, *Campo y ciudad en la geográfica española*, Barcelona, Salvat Editores, 1970.

Walton, Clifford Stevens, *The Civil Law in Spain and Spanish America*, Washington, D.C., W. H. Lowdermilk and Co., 1900.

Glossary

Aduana: the customs house

Alcabalá: sales tax imposed by the Crown

Alcaicería: the silk and silver quarter of the city

Alcalde mayor: a chief judicial officer of the city government

Alguacil mayor: head sheriff

Alhóndiga del pan: granary or warehouse for storing wheat, flour, bread

Almojarifazgo: import duty

Alumbrados: mystical sect of Christians who believed union with God was possible without a priestly intercessor

Animero: beggar who received alms in exchange for praying for souls of the dead

Arroba: wet measure equal to 2.6 to 3.6 gallons, and a dry measure of about 25 pounds

Asistente: noble appointed by the Crown to head the city council

Audiencia: judicial court of nobles appointed by the Crown

Auto de fé: ceremony for penancing people convicted by the Inquisition

Avería: export duty to raise money for defending the fleets going from Spain to the New World

Beata: holy woman, often too poor to enter a convent

Blanca de carne: sales tax on meat sold in the city

Botica: small pharmacy or shop

Botija: large cask for shipping wine or oil

Calle: street

Cambio: an exchange

Cantonera: street walker or prostitute

Casa de Contratación: royal agency to control trade and colonization with the New World

Cazuela: literally a stewing pan; popularly used to describe the women's section in the theater

Censo: mortgage on land

Cofradía: religious fraternity

Congregado: pious layman who allied with priests against brothels

Consulta: opinion, usually a recommendation to the Crown from a council

Conversos: Jews who had converted to Christianity

Corral: open courtyard

Corrida: tournament, including bull-fighting and jousting by nobles

Cortes: parliamentary body of representatives from major cities

Coto: enclosed land; used by the underworld to refer to hospitals and cemeteries

Cruzada: tax on the Church, originally imposed by the Crown to finance the Crusades and the Reconquest

Doncella: girl of marriageable age

Escarramán: a traditional dance adapted to liturgy, representing the "abortions of Hell"

Escribano: lawyer or scribe

Faena: task

Familiares: lay officials of the Inquisition

Fuero: local right or privilege recognized by the Crown

Fulidor: burglars who used small accomplices to crawl through small openings and open houses for them from the inside

Gente de hampa: ruffians and street people

Gente de mal vivir: bad people

Germanesca: derived from vagabonds and street people

Golondrero: thief who masquerades as a soldier

Guardia Civil: federal police force imposed to restore order in rural areas of Spain and still famous for their patent leather hats

Hacera: row of houses sharing common sides

Hermandad: brotherhood or fraternity

Hidalgo: noble; *hidalguía* is the granting of nobility

Hospital: common house caring for the sick, abandoned, disabled, and poor; note that it is more than a "hospital" as the word is used in English

Joya: jewel or gift

Jurado: representative elected from the parishes to the city council

Juro: loan, often made to the Crown and purchased as a bond

Limpieza de sangre: "purity of the blood," a principle that certain offices and privileges should be reserved for Old Christians, or those people whose familes had not intermarried with converted or unconverted Jews and Moors

Mal frances: syphilis

Maravedí: coin of rather small value (See appendix I)

Millones: royal sales tax, originally 0.1 percent

Morisco: Christianized Moor

Mozito: youth, younger or smaller than a *mozo,* also a youth

Mozos de cuerda: day-laborers, especially in the port

Mujeres perdidas: "lost women" or prostitutes

Pastorcillos: underworld term describing sharpened sticks

Pecado nefando: homosexual offense, usually sodomy

Pelota: usually a ball, but used by underworld people to describe women or a bag of money

Pendon Verde: a green banner captured from the Moors and a symbol of local pride

Pícaro: a rogue, usually clever and dishonest

Plebe: common people

Portero: prison trusty who took new prisoners to their cells and had access to prison keys

Postura: offical price ceiling on food

Pragmática: interpretation of the law, often a royal decree

Pregonero: town crier who called out public announcements and also sold secondhand belongings

Quadrilla: gang or small group of armed men

Real: silver coin usually worth about 34 maravedís

Regaton: street retailer

Regente: chief justice of the royal judicial court and also the king's highest minister in Seville

Romance germanesca: ballads derived from the oral tradition of vagabonds and street people

Romería: a religious pilgrimage to a rural shrine

Sabia: wise woman or folk practitioner who gave advice, prepared potions, administered medical treatment

Saludador: folk healer

Sanbenito: penitential garment worn by people penanced by the Inquisition, usually a long, one-piece robe and conspicuous conical hat

Santa Hermandad: Crown-sponsored body charged with enforcing law and order and putting down local feuds

Seises: stately dance still performed before the high altar of the cathedral on certain high feast days

Teniente: assistant

Tercia real: one third of the tithes gathered by the Church in Castile, which was given by the Church to the Crown

Tercio: military unit composed of pikesmen, cavalry, infantry, and artillery

Tratadista: economic essayist, often xenophobic, blaming Spain's declining position on the failure to develop and protect native industry and agriculture

Veinticuatro: one of the oligarchy of Seville, originally twenty-four nobles

Vito: loud music, used like the charivari to embarrass offenders of social customs

Zarabanda: traditional dance that became part of religious celebrations but was later banned as too scandalous

Index

Food policies, 39, 48–49, 52, 57, 244–245
France, 34–35, 40, 44, 47, 112, 228
Franciscans, 164, 255
Fraud, 34, 72
Fuentes, Bartolomé, 122
Fugger family, 34, 47

Galleys, 19, 43, 108, 171, 235, 239; as punishment, 87, 90–91, 102, 218; military requirements, 102
Gamarra, Francisca, 50
Gamblers, gambling, 29, 85, 107, 161; fraudulence, 12, 72, 199; in military, 101, 103, 105, 107, 112–114; juvenile, 198–199; underworld association, 12, 26, 30, 42, 66
Gang fights, 29, 70, 150, 208
García, Francisco, 140
Genoese, 34, 47, 148
Góngora, Ignacio de, 239
Granada, 6, 21
Guadalquivir River, 19, 44, 62
Guilds, 24, 27, 40, 78, 176, 240–241
Guinea, 21
Gutierrez Tello, Juan, 16, 70, 144
Guzmán family, 18, 55

Hapsburg monarchy, 1, 6–8, 44
Henriquez Ribera, Fernando, 249
Herrera, Laura de, 153
Highwaymen, 64, 92, 110, 129, 134, 143, 150; association with constables, 65, 71; concern with, 46, 69, 71
Hobsbawm, E. J., 247
Holland. See Low Countries
Homosexuality. See Sexual offenses, rape
Hospitales, 90, 132, 166, 172–178, 227–229, 238–239; confining functions, 175, 180, 182, 228–229; reduction in, 173, 177. See also Charity; Orphanages

Indies. See New World
Inquisition (Holy Office), 1, 4–5, 67, 120–122, 133, 147, 155, 220; conflicts with secular authorities, 62–64; frauds committed, 2, 64–65, 120–121; part of oligarchy, 2, 18, 64, 120, 125, 135; relationship with monarchy, 5, 63. See also Autos de fé
Irunza, Claudio, 34
Isabella. See Ferdinand and Isabella
Italica, 132
Italy, 7, 34, 83, 160–161

Jeronomites, 132–133
Jesuits, 17, 70, 75, 78, 123, 130, 132, 144; accused of heresy, 4, 121; charity, 17, 223, 235; conflicts with Dominicans, 17, 18, 121–122; drama, 17, 152; educating activities, 17, 120
Jesús María, Fray Juan de, 123
Jews, 24, 127, 205. See also Conversos
John of the Cross, 123
Josepha, María, 170
Juana, 6
Juveniles. See Children

Language, 81, 85, 117, 206, 208; religion as language, 122–127; rites of witchcraft as language, 85; underworld vocabulary, 9, 30–32, 126–127, 135, 172, 197, 201, terms for prison, 30–31, 77–78, 82–83, 89, terms for theft, 30–32, 111, 126, 129,

Library of Congress Cataloging in Publication Data

Perry, Mary Elizabeth, 1937–
    Crime and society in early modern Seville.

    Bibliography: p.
    Includes index.
        1. Crime and criminals—Spain—Seville—History.
2. Seville—Social conditions. 3. City and
town life—Spain—Seville—History. I. Title.
HV7045.S47P47   364'.96486   79–66452
ISBN 0–87451–177–1